W9-BWR-181

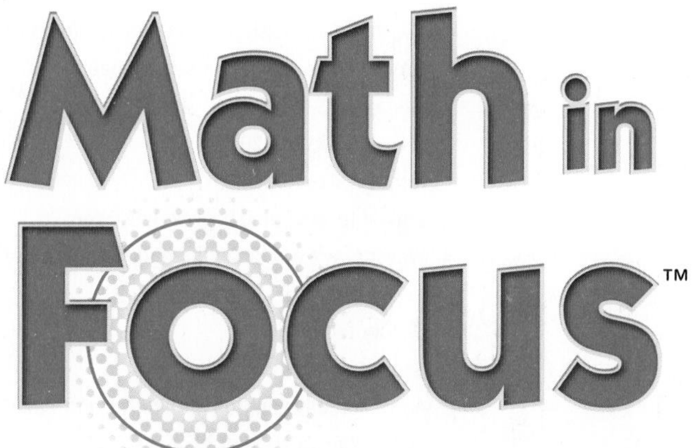

Math in Focus™

The Singapore Approach

Student Book

5A

Consultant and Author

Dr. Fong Ho Kheong

Authors

Gan Kee Soon and Chelvi Ramakrishnan

U.S. Consultants

Dr. Richard Bisk, Andy Clark,
and Patsy F. Kanter

Published by Marshall Cavendish Education
An imprint of Marshall Cavendish International (Singapore) Private Limited
A member of Times Publishing Limited

Marshall Cavendish International (Singapore) Private Limited
Times Centre, 1 New Industrial Road
Singapore 536196
Tel: +65 6411 0820
Fax: +65 6266 3677
E-mail: fps@sg.marshallcavendish.com
Website: www.marshallcavendish.com/education

Distributed by
Great Source
A division of Houghton Mifflin Harcourt Publishing Company
181 Ballardvale Street
P.O. Box 7050
Wilmington, MA 01887-7050
Tel: 1-800-289-4490
Website: www.greatsource.com

First published 2009
Reprinted 2010

Math in Focus Grade 5 Student Book A
ISBN 978-0-669-01082-4

Printed in United States of America

2 3 4 5 6 7 8 1897 16 15 14 13 12 11 10
4500219884 B C D E

Contents

1 Whole Numbers

Look for **Practice and Problem Solving**

Student Book A and Student Book B	Workbook A and Workbook B
• **Let's Practice** in every lesson • **Put on Your Thinking Cap!** in every chapter	• **Independent Practice** for every lesson • **Put on Your Thinking Cap!** in every chapter

Hundred Thousands	Ten Thousands	Thousands	Hundreds	Tens	Ones
2	3	7	9	8	1
5	0	0	6	0	0

Look for **Assessment Opportunities**

Student Book A and Student Book B	Workbook A and Workbook B
• **Quick Check** at the beginning of every chapter to assess chapter readiness • **Guided Practice** after every example or two to assess readiness to continue lesson • **Chapter Review/Test** in every chapter to review or test chapter material	• **Cumulative Reviews** six times during the year • **Mid-Year and End-of-Year Reviews** to assess test readiness

2 Whole Number Multiplication and Division

	Ten Thousands	Thousands	Hundreds	Tens	Ones
900			○○○○○ ○○○○		
900 ÷ 100					○○○○○ ○○○○
14,000	●	○○○○			
14,000 ÷ 1000				○	○○○○

3 Fractions and Mixed Numbers

Multiplying and Dividing Fractions and Mixed Numbers

Algebra

Happy Birthday

Area of a Triangle

Ratio

Welcome to

Math in Focus™

This exciting math program comes to you all the way from the country of Singapore. We are sure you will enjoy learning math with the interesting lessons you'll find in these books.

What makes *Math in Focus*™ different?

- **Two books** You don't write in the [blank] in this textbook. This book has a matching **Workbook**. When you see the pencil icon ON YOUR OWN, you will write in the **Workbook**.
- **Longer lessons** Some lessons may last more than a day, so you can really understand the math.
- **Math will make sense** Learn to use bar models to solve word problems with ease.

In this book, look for

Learn
This means you will learn something new.

Guided Practice
Your teacher will help you try some sample problems.

Let's Practice
You practice what you've learned to solve more problems. You can make sure you really understand.

Now you get to practice with lots of different problems in your own **Workbook**.

Also look forward to *Games, Hands-On Activities, Math Journals, Let's Explore,* and *Put on Your Thinking Cap!*
You will combine logical thinking with math skills and concepts to meet new problem-solving challenges. You will be talking math, thinking math, doing math, and even writing about doing math.

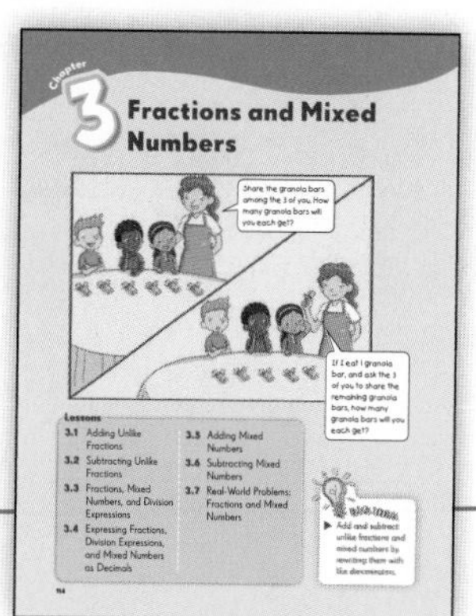

What's in the Workbook?

Math in Focus™ will give you time to learn important new concepts and skills and check your understanding. Then you will use the practice pages in the **Workbook** to try:

- Solving different problems to practice the new math concept you are learning. In the textbook, keep an eye open for this symbol ON YOUR OWN. That will tell you which pages to use for practice.
- *Put on Your Thinking Cap!*

  Challenging Practice problems invite you to think in new ways to solve harder problems.

  Problem Solving challenges you to use different strategies to solve problems.
- Math Journal activities ask you to think about thinking, and then write about that!

Students in Singapore have been using this kind of math program for many years.
Now you can too — are you ready?

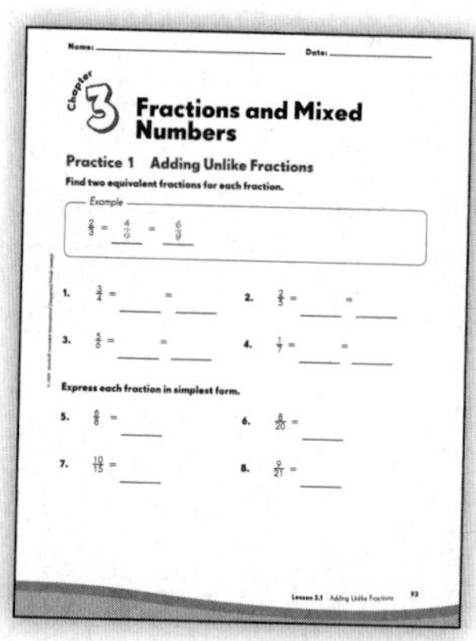
Name: ______ Date: ______

Chapter 3 **Fractions and Mixed Numbers**

Practice 1 Adding Unlike Fractions

Find two equivalent fractions for each fraction.

Example

$\frac{2}{3} = \frac{4}{6} = \frac{6}{9}$

1. $\frac{3}{4}$ = ___ = ___
2. $\frac{2}{5}$ = ___ = ___
3. $\frac{5}{6}$ = ___ = ___
4. $\frac{1}{7}$ = ___ = ___

Express each fraction in simplest form.

5. $\frac{6}{8}$ = ___
6. $\frac{8}{20}$ = ___
7. $\frac{10}{15}$ = ___
8. $\frac{9}{21}$ = ___

Lesson 3.1 Adding Unlike Fractions 93

Chapter 1

Whole Numbers

Do you know that scientists have identified more than 1 million species of insects in the world?
Some experts estimate that there may be up to 10 million species.
One of the biggest insects in the world is the Acteon beetle which can grow up to 9 cm in length!
Aaarghh!

Lessons

1.1 Numbers to 10,000,000

1.2 Place Value

1.3 Comparing Numbers to 10,000,000

1.4 Rounding and Estimating

BIG IDEA

▶ Whole numbers can be written in different ways. Numbers can be compared and rounded, according to their place value.

Recall Prior Knowledge

Writing numbers in word form, standard form and expanded form

- Write 25,193 in word form: twenty-five thousand, one hundred ninety-three
- Write forty-seven thousand, two hundred sixty-eight in standard form: 47,268
- Write 32,146 in expanded form: 30,000 + 2,000 + 100 + 40 + 6

Identifying the value of each digit in a number

Ten Thousands	Thousands	Hundreds	Tens	Ones
●	●	●	●	●
1	1	1	1	1

1 one
1 ten = 10 ones
1 hundred = 10 tens
1 thousand = 10 hundreds
1 ten thousand = 10 thousands

Comparing numbers

Ten Thousands	Thousands	Hundreds	Tens	Ones
1	0	2	3	4
	9	4	2	3

10,234 is greater than 9,423 because 1 ten thousand (10,000) is greater than 9 thousands (9,000).

Rounding to the nearest hundred

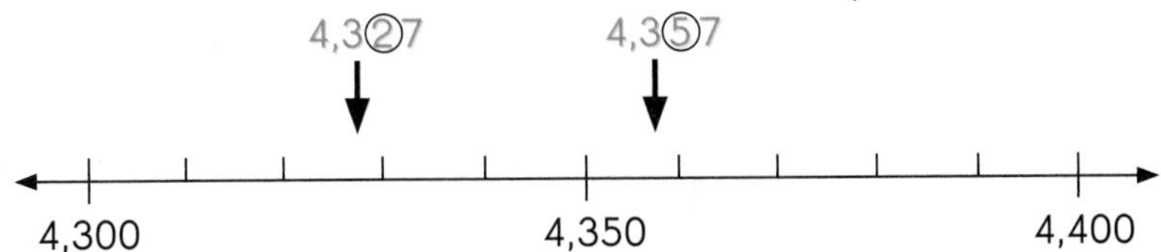

When the tens digit is 0, 1, 2, 3, or 4, round the number to the lesser hundred.

4,3②7 rounded to the nearest hundred is 4,300.

When the tens digit is 5, 6, 7, 8, or 9, round the number to the greater hundred.

4,3⑤7 rounded to the nearest hundred is 4,400.

Using rounding and front-end estimation to estimate sums and differences

Estimate the sum of 287 and 805.

Using rounding:

287 rounded to the nearest hundred is 300.
805 rounded to the nearest hundred is 800.

300 + 800 = 1,100

The estimated sum is 1,100.

Using front-end estimation:

Add the values of the leading digits.

287 → **2**00
805 → **8**00

200 + 800 = 1,000

The estimated sum is 1,000.

Estimate the difference between 686 and 417.

Using rounding:

686 rounded to the nearest hundred is 700.
417 rounded to the nearest hundred is 400.

700 – 400 = 300

The estimated difference is 300.

Using front-end estimation:

Subtract the values of the leading digits.

686 → **6**00
417 → **4**00

600 – 400 = 200

The estimated difference is 200.

Complete.

1. Write 95,718 in word form.
2. Write seventy-eight thousand, two hundred thirteen in standard form.
3. Write 31,485 in expanded form.
4. 2 tens = ___ ones
5. 3 hundreds = ___ tens
6. 5 thousands = ___ hundreds
7. 7 ten thousands = ___ thousands

Compare.

8. Which is greater, 20,345 or 21,345?
9. Which is less, 10,001 or 9,991?

Round each number to the nearest hundred.

10. 880
11. 1,249
12. 2,901
13. 8,997

Estimate by rounding to the nearest hundred.

14. 936 + 465
15. 853 – 217

Estimate by using front-end estimation.

16. 519 + 472
17. 758 – 329

Lesson 1.1

Numbers to 10,000,000

Lesson Objectives

- Count by ten thousands and hundred thousands to 10,000,000.
- Use place-value charts to show numbers to 10,000,000.
- Read and write numbers to 10,000,000 in standard form and in word form.

Vocabulary
hundred thousand
standard form
word form
periods
million

Learn

Count by ten thousands.

1 ten thousand (10,000), 2 ten thousands (20,000), 3 ten thousands (30,000), 4 ten thousands (40,000), 5 ten thousands (50,000), 6 ten thousands (60,000), 7 ten thousands (70,000), 8 ten thousands (80,000), 9 ten thousands (90,000), 10 ten thousands (100,000)

Add 1 ten thousand to 9 ten thousands to get 10 ten thousands.

10 ten thousands is the same as 1 hundred thousand. You write 1 hundred thousand as 100,000.

10 ten thousands = 1 **hundred thousand**

Hundred Thousands	Ten Thousands	Thousands	Hundreds	Tens	Ones
	●●●●● ●●●●●				

↓

Hundred Thousands	Ten Thousands	Thousands	Hundreds	Tens	Ones
●					
1	0	0	0	0	0
stands for 1 hundred thousand or 100,000	stands for 0 ten thousands or 0	stands for 0 thousands or 0	stands for 0 hundreds or 0	stands for 0 tens or 0	stands for 0 ones or 0

Guided Practice

Count by hundred thousands.

1.

One hundred thousand	100,000
Two hundred thousand	200,000
Three hundred thousand	300,000
Four hundred thousand	
Five hundred thousand	
	600,000
	700,000
Eight hundred thousand	
	900,000

A comma between the thousands digit and the hundreds digit helps you to read the number more easily.
100,000

Learn

Write numbers in standard form and word form.

What is the number in standard form and word form?

Hundred Thousands	Ten Thousands	Thousands	Hundreds	Tens	Ones
●●● ●●●	●●● ●●	●●●	●		●● ●●
stands for 6 hundred thousands	stands for 5 ten thousands	stands for 3 thousands	stands for 1 hundred	stands for 0 tens	stands for 4 ones

	Standard Form	Word Form
6 hundred thousands	600,000	six hundred thousand
5 ten thousands	50,000	fifty thousand
3 thousands	3,000	three thousand
1 hundred	100	one hundred
0 tens	0	
4 ones	4	four

Number in standard form: 653,104

Number in word form: six hundred fifty-three thousand, one hundred four

Guided Practice

Write the number shown in the place-value chart in standard form and word form.

2

Hundred Thousands	Ten Thousands	Thousands	Hundreds	Tens	Ones
stands for 5 hundred thousands	stands for 5 ten thousands	stands for 7 thousands	stands for 6 hundreds	stands for 7 tens	stands for 6 ones

	Standard Form	Word Form
☐ hundred thousands	☐	☐
☐ ten thousands	☐	☐
☐ thousands	☐	☐
☐ hundreds	☐	☐
☐ tens	☐	☐
☐ ones	☐	☐

Number in standard form : ☐

Number in word form : ☐

Hundred Thousands	Ten Thousands	Thousands	Hundreds	Tens	Ones

Number in standard form : ☐

Number in word form : ☐

Learn Read numbers to 1,000,000 by periods.

Groups of three places are called periods. You can read numbers to 1,000,000 by grouping them into periods.

Hundred Thousands	Ten Thousands	Thousands	Hundreds	Tens	Ones
4	9	7	8	3	2

First read the thousands period: four hundred ninety-seven thousand

Then read the remaining period: eight hundred thirty-two

497,832 is read as four hundred ninety-seven thousand, eight hundred thirty-two.

767,707

767,707 is read as seven hundred sixty-seven thousand, seven hundred seven.

Guided Practice

Write in word form.

4. 325,176

5. 438,834

6. 906,096

7. 680,806

8. 700,007

9. 999,999

Learn Count by hundred thousands.

1 hundred thousand (100,000), 2 hundred thousands (200,000),
3 hundred thousands (300,000), 4 hundred thousands (400,000),
5 hundred thousands (500,000), 6 hundred thousands (600,000),
7 hundred thousands (700,000), 8 hundred thousands (800,000),
9 hundred thousands (900,000), 10 hundred thousands (1,000,000)

Add 1 hundred thousand to 9 hundred thousands to get 10 hundred thousands.
10 hundred thousands is the same as 1 million. You write 1 million as 1,000,000.

10 hundred thousands = 1 **million**

Millions	Hundred Thousands	Ten Thousands	Thousands	Hundreds	Tens	Ones
	●●●●● ●●●●●					

↓

Millions	Hundred Thousands	Ten Thousands	Thousands	Hundreds	Tens	Ones

1	0	0	0	0	0	0
stands for 1 million or 1,000,000	stands for 0 hundred thousands or 0	stands for 0 ten thousands or 0	stands for 0 thousands or 0	stands for 0 hundreds or 0	stands for 0 tens or 0	stands for 0 ones or 0

Guided Practice

Count by millions.

10

One million	1,000,000
Two million	2,000,000
Three million	3,000,000
	4,000,000
Five million	5,000,000
Six million	6,000,000
Seven million	7,000,000
	8,000,000
Nine million	
Ten million	10,000,000

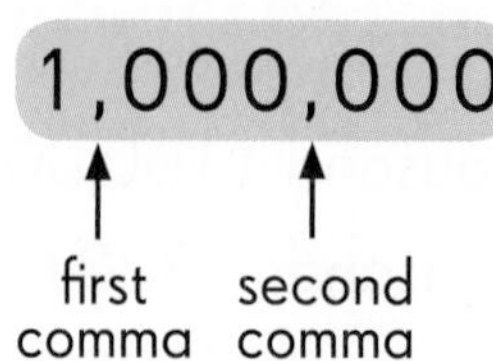

Use two commas to separate the periods. The first comma indicates the millions period. The second comma indicates the thousands period.

Learn

Write numbers in standard form and word form.

What is the number in standard form and word form?

Millions	Hundred Thousands	Ten Thousands	Thousands	Hundreds	Tens	Ones
●●●	●●● ●●	●●● ●●●	●●●● ●●●		●● ●●	●●● ●●
stands for 3 millions	stands for 5 hundred thousands	stands for 6 ten thousands	stands for 7 thousands	stands for 0 hundreds	stands for 4 tens	stands for 5 ones

	Standard Form	Word Form
3 millions	3,000,000	three million
5 hundred thousands	500,000	five hundred thousand
6 ten thousands	60,000	sixty thousand
7 thousands	7,000	seven thousand
0 hundreds	0	
4 tens	40	forty
5 ones	5	five

Number in standard form: 3,567,045

Number in word form: three million, five hundred sixty-seven thousand, forty-five

Work in groups of four or five.
Search for quantities that occur in the millions on the Internet.
Search for at least five such quantities.
Print the search results your group finds.
Present your findings to the rest of your class.

The population of Virginia is one quantity that is reported in the millions.

According to the U.S. annual population estimate by state, the population of Virginia in 2007 was about 7,700,000.

Guided Practice

Write the number shown in the place-value chart in standard form and word form.

11

Millions	Hundred Thousands	Ten Thousands	Thousands	Hundreds	Tens	Ones
stands for 4 millions	stands for 6 hundred thousands	stands for 0 ten thousands	stands for 5 thousands	stands for 3 hundreds	stands for 7 tens	stands for 9 ones

	Standard Form	Word Form
millions		
hundred thousands		
ten thousands		
thousands		
hundreds		
tens		
ones		

Number in standard form :

Number in word form :

Write the number in standard form and word form.

Millions	Hundred Thousands	Ten Thousands	Thousands	Hundreds	Tens	Ones

Number in standard form :

Number in word form :

Learn Read numbers to 10,000,000 by periods.

You can also read numbers to 10,000,000 by grouping them into periods.

Millions	Hundred Thousands	Ten Thousands	Thousands	Hundreds	Tens	Ones
5	8	2	4	4	2	8

First read the millions period: five million

Then read the thousands period: eight hundred twenty-four thousand

Finally, read the remaining period: four hundred twenty-eight

5,824,428 is read as five million, eight hundred twenty-four thousand, four hundred twenty-eight.

6,035,350

6,035,350 is read as six million, thirty-five thousand, three hundred fifty.

Guided Practice

Write in word form.

13 1,234,567

14 2,653,356

15 4,404,044

16 8,888,888

17 5,090,909

18 7,006,060

Let's Practice

Write in standard form.

1. Two hundred thousand, one hundred six
2. Nine million, five hundred twenty
3. Five million, two thousand, twelve

Write in word form.

4. 215,905
5. 819,002
6. 6,430,000
7. 5,009,300

ON YOUR OWN

Go to Workbook A: Practice 1 and 2, pages 1 – 6

Let's Explore!

Can there be numbers less than zero?

1. The table shows the minimum temperature on each day of a week in Chicago.

Day	Mon.	Tue.	Wed.	Thu.	Fri.	Sat.	Sun.
Temperature	–4°C	–14°C	–16°C	–17°C	–5°C	2°C	6°C

A temperature of 2°C means 2 degrees Celsius **above** zero.
A temperature of –4°C means 4 degrees Celsius **below** zero.

–4, –5, –14, –16, and –17 are **negative numbers**. They are used here to show temperatures below 0°C.

2, and 6 are **positive numbers**. They are used here to show temperatures above 0°C.

Positive numbers can be written with a '+' sign in front of them. For example, 2, and 6 can also be written as +2, and +6 respectively. The '+' sign helps to distinguish them from negative numbers.

2 The table shows the heights of four places in relation to sea level.

Place	New Orleans, Louisiana	Death Valley, California	Dead Sea, Israel	Marianas Trench, Pacific Ocean
Height	–6 feet	–282 feet	–1,378 feet	–35,797 feet

The negative heights mean that the places are below sea level.

How many feet below sea level is each place?

Can you think of other examples where negative numbers are used?

Use the Internet to search for more uses of negative numbers.

3 Negative numbers can be shown on a number line in each of these ways.

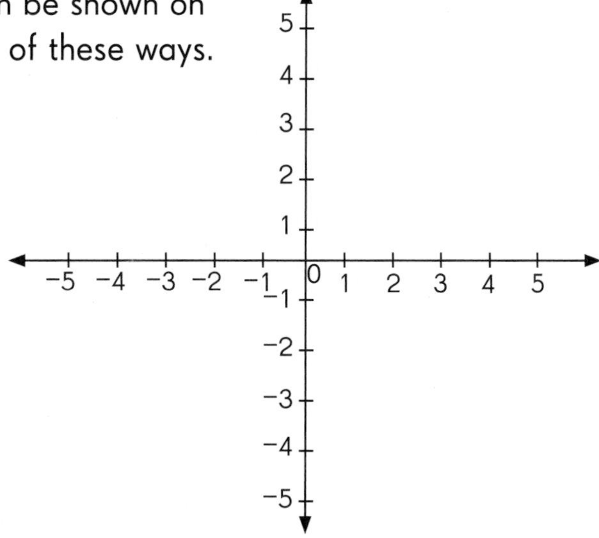

Notice that for every positive number, there is an opposite negative number. For example, 4 and –4 are opposites.

Write the opposite negative number for each positive number.

a 8 **b** 50 **c** 173 **d** 2,469

Lesson 1.2 Place Value

Lesson Objectives

- Identify the place value of any digit in numbers to 10,000,000.
- Read and write numbers to 10,000,000 in expanded form.

Vocabulary
place
value
expanded form

Learn Each digit of a number has a value and a place.

Hundred Thousands	Ten Thousands	Thousands	Hundreds	Tens	Ones
8	6	1	2	5	7

In 861,257:
the digit 8 stands for 800,000.
the value of the digit 8 is 800,000.

the digit 6 stands for 60,000.
the value of the digit 6 is 60,000.

the digit 1 stands for 1,000.
the value of the digit 1 is 1,000.

the digit 8 is in the hundred thousands place.
the digit 6 is in the ten thousands place.
the digit 1 is in the thousands place.

Guided Practice

Complete.

1. In 670,932, the value of the digit 6 is ____.
2. In 937,016, the digit ____ is in the hundreds place.
3. In 124,573, the digit in the hundred thousands place is ____.
4. In 971,465, the digit 6 is in the ____ place.
5. In 289,219, the digit 8 is in the ____ place.

Guided Practice

State the value of the digit 2 in each number.

6. 81**2**,679
7. **2**60,153
8. 8**2**7,917

For each number, state the place the digit 2 is in.

9. 18**2**,679
10. **2**60,153
11. 8**2**7,917

Learn **Numbers to 1,000,000 can be written in expanded form.**

Look at the values of the digits in 381,492. For example, the value of the digit 3 is 300,000. You can add the values of the digits to get the number.

381,492 = 300,000 + 80,000 + 1,000 + 400 + 90 + 2

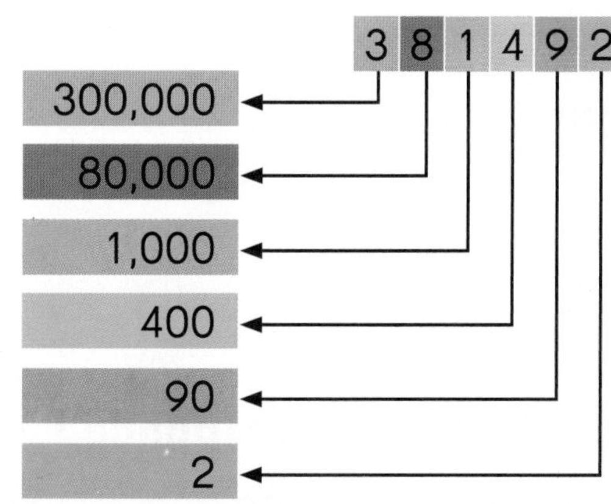

381,492 in expanded form: 300,000 + 80,000 + 1,000 + 400 + 90 + 2

Guided Practice

Complete to express each number in expanded form.

12. 761,902 = 700,000 + ☐ + 1,000 + 900 + 2
13. 124,003 = ☐ + 20,000 + 4,000 + 3
14. 900,356 = 900,000 + 300 + ☐ + 6

Learn Each digit of a number has a value and a place.

Millions	Hundred Thousands	Ten Thousands	Thousands	Hundreds	Tens	Ones
1	6	4	9	0	0	0

In 1,649,000:
the digit 1 stands for 1,000,000.
the value of the digit 1 is 1,000,000.

the digit 1 is in the millions place.
the digit 4 is in the ten thousands place.
the digit 9 is in the thousands place.

Guided Practice

Complete.

15 In 7,296,000:

a the digit ______ is in the millions place.

b the digit 2 stands for ______.

c the digit 9 is in the ______ place.

Learn Numbers to 10,000,000 can be written in expanded form.

5,000,000 ← 5,649,000 = 5,000,000 + 600,000 + 40,000 + 9,000

600,000

40,000

9,000

Complete to express each number in expanded form.

16 7,200,000 = 7,000,000 + ______

17 6,235,000 = ______ + 200,000 + 30,000 + 5,000

18 2,459,000 = 2,000,000 + 400,000 + ______ + 9,000

Let's Practice

State the value of the digit 5 in each number.

1. 64,0**5**1
2. 783,**5**62
3. 1**5**7,300
4. **5**91,368

Complete.

5. In 493,128, the digit ___ is in the ten thousands place.
6. 638,215 = ___ + 30,000 + 8,000 + 200 + 10 + 5
7. In 357,921, the value of the digit 3 is ___ and the digit 7 is in the ___ place.
8. 829,359 = 800,000 + ___ + 9,000 + 300 + 50 + 9

State the value of the digit 6 in each number.

9. **6**,390,000
10. 8,100,**6**00
11. 7,**6**20,548
12. 9,0**6**0,001

Complete.

13. In 7,005,000, the digit ___ is in the millions place.
14. In 2,321,654, the digit in the hundred thousands place is ___.
15. 9,197,328 = 9,000,000 + 100,000 + 90,000 + 7,000 + ___ + 20 + 8
16. 2,403,800 = ___ + 400,000 + 3,000 + 800

ON YOUR OWN

Go to Workbook A: Practice 3, pages 7 – 10

Lesson

1.3 Comparing Numbers to 10,000,000

Lesson Objectives

- Compare and order numbers to 10,000,000.
- Identify and complete a number pattern.
- Find a rule for a number pattern.

Vocabulary
greater than (>)
less than (<)

Learn Compare numbers by using a place-value chart.

Which number is less, 237,981 or 500,600?

When comparing numbers, look at the value of each digit from left to right. Remember, '**>**' means '**greater than**' and '**<**' means '**less than**'.

Hundred Thousands	Ten Thousands	Thousands	Hundreds	Tens	Ones
2	3	7	9	8	1
5	0	0	6	0	0

Compare the values of the digits starting from the left.
2 hundred thousands is less than 5 hundred thousands.
So, 237,981 is less than 500,600.

237,981 < 500,600

Learn Compare numbers greater than 1,000,000.

Which number is less, 3,506,017 or 5,306,007?

Millions	Hundred Thousands	Ten Thousands	Thousands	Hundreds	Tens	Ones
3	5	0	6	0	1	7
5	3	0	6	0	0	7

Compare the values of the digits starting from the left.
3 millions is less than 5 millions.
So, 3,506,017 is less than 5,306,007.

3,506,017 < 5,306,007

Guided Practice

Complete. Use the place-value chart to help you.

1 Which number is greater, 712,935 or 712,846?

Hundred Thousands	Ten Thousands	Thousands	Hundreds	Tens	Ones
7	1	2	**9**	3	5
7	1	2	**8**	4	6

Compare the values of the digits starting from the left. If they are the same, compare the next digits. Continue until the values of the digits are not the same.

Here, the values of the digits in the hundreds place are different.

Compare the values of the digits in the hundreds place.

___ hundreds is greater than ___ hundreds.

So, 712,935 is ___ than 712,846.

712,935 ◯ 712,846

Complete.

2 Which number is greater, 4,730,589 or 4,703,985?
4,7**3**0,589
4,7**0**3,985

Compare the values of the digits starting from the left. If they are the same, compare the next digits. Continue until the values of the digits are not the same.

Here, the values of the digits in the ten thousands place are different.

Compare the values of the digits in the ten thousands place.

___ ten thousands is greater than ___ ten thousands.

So, ___ is greater than ___.

___ > ___.

Compare the numbers. Fill each ◯ with < or >.

3 345,932 ◯ 435,990

4 100,400 ◯ 99,900

5 5,245,721 ◯ 524,572

6 3,143,820 ◯ 4,134,820

Order the numbers from least to greatest.

7. 324,688 32,468 3,246,880

8. 1,600,456 1,604,654 1,064,645

Learn Find rules to complete number patterns.

What is the next number in each pattern?

a. 231,590 331,590 431,590 531,590 ...

To get the next number in the pattern, add 100,000 to the previous number.

231,590 331,590 431,590 531,590 631,590

+100,000 +100,000 +100,000 +100,000

331,590 is 100,000 more than **2**31,590.

431,590 is 100,000 more than **3**31,590.

531,590 is 100,000 more than **4**31,590.

100,000 more than **5**31,590 is **6**31,590.

The next number is 631,590.

b. 755,482 705,482 655,482 605,482 ...

755,482 705,482 655,482 605,482 555,482

–50,000 –50,000 –50,000 –50,000

705,482 is 50,000 less than **75**5,482.

655,482 is 50,000 less than **70**5,482.

605,482 is 50,000 less than **65**5,482.

50,000 less than **60**5,482 is **55**5,482.

The next number is 555,482.

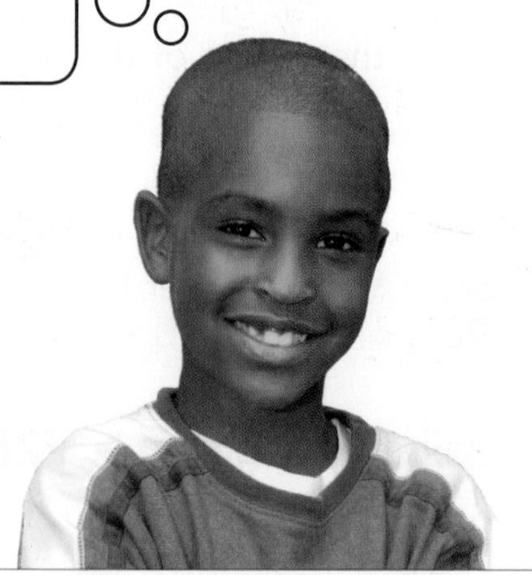

Guided Practice

Find the missing numbers.

9. 1,345,024 3,345,024 5,345,024 ...

   3,345,024 is ___ more than 1,345,024.

   5,345,024 is ___ more than 3,345,024.

   ___ more than 5,345,024 is ___.

   The next number is ___.

10. 820,346 810,346 800,346 ...

    810,346 is ___ less than 820,346.

    800,346 is ___ less than 810,346.

    ___ less than 800,346 is ___.

    The next number is ___.

Let's Practice

Answer each question.

1. Which is greater, 568,912 or 568,921?
2. Which is less, 71,690 or 100,345?
3. Which is the greatest, 81,630, 81,603 or 816,300?
4. Which is the least, 125,000, 12,500 or 25,000?

Order the numbers from least to greatest.

5. 901,736 714,800 199,981
6. 645,321 654,987 645,231

Order the numbers from greatest to least.

7. 36,925 925,360 360,925

8. 445,976 474,089 474,108

Find the missing numbers.

9. 580,356 600,356 620,356 640,356 ...

   600,356 is ____ more than 580,356.

   620,356 is ____ more than 600,356.

   640,356 is ____ more than 620,356.

   ____ more than 640,356 is ____.

10. 4,030,875 3,830,875 3,630,875 3,430,875 ...

   3,830,875 is ____ less than 4,030,875.

   3,630,875 is ____ less than 3,830,875.

   3,430,875 is ____ less than 3,630,875.

   ____ less than 3,430,875 is ____.

Find the rule. Then complete the number pattern.

11. 325,410 ____ 305,410 295,410 ____ 275,410

12. 2,390,000 3,400,000 4,410,000 ____ 6,430,000

ON YOUR OWN

Go to Workbook A: Practice 4, pages 11 – 14

Lesson 1.4 Rounding and Estimating

Lesson Objectives

- Round numbers to the nearest thousand.
- Locate numbers on a number line.
- Use rounding to estimate or check sums, differences, and products.
- Use related multiplication facts to estimate quotients.

Vocabulary
round
estimate
front-end estimation with adjustment
compatible numbers

Learn **Round** numbers to the greater thousand.

What is 6,541 rounded to the nearest thousand?

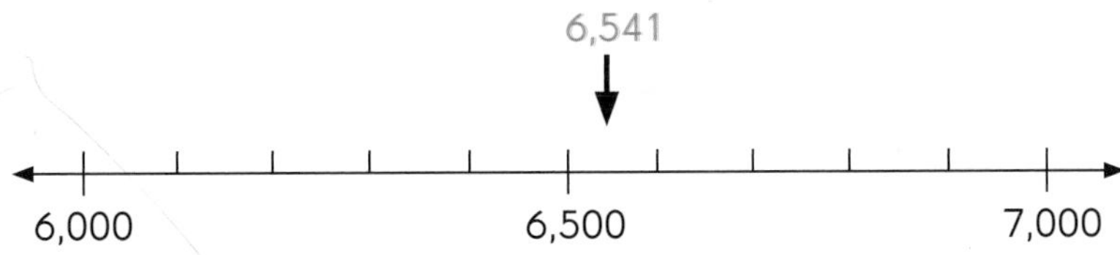

6,541 is between 6,000 and 7,000.
6,541 is nearer to 7,000 than to 6,000.
6,541 rounded to the nearest thousand is 7,000.

Guided Practice

Complete. Use the number line to help you.

1

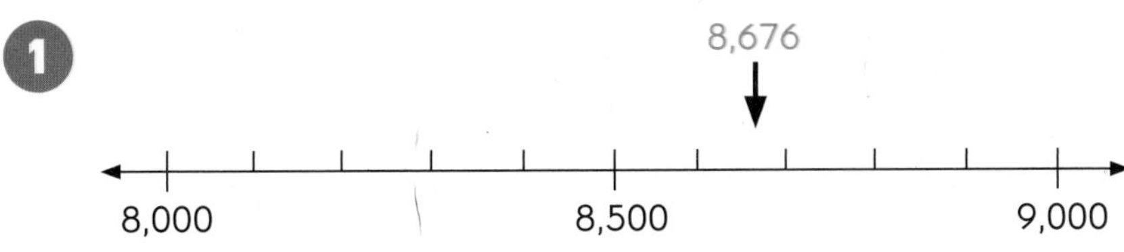

8,676 is between 8,000 and ___.
8,676 is nearer to ___ than to ___.
8,676 rounded to the nearest thousand is ___.

Learn Round numbers to the greater thousand.

What is 9,500 rounded to the nearest thousand?

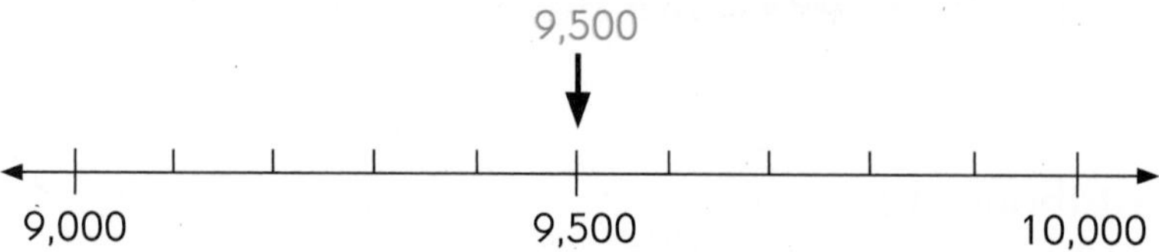

9,500 is exactly halfway between 9,000 and 10,000.
9,500 rounded to the nearest thousand is 10,000.

Guided Practice

Answer each question. Use the number line to help you.

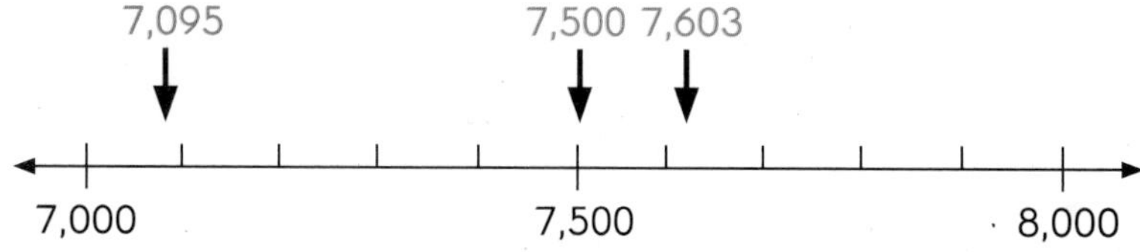

2. What is 7,095 rounded to the nearest thousand?
3. What is 7,500 rounded to the nearest thousand?
4. What is 7,603 rounded to the nearest thousand?

Learn Round numbers to the thousand that is less.

What is 85,210 rounded to the nearest thousand?

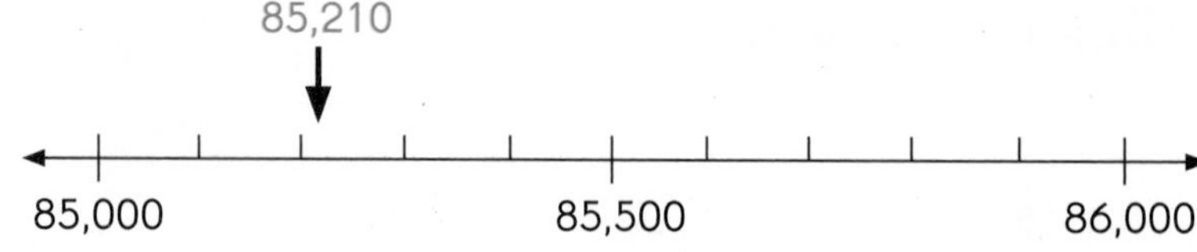

85,210 is between 85,000 and 86,000.
85,210 is nearer to 85,000 than to 86,000.
85,210 rounded to the nearest thousand is 85,000.

Guided Practice

Copy the number line. Use an X to mark the position of 125,231 and 125,780. Then round each number to the nearest thousand.

5

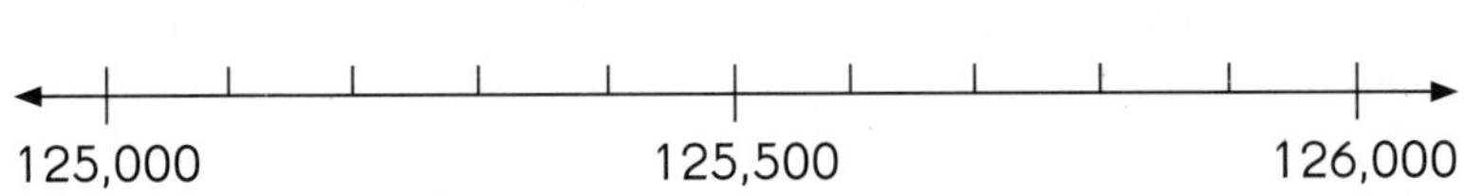

Round each number to the nearest thousand.

6 6,321 7 9,873 8 6,995 9 12,051

10 65,500 11 89,773 12 325,699 13 600,039

Answer each question. Draw a number line to help you.

14 Rounding to the nearest thousand, what is the least number that rounds to

a 4,000? b 80,000?

15 Rounding to the nearest thousand, what is the greatest number that rounds to

a 7,000? b 50,000?

Learn **Use rounding to estimate sums and differences.**

Round the numbers 6,521 and 5,079 to the nearest thousand.

6,521 rounds to 7,000.
5,079 rounds to 5,000.

Then estimate: a 6,521 + 5,079 b 6,521 − 5,079

a 6,521 + 5,079 rounds to 7,000 + 5,000 = 12,000

b 6,521 − 5,079 rounds to 7,000 − 5,000 = 2,000

Guided Practice

Round each number to the nearest thousand. Then estimate the sum or difference.

16. 7,192 + 1,642

17. 5,701 − 3,214

18. 6,290 + 5,500 + 3,719

19. 9,810 − 1,600 − 7,391

Learn Use **front-end estimation with adjustment** to estimate sums.

Estimate the sum of 4,615, 2,537, and 1,828.

Add the values of the leading digits.

4,615 ⟶ **4**,000
2,537 ⟶ **2**,000
1,828 ⟶ **1**,000

4,000 + 2,000 + 1,000 = 7,000

Then, estimate the sum of what is left over to the nearest thousand.

615 + 537 + 828 ⟶ 600 + 500 + 800 = 1,900

1,900 rounded to the nearest thousand is 2,000.

Adjust the estimate.

7,000 + 2,000 = 9,000

The estimated sum is 9,000.

Adjusting the estimate gives you a closer estimate than using only the leading digits.

Learn **Use front-end estimation with adjustment to estimate differences.**

Estimate the difference between 4,837 and 2,152.

Subtract the values of the leading digits.

4,837 → **4**,000
2,152 → **2**,000

4,000 – 2,000 = 2,000

Then, estimate the difference of what is left over to the nearest thousand.

837 – 152 → 800 – 100 = 700

700 rounded to the nearest thousand is 1,000.

Adjust the estimate.

2,000 + 1,000 = 3,000

The estimated difference is 3,000.

Estimate the difference between 5,134 and 2,918.

Subtract the values of the leading digits.

5,134 → **5**,000
2,918 → **2**,000

5,000 – 2,000 = 3,000

Then, estimate the difference of what is left over to the nearest thousand.

918 – 134 → 900 – 100 = 800

800 rounded to the nearest thousand is 1,000.

Adjust the estimate.

3,000 – 1,000 = 2,000

The estimated difference is 2,000.

Guided Practice

Use front-end estimation with adjustment to estimate each sum.

20. 4,261 + 7,879 + 6,175

Add the values of the leading digits.

4,261 → ▢

7,879 → ▢

▢ → ▢

▢ + ▢ + ▢ = ▢

Then, estimate the sum of what is left over to the nearest thousand.

261 + ▢ + ▢ → ▢ + ▢ + ▢ = ▢

▢ rounded to the nearest thousand is ▢.

Adjust the estimate.

▢ + ▢ = ▢

The estimated sum is ▢.

21. 2,619 + 7,391 + 4,738

22. 5,559 + 6,041 + 8,244

23. 3,497 + 7,198 + 8,253

24. 1,864 + 5,907 + 9,541

Guided Practice

Use front-end estimation with adjustment to estimate each difference.

25 9,872 − 2,215

Subtract the values of the leading digits.

9,872 → ____

____ → ____

____ − ____ = ____

Then, estimate the difference of what is left over to the nearest thousand.

872 – ____ → ____ − ____ = ____

____ rounded to the nearest thousand is ____.

Adjust the estimate.

____ + ____ = ____

The estimated difference is ____.

26 3,842 − 1,206

27 5,770 − 2,216

28 8,671 − 4,329

29 6,983 − 3,507

30 7,966 − 2,643

Guided Practice

Use front-end estimation with adjustment to estimate each difference.

31 8,275 − 3,860

Subtract the values of the leading digits.

8,275 → ___

___ → ___

___ − ___ = ___

Then, estimate the difference of what is left over to the nearest thousand.

860 − ___ → ___ − ___ = ___

___ rounded to the nearest thousand is ___.

Adjust the estimate.

___ − ___ = ___

The estimated difference is ___.

32 5,016 − 2,770

33 6,392 − 2,931

34 7,210 − 4,932

35 9,550 − 1,697

Learn Use rounding to estimate products.

Estimate the value of 7,120 × 5.

First, round 7,120 to the nearest thousand.

7,120 rounds to 7,000.

7,000 × 5 = 35,000

7,120 × 5 is about 35,000.

Guided Practice

Estimate the value of 6,327 × 7.

Round the 4-digit
number to the nearest
thousand first.

 6,327 rounds to ____.

 × 7 = ____

6,327 × 7 is about ____.

Estimate each product.

 2,145 × 7

 8,756 × 6

Learn

Use **compatible numbers** to estimate quotients.

Compatible numbers are numbers that are easy to add, subtract, multiply, or divide. They can be used to estimate sums, differences, products, or quotients.

In division, compatible numbers are number pairs that are easy to divide. Such number pairs are obtained from basic facts for division. You can use compatible numbers to estimate quotients.

Estimate the value of 3,465 ÷ 6.

Look for compatible numbers close to 3,465 and 6.

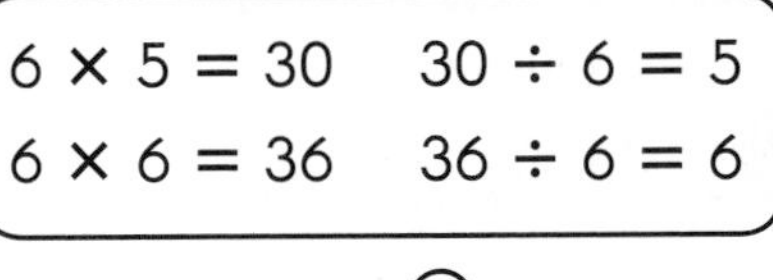

3,000 ÷ **6** = **5**00

3,600 ÷ **6** = **6**00

Compatible number pairs are:

3,000 and 6 or 3,600 and 6

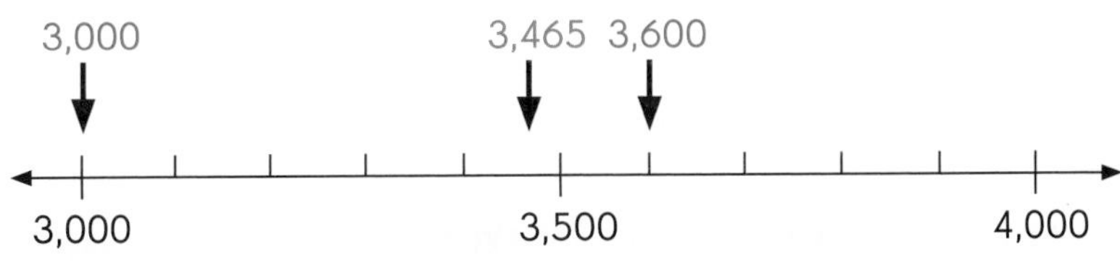

3,465 is nearer to 3,600 than to 3,000.

Choose 3,600 to make this estimate.

3,600 ÷ 6 = 600

3,465 ÷ 6 is about 600.

Guided Practice

Estimate the value of 6,742 ÷ 8.

39

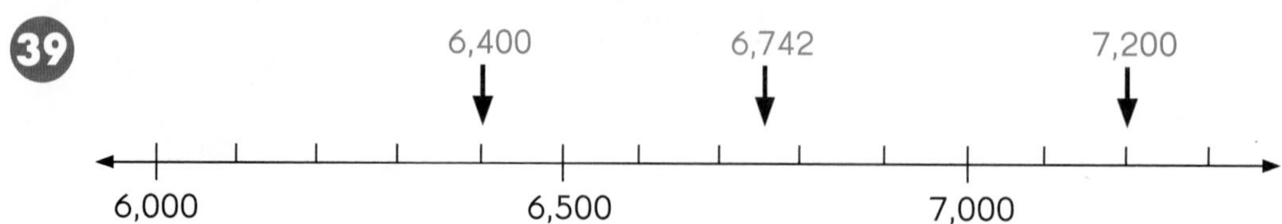

Choose ___ to make the estimate.

___ ÷ 8 = ___

6,742 ÷ 8 is about ___.

Look for compatible numbers.

6,742 ÷ 8 → 6,400 ÷ 8
6,742 ÷ 8 → 7,200 ÷ 8

6,742 is nearer to ___ than to ___.

Estimate each quotient.

40 1,745 ÷ 3

41 4,467 ÷ 6

Let's Practice

Round each number to the nearest thousand.

1 80,295

2 229,078

3 549,947

Answer the question. Draw number lines to help you.

4 Rounding to the nearest thousand, what is

a the least number that rounds to 8,000?

b the greatest number that rounds to 60,000?

Round each number to the nearest thousand. Then estimate the sum or difference.

5 3,670 − 2,189

6 3,638 + 7,917 + 6,148

Use front-end estimation with adjustment to estimate each sum or difference.

7. 7,958 + 5,233 + 4,068
8. 3,725 + 1,882 + 6,536
9. 9,978 − 4,209
10. 8,134 − 4,917

Estimate each product.

11. 3,322 × 8
12. 9,245 × 5

Estimate each quotient.

13. 6,581 ÷ 7
14. 8,502 ÷ 9

ON YOUR OWN
Go to Workbook A:
Practice 5, page 15 – 24

CRITICAL THINKING SKILLS

Put On Your Thinking Cap!

PROBLEM SOLVING

1. Three cards have different whole numbers on them.
   Each number, when rounded to the nearest ten, is 30.
   What can the three numbers be?
2. Without adding the 99s, use a quicker way to find the value of:
   a. 99 + 99
   b. 99 + 99 + 99 + 99 + 99 + 99
   c. What is the value of the digit in the ones place in each case?
   d. What is the least number of 99s which must be added to get a 1 in the ones place?

ON YOUR OWN
Go to Workbook A:
Put on Your Thinking Cap!
pages 25 – 26

Chapter Wrap Up

Study Guide

You have learned...

Numbers to 10,000,000

Write

Standard form:
6,245,781

Word form:
six million, two hundred forty-five thousand, seven hundred eighty-one

Expanded form:
6,245,781 =
6,000,000 +
200,000 + 40,000 +
5,000 +700 + 80 + 1

Compare

Greater than:
9,195,079 > 8,753,426

Less than:
5,187,326 < 7,946,704

Using rounding

Addition:
2,381 + 4,502 rounds to
2,000 + 5,000 = 7,000

Subtraction:
7,185 − 2,738 rounds to
7,000 − 3,000 = 4,000

Multiplication:
3,856 × 7 rounds to
4,000 × 7 = 28,000

Show

Millions	Hundred Thousands	Ten Thousands	Thousands	Hundreds	Tens	Ones
●●● ●●●	● ●	●● ●●	●●● ●●	●●●● ●●●	●●●● ●●●●	●
6	2	4	5	7	8	1

▶ Whole numbers can be written in different ways. Numbers can be compared and rounded, according to their place value.

Find patterns

505,347 605,347 705,347 ...
605,347 is 100,000 more than 505,347.
705,347 is 100,000 more than 605,347.
Rule: Add 100,000 to a number in the pattern to get the next number.

Estimate

Using compatible numbers

Division:
5,456 ÷ 6

4,800 ÷ 6 = 800
5,400 ÷ 6 = 900

5,456 ÷ 6
→ 5,400 ÷ 6 = 900

Using front-end estimation with adjustment

Sum:
5,174 + 1,546 + 7,301
→ 5,000 + 1,000 + 7,000 = 13,000
174 + 546 + 301
→ 100 + 500 + 300 = 900
→ 1,000
13,000 + 1,000 = 14,000

Difference:
5,915 − 3,250
→ 5,000 − 3,000 = 2,000
915 – 250 → 900 − 200 = 700
→ 1,000
2,000 + 1,000 = 3,000

Chapter Review/Test

Vocabulary

Fill in the blanks.

- hundred thousand
- standard form
- word form
- periods
- million
- place-value
- expanded form
- greater than (>)
- less than (<)
- round
- estimate
- front-end estimation with adjustment
- compatible numbers

1. You can read numbers up to 10,000,000 by grouping them into ____ which are groups of three places.

2. The number 2,002,002 in ____ is two ____, two thousand, two.

3. The method shown for estimating 3,924 + 7,806 is called ____.

   3,924 → 3,000
   7,806 → 7,000
   3,000 + 7,000 = 10,000 ← Add the values of the leading digits.

   924 + 806
   → 900 + 800 = 1,700
   → 2,000 ← Estimate the sum of what is left over to the nearest thousand.

   10,000 + 2,000 = 12,000 ← Adjust the estimate.

4. Numbers that are easy to add, subtract, multiply or divide are called ____. In division, they are number pairs that are easy to divide.

Concepts and Skills

Look at the place-value chart. Then complete the sentences.

Millions	Hundred Thousands	Ten Thousands	Thousands	Hundreds	Tens	Ones
●●●●●	●●●●●●●●	●●●●●●●●●	●●●●●●	●●●●	●	●●●

5. Number in standard form: ____

6. Number in word form: ____

7. Number in expanded form: ____

Complete.

Millions	Hundred Thousands	Ten Thousands	Thousands	Hundreds	Tens	Ones
2	9	3	7	0	4	5

In 2,937,045:

8 The digit 9 stands for ____.

9 The value of the digit 2 is ____.

10 The digit 3 is in the ____ place.

Compare the numbers. Fill each ◯ with > or <.

11 8,417,855 ◯ 8,045,762

12 604,259 ◯ 1,105,873

Find the rule. Then complete the number pattern.

13 8,584,671 8,084,671 7,584,671 ____ ____

14 300,534 1,400,534 2,500,534 ____ ____

Round each number to the nearest thousand.

15 1,939

16 527,138

Estimate each sum or difference.

17 8,068 + 2,643

18 5,632 + 2,165 + 7,464

19 3,815 − 1,113

20 5,325 − 1,689

Estimate each product.

21 9,301 × 5

22 3,876 × 6

Estimate each quotient.

23. 6,783 ÷ 8

24. 4,463 ÷ 5

Problem Solving

Use the table to answer each question.

The land areas of some countries are shown below.

Country	Land area (square miles)
Canada	3,851,808
France	211,209
Hong Kong	426
Singapore	268
Thailand	198,456
United States	3,717,811

25. Write the land area of Canada in word form.

26. Order the countries from greatest to least land area.

27. Which countries have a land area greater than 1,000,000 square miles?

28. Which countries have a land area of 200,000 square miles when their land areas are rounded to the nearest hundred thousand square miles?

Whole Number Multiplication and Division

Lessons

2.1 Using a Calculator
2.2 Multiplying by Tens, Hundreds, or Thousands
2.3 Multiplying by 2-Digit Numbers
2.4 Dividing by Tens, Hundreds, or Thousands
2.5 Dividing by 2-Digit Numbers
2.6 Order of Operations
2.7 Real-World Problems: Multiplication and Division

- Patterns can be used to help you multiply and divide numbers.
- Numeric expressions can be simplified using the order of operations.
- Multiplication and division can be used to solve real-world problems.

Recall Prior Knowledge

Writing numbers in expanded form and word form

Write 4,937,512 in expanded form and word form.

Expanded form:
4,000,000 + 900,000 + 30,000 + 7,000 + 500 + 10 + 2

Word form:
Four million, nine hundred thirty-seven thousand, five hundred twelve

Using bar models to show the four operations

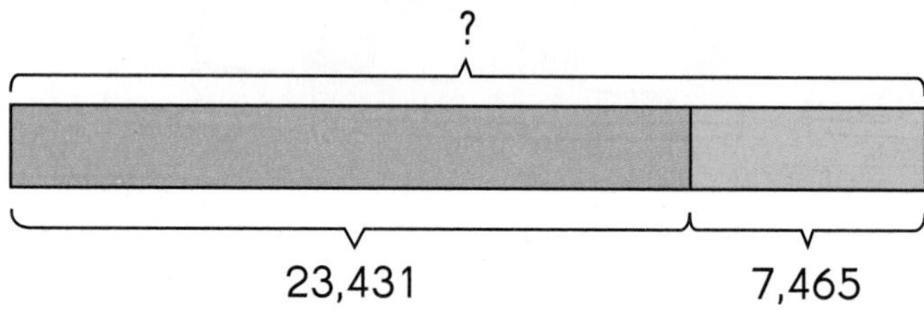

? = 23,431 + 7,465
= 30,896

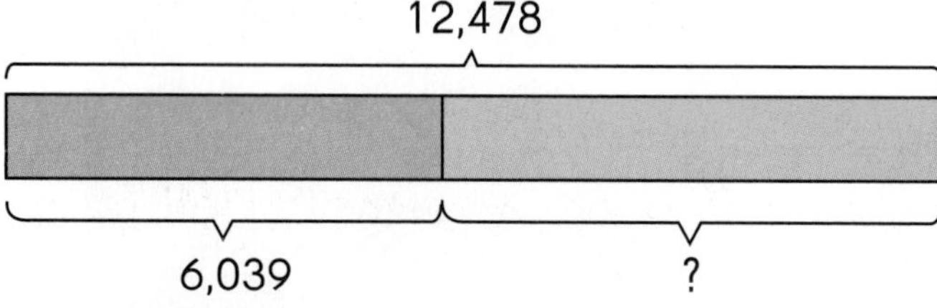

? = 12,478 − 6,039
= 6,439

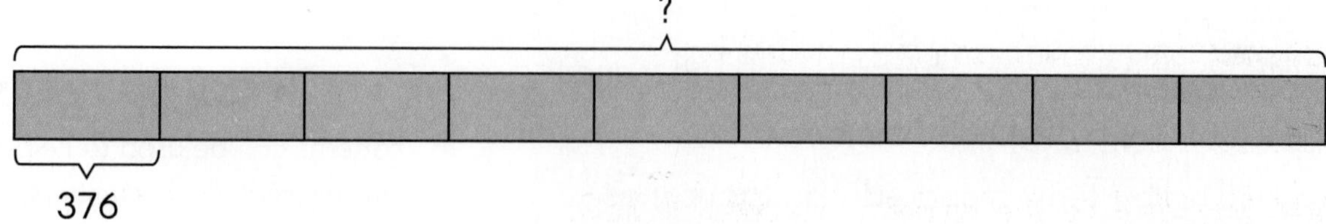

? = 9 × 376
= 3,384

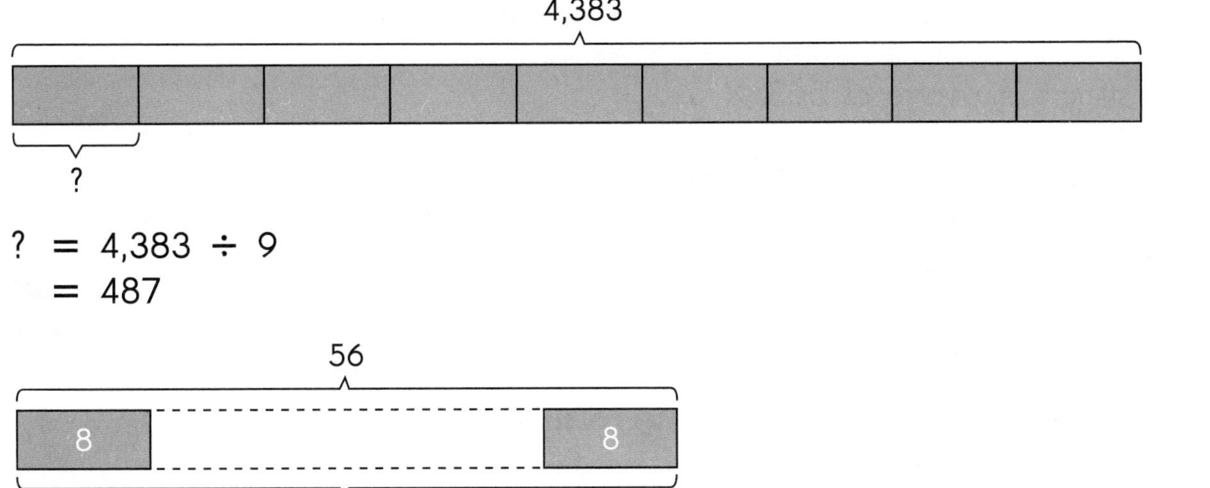

$? = 4{,}383 \div 9$
$= 487$

$? = 56 \div 8$
$= 7$

Rounding to the nearest thousand

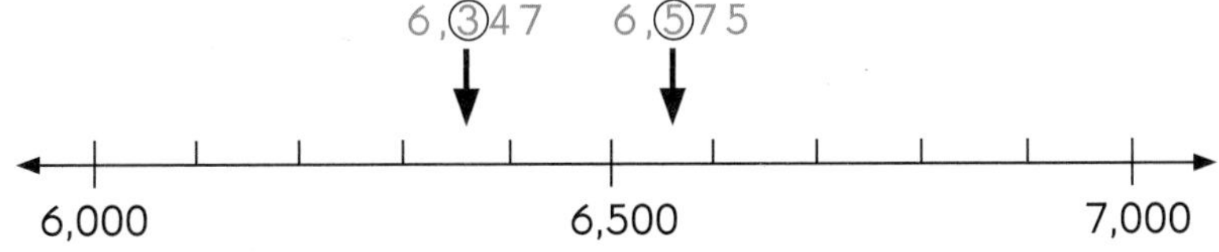

When the hundreds digit is 0, 1, 2, 3, or 4, round the number to the lesser thousand.

6,③47 rounded to the nearest thousand is 6,000.

When the hundreds digit is 5, 6, 7, 8, or 9, round the number to the greater thousand.

6,⑤75 rounded to the nearest thousand is 7,000.

Estimating products by rounding

Estimate the value of 684×9.

684 rounded to the nearest hundred is 700.

$700 \times 9 = 6{,}300$

684×9 is about 6,300.

Estimating products by using front-end estimation

Estimate the value of 563×7.

$563 \rightarrow 500$

$500 \times 7 = 3,500$

563×7 is about 3,500.

Estimating quotients by using related multiplication facts

Estimate the value of $156 \div 4$.

Look for compatible numbers close to 156 and 4.

$4 \times 30 = 120$

$4 \times 40 = 160$

156 is nearer to 160 than to 120.

Choose 160 to make this estimate.

$160 \div 4 = 40$

$156 \div 4$ is about 40.

✔ Quick Check

Write the numbers in expanded form and in word form.

1 8,753,924

Expanded form: ___ + ___ + ___ + ___ + ___ + ___ + ___

Word form: ___

2 5,905,478

Expanded form: ___ + ___ + ___ + ___ + ___ + ___

Word form: ___

Find each missing symbol or number.

3

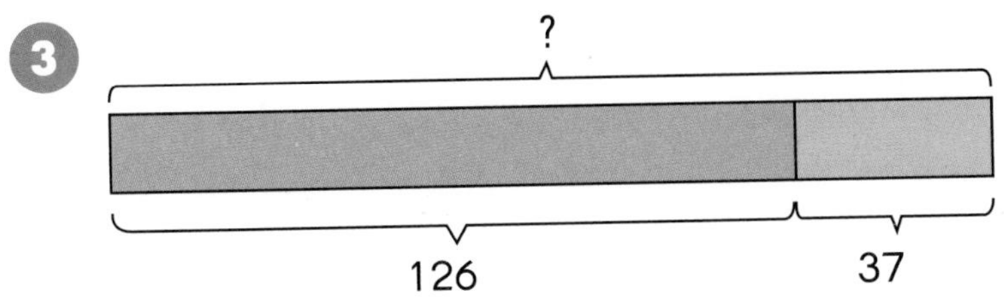

? = 126 ◯ 37

= ▭

4

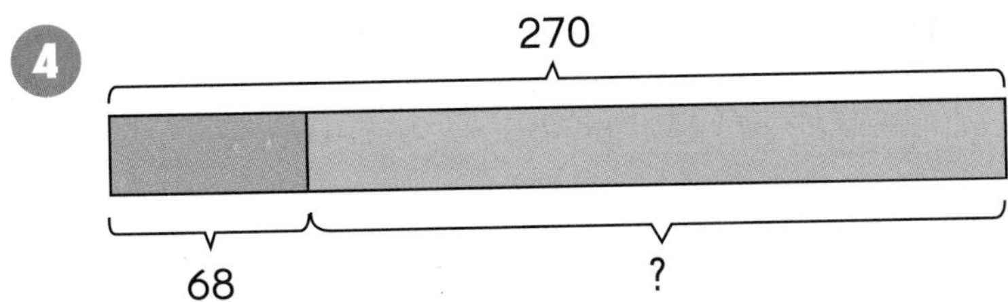

? = 270 ◯ 68

= ▭

5

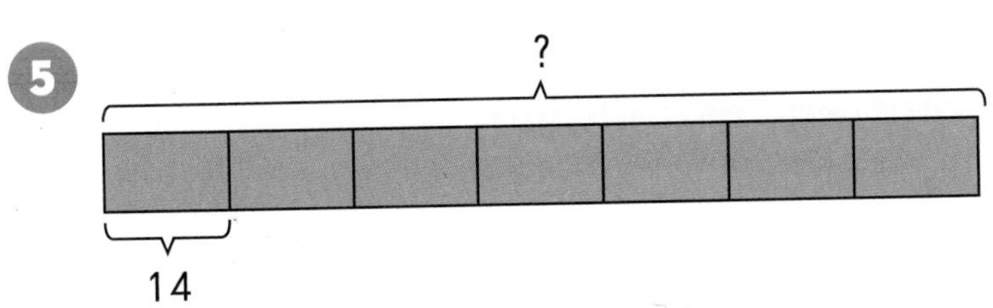

? = 7 ◯ 14

= ▭

6

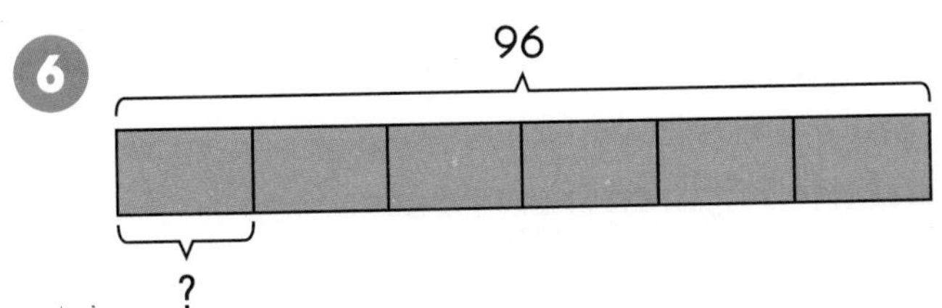

? = 96 ◯ 6

= ▭

7

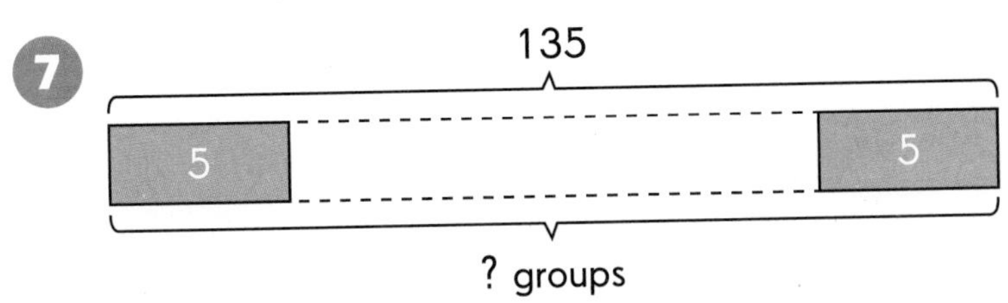

? = 135 ◯ 5

= ▭

Round to the nearest thousand.

8. 750

9. 10,497

10. 14,568

Estimate each product by rounding.

11. 203 × 6

12. 792 × 4

13. 857 × 3

Estimate each product by using front-end estimation.

14. 142 × 9

15. 967 × 5

16. 374 × 6

Estimate each quotient by using related multiplication facts.

17. 178 ÷ 3

18. 265 ÷ 5

19. 532 ÷ 6

Lesson 2.1 Using a Calculator

Lesson Objective

- Use a calculator to add, subtract, multiply, and divide whole numbers.

Learn Get to know your calculator.

Turn on your calculator.

Follow the steps to enter numbers on your calculator.

To enter 12,345, press: [1] [2] [3] [4] [5]

To clear the display on your calculator, press: [C]

Hands-On Activity

Enter these numbers on your calculator. Clear the display on your calculator before entering the next number.

1. 735
2. 9,038
3. 23,104
4. 505,602

Check each number on your calculator with your partner's number. Do both calculators show the same number on the display screen?

Find the missing factors.

7. $8 \times$ ☐ $= 80$

8. $22 \times$ ☐ $= 220$

9. ☐ $\times 10 = 5{,}280$

10. ☐ $\times 10 = 74{,}600$

Learn: Break apart a number to help you multiply by tens.

6 × 20

20		20		20		20		20		20	
10	10	10	10	10	10	10	10	10	10	10	10

$$\begin{aligned}6 \times 20 &= 6 \times 2 \text{ tens}\\ &= (6 \times 2) \times 10\\ &= 12 \times 10\\ &= 120\end{aligned}$$

$$\begin{aligned}27 \times 30 &= 27 \times 3 \text{ tens}\\ &= (27 \times 3) \times 10\\ &= 81 \times 10\\ &= 810\end{aligned}$$

Multiplying a number by 20 is the same as multiplying it by 2 and then by 10.

Multiplying a number by 30 is the same as multiplying it by 3 and then by 10.

Hands-On Activity

Copy and complete the table by multiplying each number by 6 and by 60. An example is shown.

	× 6	× 60
42	252	2,520
65		
861		

Look at the answers in the table. Find the missing numbers.

1. 42 × 60 = (42 × 6) × ▢
2. 65 × 60 = (65 × ▢) × ▢
3. 861 × 60 = (861 × ▢) × ▢

Guided Practice

Find the missing numbers.

11. 62 × 40 = (62 × 4) × 10
    = ▢ × 10
    = ▢

12. 307 × 80 = (307 × ▢) × 10
    = ▢ × 10
    = ▢

Multiply.

13. 274×50

14. $1{,}970 \times 90$

15. $8{,}145 \times 40$

Learn: Look for a pattern in the products when 100 or 1,000 is a factor.

100	100	100	100	100

$5 \times 100 = 500$

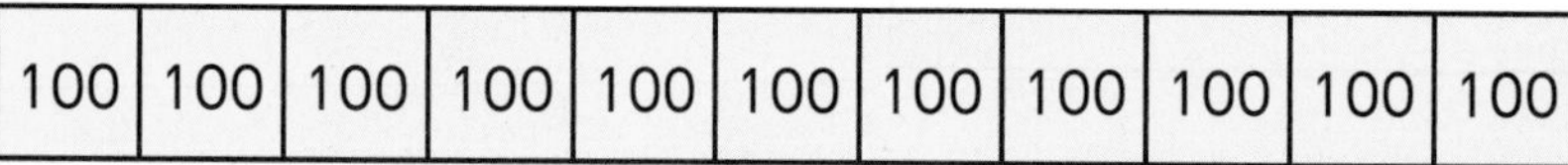

100	100	100	100	100	100	100	100	100	100	100

$11 \times 100 = 1{,}100$

$5 \times 100 = 5$ hundreds
$= 500$

$11 \times 100 = 11$ hundreds
$= 1{,}100$

1,000	1,000	1,000	1,000	1,000

$5 \times 1{,}000 = 5{,}000$

$5 \times 1{,}000 = 5$ thousands
$= 5{,}000$

$11 \times 1{,}000 = 11$ thousands
$= 11{,}000$

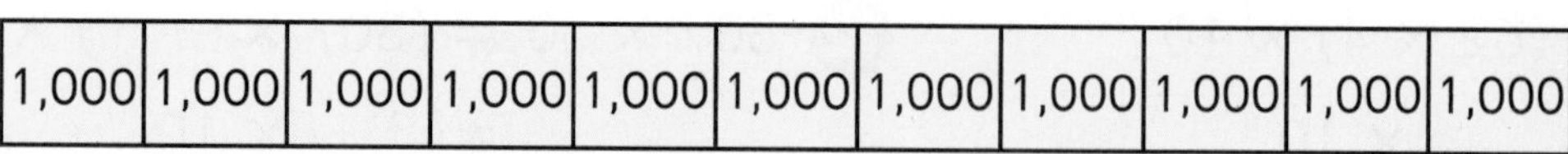

1,000	1,000	1,000	1,000	1,000	1,000	1,000	1,000	1,000	1,000	1,000

$11 \times 1{,}000 = 11{,}000$

Look at the place-value chart.

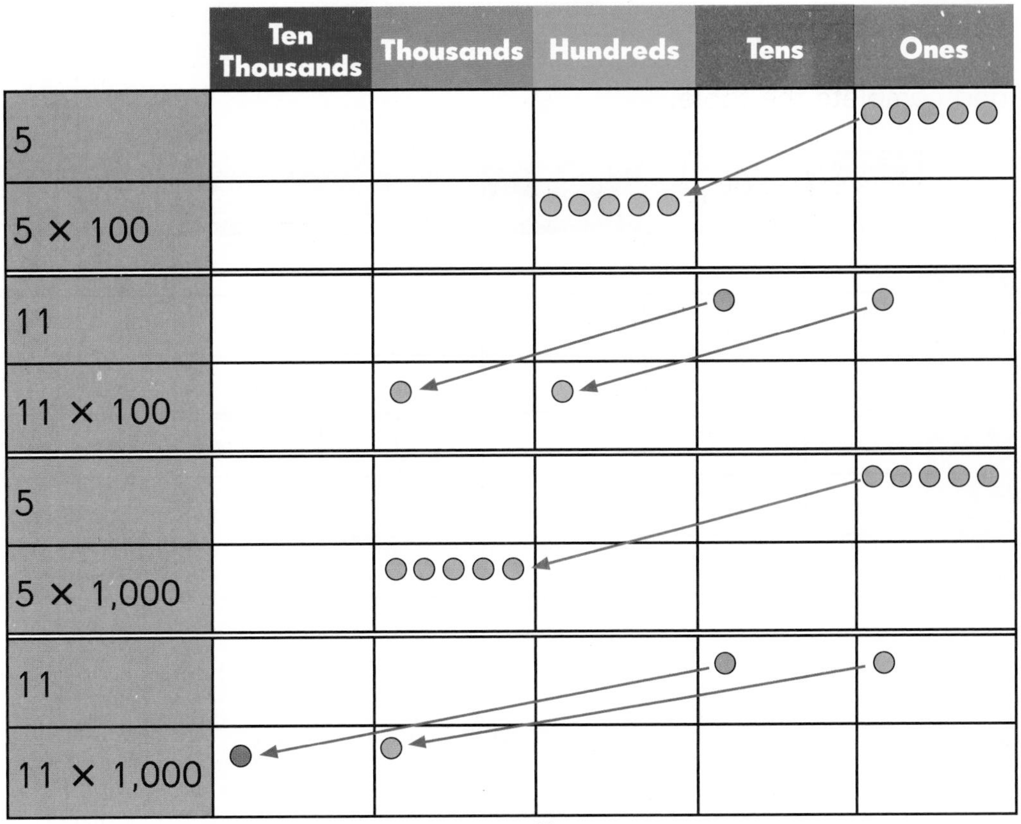

	Ten Thousands	Thousands	Hundreds	Tens	Ones
5					●●●●●
5 × 100			●●●●●		
11				●	●
11 × 100		●	●		
5					●●●●●
5 × 1,000		●●●●●			
11				●	●
11 × 1,000	●	●			

	Ten Thousands	Thousands	Hundreds	Tens	Ones
5					5
5 × 100			5	0	0
11				1	1
11 × 100		1	1	0	0
5					5
5 × 1,000		5	0	0	0
11				1	1
11 × 1,000	1	1	0	0	0

Each digit moves two places to the left when the number is multiplied by 100.
Each digit moves three places to the left when the number is multiplied by 1,000.

Hands-On Activity

Copy and complete the table.

	Millions	Hundred Thousands	Ten Thousands	Thousands	Hundreds	Tens	Ones
174					1	7	4
174 × 100			1	7	4	0	0
174 × 1,000		1	7	4	0	0	0
3,298				3	2	9	8
3,298 × 100							
3,298 × 1,000							

Write the products.

1. 174 × 100
2. 174 × 1,000
3. 3,298 × 100
4. 3,298 × 1,000

What rule can you use when you multiply a whole number by 100?

What rule can you use when you multiply a whole number by 1,000?

Guided Practice

Multiply.

16. 27 × 100
17. 615 × 100
18. 9,670 × 100
19. 18 × 1,000
20. 487 × 1,000
21. 5,346 × 1,000

Find the missing factors.

22. 26 × ___ = 2,600
23. 195 × ___ = 195,000
24. ___ × 100 = 49,000
25. ___ × 1,000 = 168,000

Learn

Break apart a number to help you multiply by hundreds or thousands.

7 × 200

200		200		200		200		200		200		200	
100	100	100	100	100	100	100	100	100	100	100	100	100	100

7 × 200 = 7 × 2 hundreds
= (7 × 2) × 100
= 14 × 100
= 1,400

67 × 5,000 = 67 × 5 thousands
= (67 × 5) × 1,000
= 335 × 1,000
= 335,000

Multiplying a number by 200 is the same as multiplying it by 2 and then by 100.

Multiplying a number by 5,000 is the same as multiplying it by 5 and then by 1,000.

Hands-On Activity

Copy and complete the table by multiplying each number by 7, 700, and 7,000. An example is shown.

	× 7	× 700	× 7,000
78	546	54,600	546,000
113			
251			

Look at the answers in the table. Find the missing numbers.

1. 78 × 700 = (78 × 7) × ▭
2. 113 × 700 = (113 × ▭) × ▭
3. 251 × 700 = (251 × ▭) × ▭
4. 78 × 7,000 = (78 × 7) × ▭
5. 113 × 7,000 = (113 × ▭) × ▭
6. 251 × 7,000 = (251 × ▭) × ▭

Guided Practice

Find the missing numbers.

26. 72 × 400 = (72 × 4) × 100
    = ▭ × 100
    = ▭

27. 123 × 700 = (123 × ▭) × ▭
    = ▭ × 100
    = ▭

Find the missing numbers.

28. $6 \times 5{,}000 = (6 \times 5) \times 1{,}000$
$= \square \times 1{,}000$
$= \square$

29. $18 \times 6{,}000 = (18 \times \square) \times \square$
$= \square \times 1{,}000$
$= \square$

Multiply.

30. 81×500

31. 932×800

32. $6{,}455 \times 900$

33. $6{,}007 \times 800$

34. $73 \times 4{,}000$

35. $905 \times 8{,}000$

36. $654 \times 3{,}000$

37. $807 \times 9{,}000$

Learn

Round factors to the nearest ten or hundred to estimate products.

Estimate the product of 632 and 26.

Round 632 to the nearest hundred.

Round 26 to the nearest ten.

632 rounds to 600, and 26 rounds to 30.

$600 \times 30 = (600 \times 3) \times 10$
$= 1{,}800 \times 10$
$= 18{,}000$

The product is about 18,000.

Guided Practice

Estimate.

38 Estimate the product of 228 and 57.

Round 228 to the nearest hundred.
Round 57 to the nearest ten.
228 rounds to ___, and 57 rounds to 60.

___ × 60 = (___ × 6) × 10
= ___ × 10
= ___

39 702 × 15

40 27 × 364

41 38 × 246

42 851 × 19

43 511 × 62

44 35 × 424

Learn **Round factors to the nearest ten or thousand to estimate products.**

A museum gift shop sold 1,215 sets of dinosaur models.
There were 26 dinosaur models in each set.
Estimate the total number of dinosaur models the shop sold.

Round 1,215 to the nearest thousand.
Round 26 to the nearest ten.
1,215 rounds to 1,000, and 26 rounds to 30.

1,000 × 30 = (1,000 × 3) × 10
= 3,000 × 10
= 30,000

The shop sold about 30,000 dinosaur models.

Guided Practice

Estimate.

45 Estimate the product of 1,238 and 56.

Round 1,238 to the nearest thousand.
Round 56 to the nearest ten.
1,238 rounds to 1,000, and 56 rounds to ___.

1,000 × ___ = (1,000 × ___) × ___

= ___ × ___

= ___

46 99 × 38

47 67 × 439

48 9,281 × 32

49 2,065 × 41

Let's Practice

Multiply.

1 412 × 10

2 792 × 100

3 740 × 1,000

4 703 × 60

5 815 × 700

6 169 × 3,000

Estimate each product.

7 3,711 × 9

8 2,087 × 37

9 1,985 × 302

Solve.

10 A factory produces 452 beads in 1 minute.
Estimate the number of beads the factory produces in 56 minutes.

ON YOUR OWN
**Go to Workbook A:
Practice 2, pages 29–36**

Multiply. Estimate to check if your answers are reasonable.

11. 681 × 60
12. 210 × 80
13. 651 × 70
14. 413 × 12
15. 516 × 21
16. 294 × 48

Learn Multiply a 4-digit number by tens.

Multiply 7,360 by 20.

Method 1

$$7{,}360 \times 20 = (7{,}360 \times 2) \times 10$$
$$= 14{,}720 \times 10$$
$$= 147{,}200$$

7,360 × 20 is the same as 7,360 × 2 tens.

7,360 × 2 tens = 14,720 tens
= 14,720 × 10
= 147,200

Method 2

```
      7, 3 6 0
×          2 0
--------------
  1 4 7, 2 0 0
```

```
      1
   7, 3 6 0
×         2
-----------
 1 4, 7 2 0
```

Learn Multiply a 4-digit number by a 2-digit number.

Multiply 5,362 by 76.

```
     2  4  1
     2  3  1
     5, 3  6  2
×           7  6
----------------
   3 2, 1  7  2  ← multiply 5,362 by 6 ones
 3 7 5, 3  4  0  ← multiply 5,362 by 7 tens
----------------
 4 0 7, 5  1  2  ← add
```

Estimate the value of 5,362 × 76.
5,362 rounds to 5,000.
76 rounds to 80.
5,000 × 80 = 400,000
The estimate shows the answer 407,512 is reasonable.

Guided Practice

Multiply. Show your work.

17
$$\begin{array}{r} 9\,2\,0\,5 \\ \times \quad 2\,4 \\ \hline \square \\ \square \\ \hline \square \end{array}$$

← multiply 9,205 by ___ ones
← multiply 9,205 by ___ tens
← add

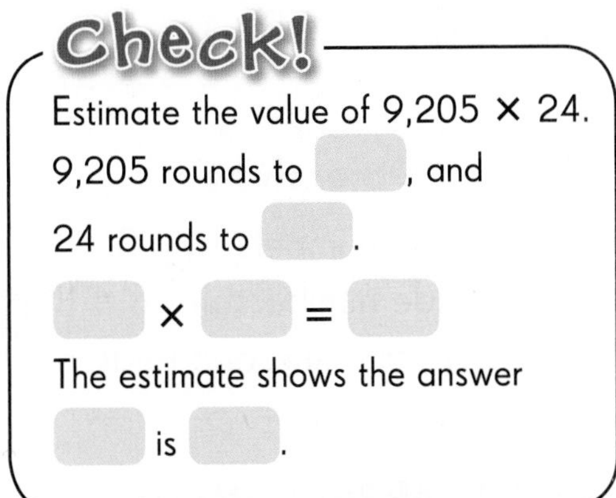

Check!
Estimate the value of 9,205 × 24.
9,205 rounds to ___, and
24 rounds to ___.
___ × ___ = ___
The estimate shows the answer
___ is ___.

Multiply. Estimate to check if your answers are reasonable.

18 1,246 × 50

19 5,913 × 60

20 3,352 × 14

21 9,540 × 36

22 1,598 × 72

23 2,535 × 47

Let's Practice

Multiply. Estimate to check if your answers are reasonable.

1 20 × 30

2 41 × 70

3 300 × 50

4 430 × 80

5 413 × 90

6 2,000 × 70

7 3,700 × 40

8 2,550 × 60

9 56 × 32

10 26 × 76

11 589 × 77

12 817 × 69

13 3,438 × 81

14 1,256 × 45

ON YOUR OWN

Go to Workbook A: Practice 3, pages 37–42

Lesson 2.4 Dividing by Tens, Hundreds, or Thousands

Lesson Objectives

- Divide numbers by 10, 100, or 1,000 using patterns.
- Divide numbers up to 4 digits by multiples of 10, 100, or 1,000.
- Use rounding and related multiplication facts to estimate quotients.

Vocabulary
quotients
dividend
divisor

Learn Look for patterns when dividing by 10.

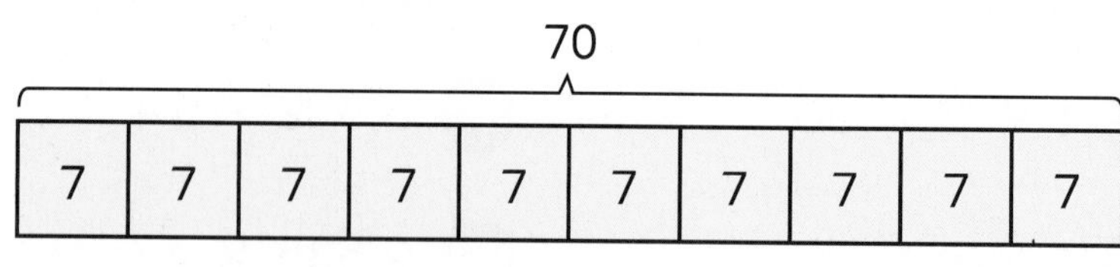

7 × 10 = 70
So, 70 ÷ 10 = 7.

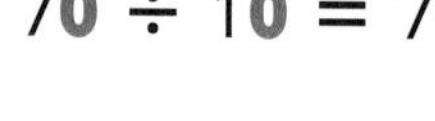

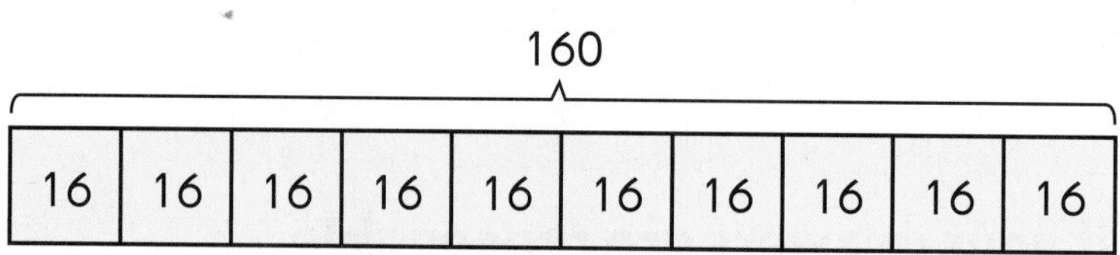

160 ÷ 10 = 16

16 × 10 = 160
So, 160 ÷ 10 = 16.

180	180	180	180	180	180	180	180	180	180

(Total: 1,800)

1,800 ÷ 10 = 180

180 × 10 = 1,800
So, 1,800 ÷ 10 = 180.

Look at the place-value chart.

	Thousands	Hundreds	Tens	Ones
70			●●●●●●●	
70 ÷ 10				●●●●●●●
160		●	●●●●●●	
160 ÷ 10			●	●●●●●●
1,800	●	●●●●●●●●		
1,800 ÷ 10		●	●●●●●●●●	

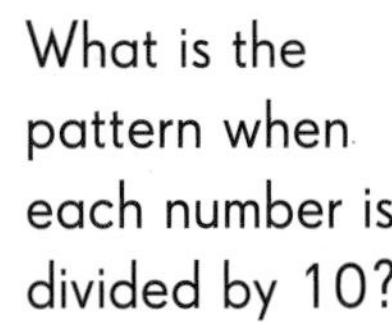

What is the pattern when each number is divided by 10?

	Thousands	Hundreds	Tens	Ones
70			7	0
70 ÷ 10				7
160		1	6	0
160 ÷ 10			1	6
1,800	1	8	0	0
1,800 ÷ 10		1	8	0

Each digit moves one place to the right when the number is divided by 10.

Hands-On Activity

Copy and complete the table.

	Thousands	Hundreds	Tens	Ones
360		3	6	0
360 ÷ 10			3	6
1,580	1	5	8	0
1,580 ÷ 10				

Write the quotients.

1. 360 ÷ 10
2. 1,580 ÷ 10

Guided Practice

To divide a whole number with 0 in the ones place by 10, just drop the zero.
3,740 ÷ 10 = 374

Divide.

1. 90 ÷ 10
2. 380 ÷ 10
3. 1,900 ÷ 10
4. 43,650 ÷ 10
5. 23,040 ÷ 10
6. 53,600 ÷ 10

Find the missing numbers.

7. 2,600 ÷ ___ = 260
8. 19,500 ÷ ___ = 1,950
9. ___ ÷ 10 = 4,900
10. ___ ÷ 10 = 1,680

Learn Break apart a number to help you divide by tens.

$$60 \div 30 = (60 \div 10) \div 3$$
$$= 6 \div 3$$
$$= 2$$

Dividing a number by 30 is the same as dividing it by 10 and then by 3.

$$420 \div 70 = (420 \div 10) \div 7$$
$$= 42 \div 7$$
$$= 6$$

Hands-On Activity

Copy and complete the table by dividing each number by 9 and by 90. An example is shown.

	÷9	÷90
540	60	6
720		
810		

Look at the answers in the table. Find the missing numbers.

1. $540 \div 90 = (540 \div \square) \div 9$
2. $720 \div 90 = (720 \div \square) \div \square$
3. $810 \div 90 = (810 \div \square) \div \square$

Guided Practice

Find the missing numbers.

11 $850 \div 50 = (850 \div 10) \div 5$

$= \square \div 5$

$= \square$

12 $7{,}200 \div 80 = (7{,}200 \div \square) \div \square$

$= \square \div 8$

$= \square$

Divide.

13 $160 \div 40$

14 $700 \div 50$

15 $6{,}320 \div 20$

16 $8{,}400 \div 60$

Learn

Look for patterns when dividing by 100 or 1,000.

$9 \times 100 = 900$

So, $900 \div 100 = 9$.

$14 \times 100 = 1{,}400$

So, $1{,}400 \div 100 = 14$.

$9 \times 1{,}000 = 9{,}000$

So, $9{,}000 \div 1{,}000 = 9$.

$14 \times 1{,}000 = 14{,}000$

So, $14{,}000 \div 1{,}000 = 14$.

Look at the place-value chart.

	Ten Thousands	Thousands	Hundreds	Tens	Ones
900			○○○○○ ○○○○		
900 ÷ 100					○○○○○ ○○○○
1,400		○	○○○○		
1,400 ÷ 100				○	○○○○
9,000		○○○○○ ○○○○			
9,000 ÷ 1,000					○○○○○ ○○○○
14,000	○	○○○○			
14,000 ÷ 1,000				○	○○○○

What is the pattern when each number is divided by **100** and by **1,000**?

	Ten Thousands	Thousands	Hundreds	Tens	Ones
900			9	0	0
900 ÷ 100					9
1,400		1	4	0	0
1,400 ÷ 100				1	4
9,000		9	0	0	0
9,000 ÷ 1,000					9
14,000	1	4	0	0	0
14,000 ÷ 1,000				1	4

Each digit moves two places to the right when the number is divided by 100.
Each digit moves three places to the right when the number is divided by 1,000.

Hands-On Activity

Copy and complete the table.

	Ten Thousands	Thousands	Hundreds	Tens	Ones
700			7	0	0
700 ÷ 100					7
3,600		3	6	0	0
3,600 ÷ 100					
8,000		8	0	0	0
8,000 ÷ 1,000					
54,000	5	4	0	0	0
54,000 ÷ 1,000					

Write the quotients.

1. 700 ÷ 100
2. 3,600 ÷ 100
3. 8,000 ÷ 1,000
4. 54,000 ÷ 1,000

What rule can you use when you divide a multiple of 100 by 100?

What rule can you use when you divide a multiple of 1,000 by 1,000?

Guided Practice

Divide.

17. $400 \div 100$
18. $1{,}500 \div 100$
19. $20{,}500 \div 100$
20. $10{,}000 \div 1{,}000$
21. $124{,}000 \div 1{,}000$
22. $3{,}230{,}000 \div 1{,}000$

Learn

Break apart a number to help you divide by hundreds or thousands.

$$600 \div 300 = (600 \div 100) \div 3$$
$$= 6 \div 3$$
$$= 2$$

$$6{,}000 \div 2{,}000 = (6{,}000 \div 1{,}000) \div 2$$
$$= 6 \div 2$$
$$= 3$$

Dividing a number by 300 is the same as dividing it by 100 and then by 3.

Dividing a number by 2,000 is the same as dividing it by 1,000 and then by 2.

Hands-On Activity

Copy and complete the table by dividing each number by 6 and by 600. An example is shown.

	÷6	÷600
1,200	200	2
4,200		
5,400		

Look at the answers in the table. Find the missing numbers.

1. 1,200 ÷ 600 = (1,200 ÷ ___) ÷ 6
2. 4,200 ÷ 600 = (4,200 ÷ ___) ÷ ___
3. 5,400 ÷ 600 = (5,400 ÷ ___) ÷ ___

Copy and complete the table by dividing each number by 8 and by 8,000. An example is shown.

	÷8	÷8,000
32,000	4,000	4
48,000		
64,000		

Look at the answers in the table. Find the missing numbers.

1. 32,000 ÷ 8,000 = (32,000 ÷ ___) ÷ 8
2. 48,000 ÷ 8,000 = (48,000 ÷ ___) ÷ ___
3. 64,000 ÷ 8,000 = (64,000 ÷ ___) ÷ ___

Guided Practice

Find the missing numbers.

23 2,400 ÷ 400

= (2,400 ÷ 100) ÷ 4

= ___ ÷ 4

= ___

24 35,000 ÷ 7,000

= (35,000 ÷ 1,000) ÷ 7

= ___ ÷ 7

= ___

Divide.

25 800 ÷ 200

26 5,400 ÷ 600

27 7,200 ÷ 900

28 18,000 ÷ 3,000

29 45,000 ÷ 5,000

30 102,000 ÷ 2,000

Learn **Round numbers to estimate quotients.**

Estimate 1,728 ÷ 38.

divisor → $38\overline{)1,728}$ ← dividend

The number that is being divided is the **dividend**.
The number that the dividend is being divided by is the **divisor**.

To estimate 1,728 ÷ 38, round the divisor 38 to 40, and choose a number close to the dividend 1,728 that can be evenly divided by 40.

38 rounds to 40.
1,728 is nearer to 1,600 than to 2,000.

1,600 ÷ 40 = (1,600 ÷ 10) ÷ 4
= 160 ÷ 4
= 40

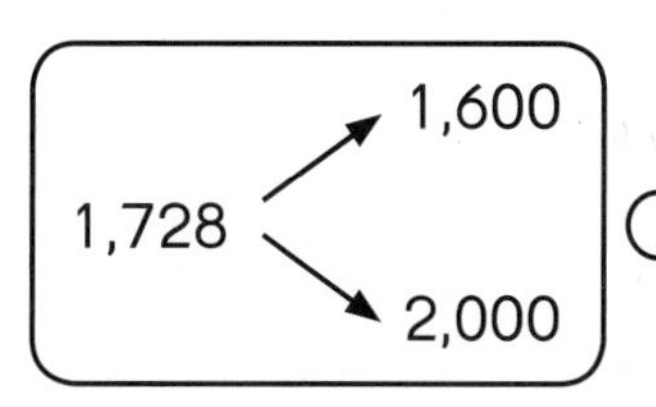

1,728 ÷ 38 is about 40.

Guided Practice

Estimate.

31 Estimate the quotient of 4,367 divided by 670.
670 rounds to 700.
4,367 is nearer to 4,200 than to 4,900.

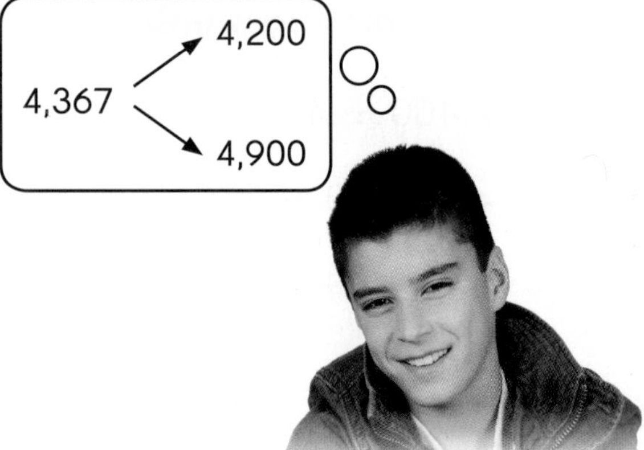

▢ ÷ 700 = (▢ ÷ ▢) ÷ 7
= ▢

32 987 ÷ 17

33 6,106 ÷ 28

34 4,932 ÷ 96

35 3,785 ÷ 379

Hands-On Activity

Find three whole numbers that can evenly divide each number shown. The whole numbers or divisors must be multiples of ten, a hundred, or a thousand. Use different divisors for each number in the list.

4,500 420 2,000 40 88,000

An example is shown.

Number	Can be divided by	Answer
4,500	10	4,500 ÷ 10 = 450
4,500	30	4,500 ÷ 30 = 150
4,500	500	4,500 ÷ 500 = 9

Discuss with your partner how you can find these quotients.

1. 43 ÷ 10
2. 735 ÷ 100

Use the following table to help you.

Thousands	Hundreds	Tens	Ones	Tenths	Hundredths

Let's Practice

Divide.

1. 870 ÷ 10
2. 9,000 ÷ 10
3. 7,100 ÷ 100
4. 82,000 ÷ 100
5. 3,000 ÷ 1,000
6. 97,000 ÷ 1,000
7. 500 ÷ 20
8. 7,070 ÷ 70
9. 8,100 ÷ 300
10. 65,600 ÷ 800
11. 6,000 ÷ 3,000
12. 54,000 ÷ 9,000

Estimate.

13. 6,726 ÷ 19
14. 4,008 ÷ 12

ON YOUR OWN

Go to Workbook A: Practice 4, pages 43–48

Lesson 2.5 Dividing by 2-Digit Numbers

Lesson Objective

- Divide a 2-, 3-, or 4-digit number by a 2-digit number.

Vocabulary
remainder

Learn Use different methods to divide by tens.

Divide 180 by 20.

Method 1

18~~0~~ ÷ 2~~0~~ = 9

18 tens ÷ 2 tens
= 18 ÷ 2
= 9

Method 2

```
         9
2 0 ) 1 8 0
      1 8 0  ← 9 × 20
      -----
          0
```

Use Method 2 when the dividend cannot be evenly divided by the divisor.
For 180 ÷ 40, dropping the zeros gives an incorrect **remainder**.

Incorrect

2 is the remainder.
18~~0~~ ÷ 4~~0~~ = 4 R 2

```
      4
4 ) 1 8
    1 6
    ---
      2
```

Correct

20 is the remainder.
180 ÷ 40 = 4 R 20

```
          4
4 0 ) 1 8 0
      1 6 0
      -----
        2 0
```

Guided Practice

Divide.

 1. 240 ÷ 80 = ___  2. 4,000 ÷ 50 = ___  3. 5,200 ÷ 90 = ___

Learn Divide a 2-digit number by a 2-digit number.

Divide 83 by 15.

15 rounds to 20.

Estimate the quotient.
$4 \times 20 = 80$

$$20\overline{)83} \quad \text{quotient } 4$$

$$\begin{array}{r} 4 \\ 15\overline{)83} \\ 60 \\ \hline 23 \end{array}$$

← This should be less than 15.

The estimated quotient is too small. Try 5.

$$\begin{array}{r} 5 \text{ R } 8 \\ 15\overline{)83} \\ 75 \\ \hline 8 \end{array}$$

The quotient is 5 and the remainder is 8.

Divide 88 by 23.

23 rounds to 20.

Estimate the quotient.
$4 \times 20 = 80$

$$20\overline{)88} \quad \text{quotient } 4$$

$$\begin{array}{r} 4 \\ 23\overline{)88} \\ 92 \\ \hline \end{array}$$

← This should be less than 88.

The estimated quotient is too big. Try 3.

$$\begin{array}{r} 3 \text{ R } 19 \\ 23\overline{)88} \\ 69 \\ \hline 19 \end{array}$$

The quotient is 3 and the remainder is 19.

Guided Practice

4 **Divide 65 by 16.**

16 rounds to ___.

Estimate the quotient.

3 × ___ = ___

```
        3
___ ) 6 5
```

```
         3
1 6 ) 6 5
      ___
      ___
```

The estimated quotient is too ___. Try ___.

```
      ___ R ___
1 6 ) 6 5
      ___
      ___
```

The quotient is ___ and the remainder is ___.

5 **Divide 94 by 32.**

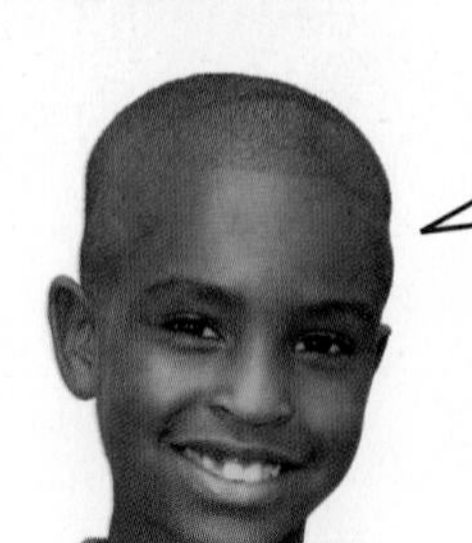

32 rounds to ___.

Estimate the quotient.

3 × ___ = ___

```
        3
___ ) 9 4
```

```
         3
3 2 ) 9 4
      ___
```

The estimated quotient is too ___. Try ___.

```
      ___ R ___
3 2 ) 9 4
      ___
      ___
```

The quotient is ___ and the remainder is ___.

Guided Practice

Divide.

6. 65 ÷ 16
7. 69 ÷ 17
8. 64 ÷ 12

Learn Divide a 3-digit number by a 2-digit number.

Divide 235 by 32.

```
        7 R 11
3 2 ) 2 3 5
      2 2 4  ← 7 × 32
      -----
        1 1
```

The quotient is 7 and the remainder is 11.

32 rounds to 30.

Estimate the quotient.
$7 \times 30 = 210$
$8 \times 30 = 240$

The quotient is about 7.

Guided Practice

Divide. Show your work.

9.
```
           ___ R ___
7 5 )  6    1    2
      ___  ___  ___
      -------------
           ___  ___
```

The quotient is ___ and the remainder is ___.

75 rounds to 80.

Estimate the quotient.
$7 \times 80 = 560$
$8 \times 80 = 640$

The quotient is about ___.

Divide.

10. 153 ÷ 27
11. 270 ÷ 39
12. 661 ÷ 74
13. 802 ÷ 92

Learn Divide the tens before dividing the ones.

Divide 765 by 23.

```
        3 3 R 6
 2 3 ) 7 6 5
       6 9     ← 23 × 3 tens
       -----
         7 5
         6 9   ← 23 × 3
       -----
           6
```

7 hundreds 6 tens = 76 tens
76 tens ÷ 23 = 3 tens R 7 tens

7 tens 5 ones = 75 ones
75 ÷ 23 = 3 R 6

The quotient is 33 and the remainder is 6.

Guided Practice

Divide. Show your work.

14

```
          ___ ___ R ___
 2 1 )  3   1   7
       ___ ___       ← 21 × ___ tens
       -----------
       ___ ___ ___
       ___ ___ ___   ← 21 × ___
       -----------
               ___
```

The quotient is ___ and the remainder is ___.

Divide.

15 153 ÷ 11

16 271 ÷ 14

17 837 ÷ 67

18 963 ÷ 27

Learn Divide a 4-digit number by a 2-digit number.

Divide 6,118 by 75.

```
       8 1 R 43
75 ) 6,1 1 8
     6 0 0   ← 75 × 8 tens
     -----
       1 1 8
         7 5 ← 75 × 1
       -----
         4 3
```

6 thousands 1 hundred 1 ten = 611 tens
611 tens ÷ 75 = 8 tens R 11 tens

11 tens 8 ones = 118 ones
118 ÷ 75 = 1 R 43

The quotient is 81 and the remainder is 43.

Guided Practice

Divide. Show your work.

19

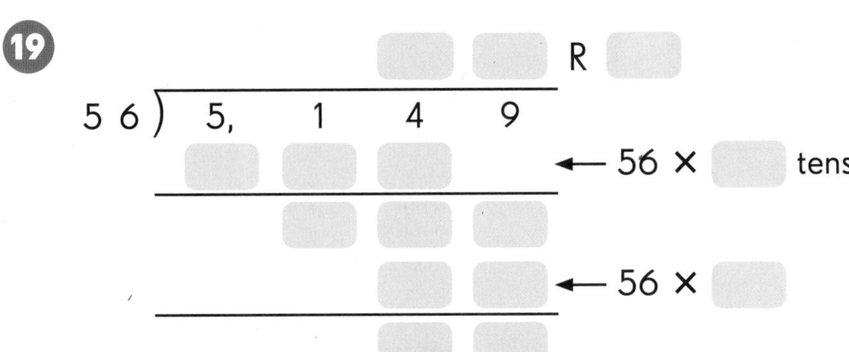

The quotient is ___ and the remainder is ___.

Divide.

20 4,531 ÷ 50

21 2,304 ÷ 29

22 3,650 ÷ 82

23 8,432 ÷ 96

Learn Divide the hundreds, then the tens, and then the ones.

Divide 5,213 by 15.

```
      3 4 7 R 8
1 5 ) 5,2 1 3
      4 5       ← 15 × 3 hundreds
      -----
        7 1
        6 0     ← 15 × 4 tens
      -----
        1 1 3
        1 0 5   ← 15 × 7
      -------
            8
```

5 thousands 2 hundreds = 52 hundreds
52 hundreds ÷ 15 = 3 hundreds R 7 hundreds

7 hundreds 1 ten = 71 tens
71 tens ÷ 15 = 4 tens R 11 tens

11 tens 3 ones = 113 ones
113 ÷ 15 = 7 R 8

The quotient is 347 and the remainder is 8.

Guided Practice

Divide. Show your work.

24

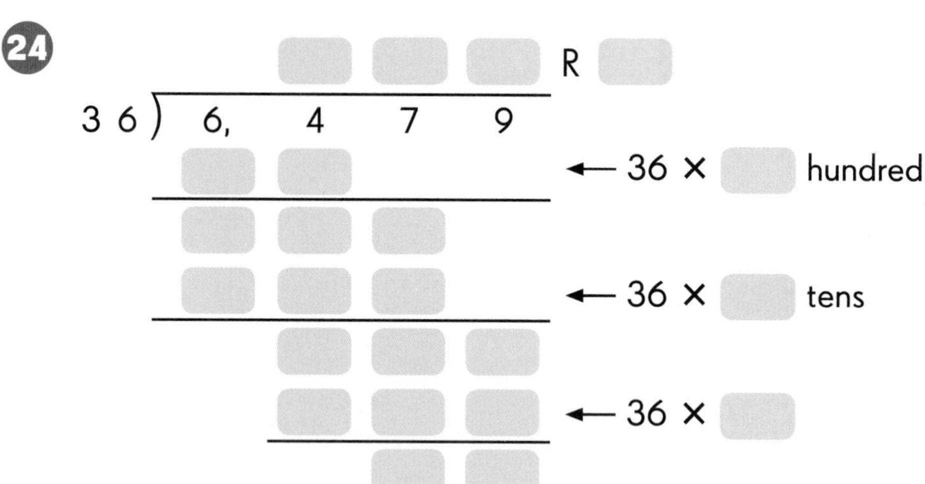

The quotient is ___ and the remainder is ___.

Divide.

25 6,025 ÷ 18

26 1,822 ÷ 11

27 5,283 ÷ 37

28 9,532 ÷ 81

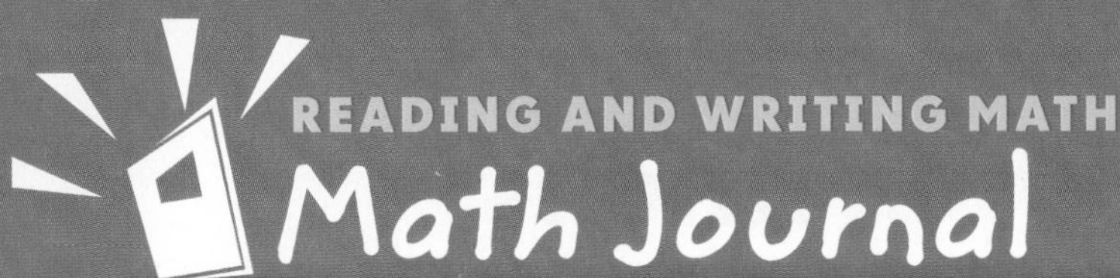

Angela wants to work out the division below:

187 ÷ 32

The first step of her working is as shown:

STEP 1 Round 32 to the nearest ten.

How should she continue from here? Show the rest of the steps.

Let's Practice

Divide.

1. 90 ÷ 30
2. 60 ÷ 40
3. 56 ÷ 34
4. 270 ÷ 20
5. 720 ÷ 90
6. 981 ÷ 90
7. 105 ÷ 12
8. 600 ÷ 73
9. 6,300 ÷ 70
10. 3,541 ÷ 20
11. 6,400 ÷ 51
12. 5,283 ÷ 36

ON YOUR OWN

Go to Workbook A: Practice 5, pages 49–54

Lesson 2.6 Order of Operations

Lesson Objective

- Use order of operations to simplify a numeric expression

Vocabulary
numeric expression
order of operations

Learn

Work from left to right when a numeric expression uses only addition and subtraction.

96 commuters are on a train. At the next station, 26 commuters get off and 48 commuters get on. How many commuters are on the train now?

First expression $96 - 26 + 48$ ← Work from left to right.

Second expression $70 + 48$

118

$96 - 26 + 48$ is a numeric expression.
A numeric expression contains only numbers and operation symbols. There is no equal sign.

Now there are 118 commuters on the train.

Guided Practice

Simplify.

1. $37 + 8 - 25$
2. $67 - 21 + 20$
3. $32 - 12 + 26 - 15$
4. $50 + 27 - 19 - 35$

Learn

Work from left to right when a numeric expression uses only multiplication and division.

Rogers & Co. orders 40 cartons of paper towels from Diego's paper store. Each carton contains 24 rolls of paper towels. The paper store delivers 60 rolls of paper towels each day. How many days will it take for the paper store to deliver all the paper towels?

First expression $40 \times 24 \div 60$ ← Work from left to right.

Second expression $960 \div 60$

16

It will take 16 days for the paper store to deliver all the paper towels.

Guided Practice

Simplify.

5. $12 \times 20 \div 6$
6. $63 \div 9 \times 12$
7. $28 \times 5 \div 10 \div 7$
8. $48 \div 8 \times 60 \div 3$

Learn

Always work from left to right. Multiply and divide first. Then add and subtract.

There are 28 children and 56 men at a park. The number of men is 4 times the number of women. How many children and women are at the park?

First expression $28 + 56 \div 4$ ← Divide first.

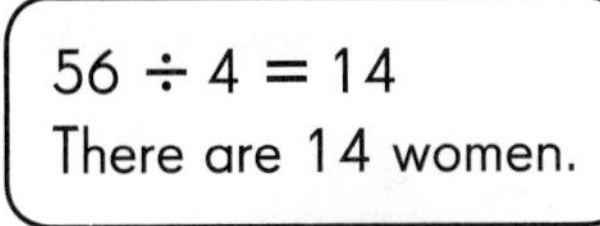
56 ÷ 4 = 14
There are 14 women.

Second expression $28 + 14$ ← Then add.

42

There are 42 children and women at the park.

Continued on next page

Sarah has 900 stamps in her collection. She arranges 25 stamps on each page of a stamp album. The album has 30 pages. How many stamps are left?

First expression $900 - \mathbf{30} \times \mathbf{25}$ ← Multiply first.

Second expression $900 - \mathbf{750}$ ← Then subtract.

150

There are 150 stamps left.

30 × 25 = 750
Sarah puts 750 stamps into the album.

Guided Practice

Simplify.

9. $13 + 20 \times 7$
10. $70 - 75 \div 5$
11. $15 + 18 \times 5 \div 9$
12. $80 - 54 \div 9 \times 11$
13. $48 - 6 \times 6 + 34$
14. $33 + 210 \div 30 - 25$

Learn **Carry out any operations in parentheses first.**

There are 670 boys and 530 girls at a track and field event. Each student participates in one event. Each event has 40 students participating. How many events are there?

First expression $(\mathbf{670} + \mathbf{530}) \div 40$ ← Perform all operations in the parentheses first.

Second expression $\mathbf{1{,}200} \div 40$ ← Then divide.

30

There are 30 events.

Guided Practice

Simplify.

15. $17 - (38 - 29)$
16. $690 \div (15 \times 2)$
17. $(44 - 33) \times 7$
18. $80 \div (40 - 32)$

Learn: Order of operations

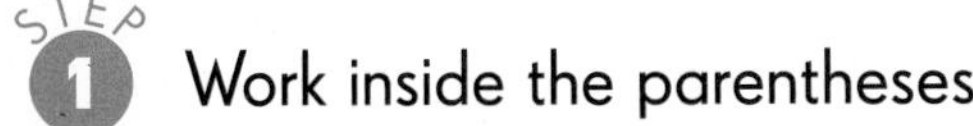

STEP 1 Work inside the parentheses.

STEP 2 Multiply and divide from left to right.

STEP 3 Add and subtract from left to right.

Jimmy has 60 ounces of pecans and 64 ounces of macadamias. He mixes and packs them into 9-ounce packets. He packs 8 packets. How many ounces of nuts does he have left?

First expression $(60 + 64) - 8 \times 9$ ← Perform all operations in the parentheses first.

Second expression $124 - 8 \times 9$ ← Then multiply.

Third expression $124 - 72$ ← Finally, subtract.

52

He has 52 ounces of nuts left.

Guided Practice

Simplify.

19. $107 + (44 - 33) \times 7$
20. $80 \times (40 \div 5) \div 10$
21. $(64 + 32) \div 8 - 3$
22. $98 - (34 - 26) \times 7$

Hands-On Activity

Use copies of the cards to form a numeric expression with two or more operations.

0 1 2 3 4 5 6 7 8 9

+ − × ÷ ( )

Example

3 2 8 × 5 4 ÷ 3 6

Simplify the expression and compare your answer with your partner's.

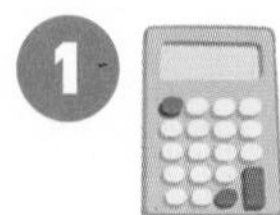

Let's Explore!

1. To find the value of $350 \times 20 \div 4$, use your calculator to find 350×20 first. Then, divide the result by 4.
Next, use your calculator to find $20 \div 4$ first. Then, multiply the result by 350. What do you notice?
Try this activity with other numbers and operations.

2 

WORK IN PAIRS

Look at the five expressions in the table below.
The first partner is to simplify each expression from left to right.
The second partner is to simplify the expression using the order of operations.
Use a copy of this table and record your answers. Discuss your results.

Number sentence	Partner A's answers	Partner B's answers
$9 + 6 - 5$		
$48 \div 4 \times 2$		
$36 \div 6 - 3$		
$14 + 4 \times 2$		
$50 - 8 \div 2$		

Let's Practice

Simplify.

1. $96 - 50 + 64$
2. $175 + 25 - 95$
3. $6 \times 40 \div 3$
4. $250 \div 5 \times 53$
5. $79 + 27 \times 2$
6. $280 - 72 \div 8$
7. $35 \times (560 \div 70)$
8. $540 \div (293 - 203)$

ON YOUR OWN

Go to Workbook A: Practice 6, pages 55–62

Lesson 2.7 Real-World Problems: Multiplication and Division

Lesson Objectives

- Use efficient strategies to solve multi-step problems involving multiplication and division.
- Express and interpret the product or quotient appropriately.

Learn **The remainder can be part of an answer.**

Rena has a roll of ribbon 250 centimeters long. She cuts it into a number of pieces that measures 20 centimeters each. How many pieces does she cut?
What is the length of the remaining ribbon?

Length of ribbon = 250 cm
Length of each piece = 20 cm
Number of pieces = 250 ÷ 20
= 12 R 10

$$\begin{array}{r} 12\text{ R }10 \\ 20\overline{)250} \\ \underline{20} \\ 50 \\ \underline{40} \\ 10 \end{array}$$

Rena cuts the ribbon into 12 pieces.
The length of the remaining ribbon is 10 centimeters.

Guided Practice

Solve. Show your work.

1. A bin of potatoes weighs 100 pounds. The potatoes are packed into bags weighing 15 pounds each. How many bags of potatoes are there? How many pounds are left?

Weight of potatoes = 100 lb
Weight of each bag = 15 lb

Number of bags = ___ ÷ ___
= ___

There are ___ bags of potatoes. ___ pounds of potatoes are left.

Learn

Increase the quotient when it includes the remainder.

A school has 120 fifth-graders who are going by bus on a field trip. Each bus holds 35 students. What is the number of buses needed?

Number of fifth-graders = 120

Number of fifth-graders in 1 bus = 35

Number of buses = 120 ÷ 35

= 3 R 15

$$\begin{array}{r} 3\text{ R }15 \\ 35\overline{)120} \\ 105 \\ \hline 15 \end{array}$$

The 15 remaining fifth-graders would need 1 more bus.

Add 1 more to the quotient: 3 + 1 = 4

The number of buses needed is 4.

Guided Practice

2 Julie has 172 stamps. She wants to put them in an album. Each page of the album holds 25 stamps. How many pages of the album will Julie need to stick all her stamps?

Number of stamps = ___

Number of stamps on 1 page = ___

Number of pages = ___ ÷ ___

= ___ R ___

Julie will need ___ more page to stick the remaining ___ stamps.

Add ___ more to the quotient: ___ + ___ = ___

The number of pages Julie will need is ___.

Learn Some problems require two steps to solve.

The Fairfield Elementary School library is in the shape of a rectangle. It measures 36 yards by 21 yards. The school's principal, Mr. Jefferson, wants to carpet the library floor. Find the cost of carpeting the library fully if a 1-square-yard carpet tile costs $16.

First, find the floor area of the library.

Area = length × width
= 36 × 21
= 756 yd^2

Estimate the answer.
36 rounds to 40.
21 rounds to 20.
40 × 20 = 800
756 is a reasonable answer.

The floor area of the library is 756 square yards.

Then, find the cost of carpeting.

Cost of carpeting
= area × cost of 1 yd^2
= 756 × $16
= $12,096

Estimate to check if the answer is reasonable.

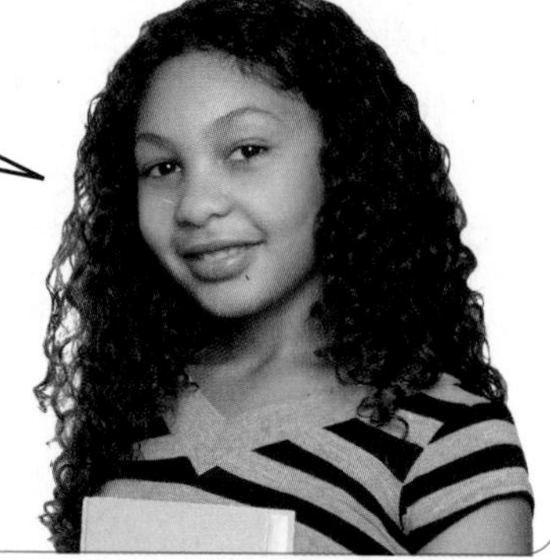

It will cost $12,096 to carpet the library fully.

Guided Practice

Solve. Show your work.

3 Rob fills 250-gallon fuel tanks at $3 per gallon at a gas station. How much money does he need to pay for filling 9 such tanks?

Total amount of fuel = 9 × 250 = ____

Cost of fuel = ____ × $3 = $____

He needs to pay $____.

Learn Some problems require more than two steps to solve.

A group of volunteers buys 32 cartons of 40 apples. The volunteers pack the apples into bags of 5 each and sell each bag for \$4 to raise funds for a charity. How much do they collect after selling all the apples?

First, find the total number of apples.

Total number of apples = number of cartons × number of apples in a carton
= 32 × 40
= 1,280

There are 1,280 apples.

Next, find the number of bags.

Number of bags = total number of apples ÷ number of apples in a bag
= 1,280 ÷ 5
= 256

There are 256 bags of apples.

Then, find how much money they collected.

Amount collected = number of bags × price of a bag
= 256 × \$4
= \$1,024

The volunteers collected \$1,024.

Guided Practice

Solve. Show your work.

  Ms. Hernandez buys a car and pays for it in equal payments of \$478. After 45 payments, she still owes \$3,090. How much would each payment be if she pays for the car in 60 equal payments?

First, find the total amount paid in equal payments.

Amount paid = number of payments × amount for each payment

= 45 × \$478

= \$

Then, find the cost of the car.

Cost of car = total amount paid + amount she still has to pay

= \$ + \$3,090

= \$

Cost of the car:

(45 × \$478) + \$3,090

= \$

Which operation will you use to find how much she would pay for each of the 60 payments?

She would pay  for each of the 60 equal payments.

Learn: Read a table to find the information for a question.

The table shows the wages of workers in a plumbing company.
Ms. Jensen works Tuesday through Sunday. How much is she paid?

Weekdays	$170 per day
Saturdays and Sundays	$315 per day

First, find the number of weekdays and the number of Saturdays and Sundays she worked.

Number of weekdays worked = 4 days

Number of Saturdays and Sundays worked = 2 days

Ms. Jensen's wages for 4 weekdays = 4 × $170
= $680

Her wages for Saturday and Sunday = 2 × $315
= $630

Total wages = $680 + $630
= $1,310

Ms. Jensen is paid $1,310.

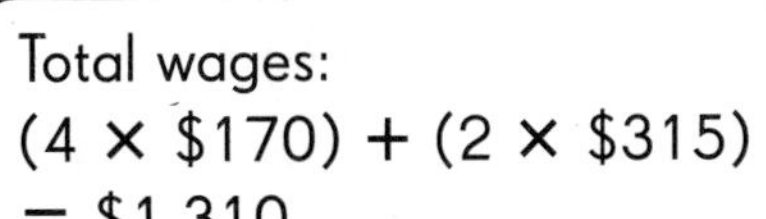
Total wages:
(4 × $170) + (2 × $315)
= $1,310

Guided Practice

Solve. Show your work.

5 The table shows the charges at a parking garage.

First Hour	Second Hour	After the Second Hour
$7	$5	$3 per hour

Mr. Lee parked his car here from 9 A.M. to 2 P.M. one day. How much did he pay?

Total number of hours = ___ h

Parking fee for the first hour = $___

Parking fee for the second hour = $___

Parking fee from 11 A.M. to 2 P.M. = ___ × $___ = $___

Total parking fee = $___ + $___ + $___ = $___

Mr. Lee paid $___.

Let's Practice

Solve. Show your work.

1. A water tank contains 1,250 gallons of water. The water is used to fill some 30-gallon barrels. What is the number of barrels that can be completely filled and how much water is left?

2. Some students in a stamp club collected a total of 6,707 stamps. They gave away 569 of the stamps. Then the students put equal numbers of the remaining stamps into 18 albums. How many stamps were in each album?

3. A grocer had 49 boxes of strawberries. Each box contained 75 strawberries. The strawberries were repacked into small boxes with 15 strawberries. How many small boxes of strawberries were there?

4. Mr. Tan paid $2 for each package of 12 granola bars. He sold each granola bar for $0.50. In a week, he sold a total of 4,385 granola bars.
   a. What is the least number of packages of granola bars?
   b. How much did he pay for this number of packages of granola bars?
   c. How much money did he make after he sold 4,385 granola bars?

5. A restaurant owner bought 245 cartons of canned corn. Each carton held 28 cans of corn. There were 2,198 cans of yellow corn and the rest were white corn. All the cans of white corn were used equally over 42 months. How many cans of white corn did the restaurant owner use each month?

6. The table shows the cost of beads by weight at a store. Chyna and Desmond bought some beads from the store.

Weight	Cost
First 2 ounces	70¢
Each additional ounce	30¢

   a. Chyna bought beads weighing 5 ounces in all. Find the cost of the beads.
   b. Desmond paid $6.10 for his beads. Find the total weight of the beads that he bought.

ON YOUR OWN

Go to Workbook A: Practice 7, pages 63–68

Learn Solve problems by drawing bar models.

Hector, Teddy, and Jim scored a total of 4,670 points playing a video game. Teddy scored 316 points less than Hector. Teddy scored 3 times as many points as Jim. How many points did Teddy score?

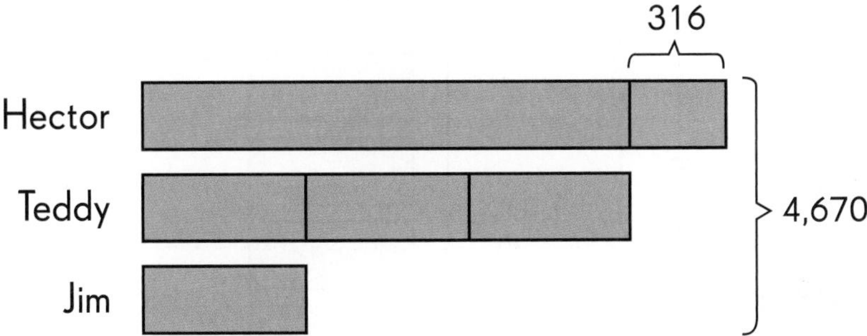

First, subtract 316 points from Hector's score so that he will have the same number of points as Teddy.

This also means subtracting 316 points from the total number of points.

4,670 − 316 = 4,354

The drawing shows there are 7 equal units after subtracting the 316 points. Divide the remaining points by 7 to find the number of points that represent one unit.

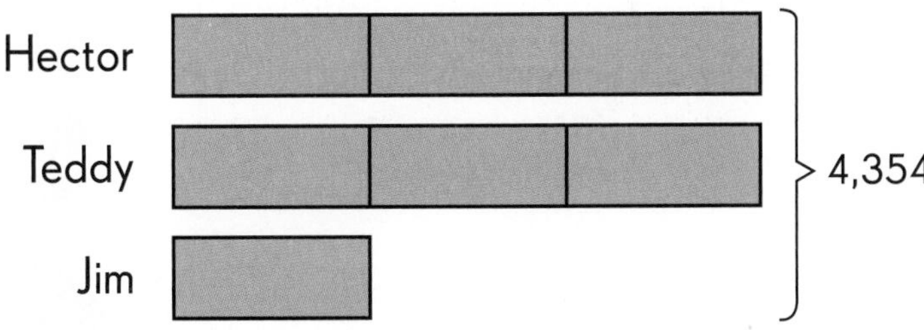

7 units → 4,354 points

1 unit → 4,354 ÷ 7 = 622 points

3 units → 3 × 622 = 1,866 points

Teddy scored 1,866 points.

Guided Practice

Solve. Show your work.

6 The cost of 4 belts and 5 ties is \$247. Each tie costs 3 times as much as a belt. What is the total cost of a tie and a belt?

Draw models.
Represent 1 belt with 1 unit and 1 tie with 3 units.

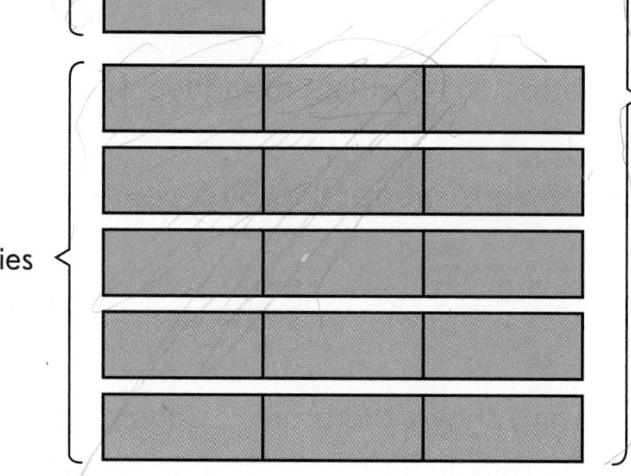

___ units → \$247

1 unit → \$247 ÷ ___ = \$___

Each belt costs \$___.

3 units → 3 × \$___ = \$39

Each tie costs \$___.

\$___ + \$___ = \$___

The total cost of a belt and a tie is \$___.

7 A florist had an equal number of red and yellow tulips. She sold 624 red tulips. Then she had 4 times as many yellow tulips as red tulips. How many tulips did she have at first?

Before

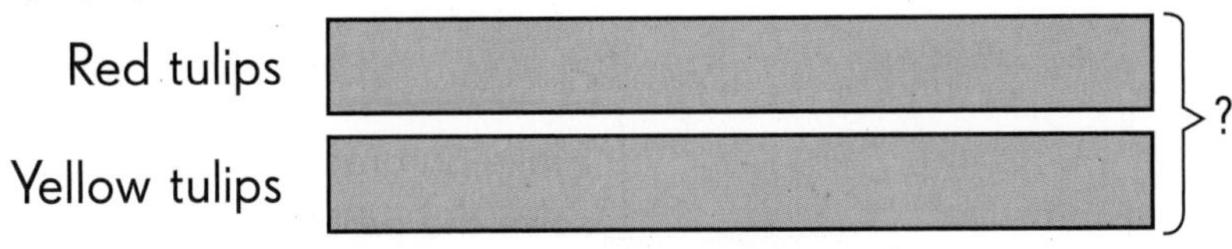

After

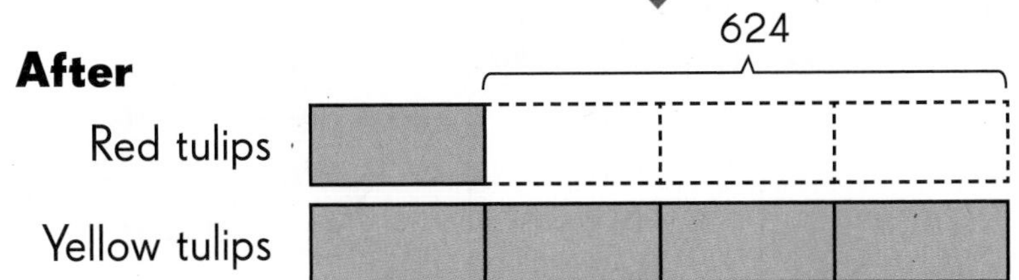

1 unit represents the number of red tulips left and 4 units represent the number of yellow tulips.

3 units → 624 tulips

1 unit → $624 \div 3 = 208$ tulips

8 units → $8 \times$ ____ = ____ tulips

She had ____ tulips at first.

8 Ella and Michelle had \$1,250. Ella and Surya had \$830. Michelle had 4 times as much as Surya. How much did Ella have?

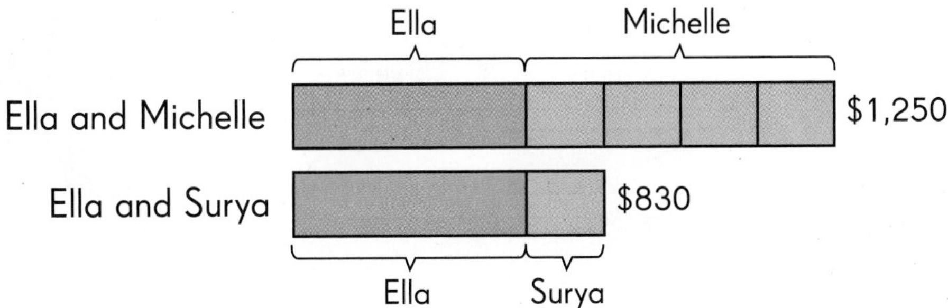

\$1,250 − \$830 = \$420

The difference between the amount Michelle and Surya had was \$420.

3 units → \$420

1 unit → \$420 ÷ 3 = \$____

Surya had \$____.

\$830 − \$____ = \$____

Ella had \$____.

Learn: Some problems can be solved using other strategies.

Mandy is 12 years old and Nacha is 15 years older. In how many years will Nacha be twice as old as Mandy?

Method 1

12 + 15 = 27

Nacha is 27 years old now.

Make an organized list to solve the problem.

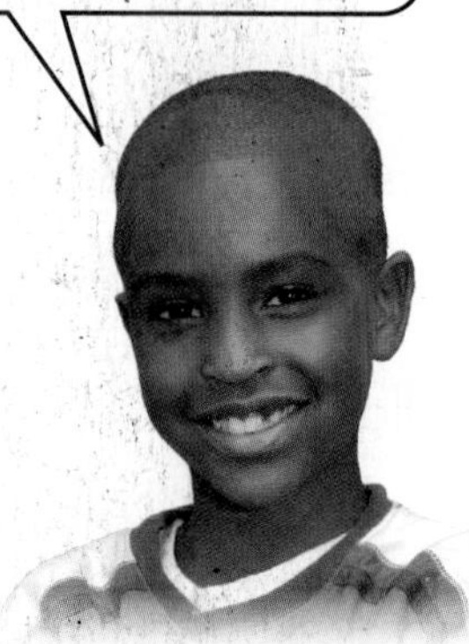

Mandy's Age	Nacha's Age	Is it twice?
12 (now)	27 (now)	No
13	28	No
14	29	No
15	30	Yes

Nacha will be twice Mandy's age in 3 years' time.

Method 2

Draw a bar model to solve the problem.

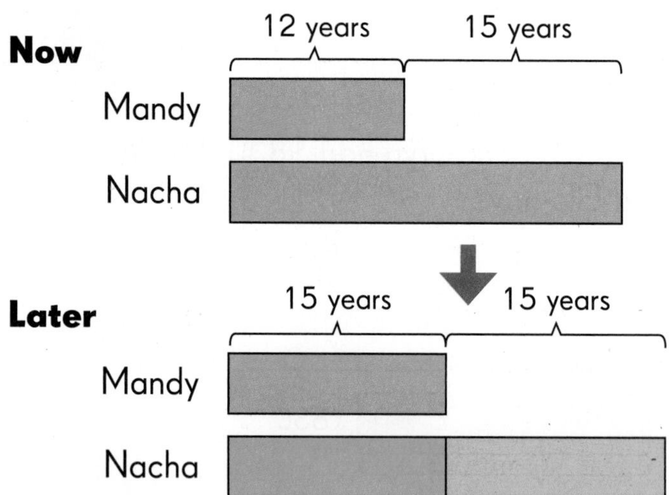

1 unit ⟶ 15 years

15 − 12 = 3

Nacha will be twice Mandy's age in 3 years' time.

Guided Practice

Solve. Show your work.

9 There are 20 cars and motorcycles altogether in a parking lot. The total number of wheels is 50. How many motorcycles are there?

Use the data — number of vehicles and number of wheels — to make an organized list.
Remember, the number of cars and motorcycles must always add up to 20.

Number of Cars	Number of Motorcycles	Number of Wheels	Are there 50 Wheels?
10	10	40 + 20 = 60	No (too many)
9	11	36 + ___ = 58	No (too many)
___	12	32 + 24 = 56	No (too many)
5	15	20 + 30 = 50	___

There are ___ motorcycles.

Let's Practice

Solve. Show your work.

1 Mrs. Atkins pays $1,800 for a new refrigerator, washer, and dryer. The refrigerator costs $250 more than the washer. The dryer costs half as much as the washer. How much does the washer cost?

2. Apples are sold at 3 for $2 at Busy Mart. At Big Foods, the same apples are sold at 5 for $2. Kassim buys 15 apples from Big Foods instead of Busy Mart. How much does he save?

3. Margaret paid $87 for a skirt and a blouse. The skirt costs twice as much as the blouse. What was the cost of the skirt?

4. A shopkeeper sold a total of 15 boxes of pencils on Monday and Tuesday. He sold 3 more boxes on Monday than on Tuesday. There were 12 pencils in each box. How many pencils did he sell on Monday?

5. Jane had $7 and her sister had $2. Their parents gave each of them an equal amount of money. Then, Jane had twice as much money as her sister. How much money did their parents give each of them?

6. On a farm, there are some cows and some chickens. If the animals have a total of 40 heads and 112 legs, how many cows are there?

7. Naomi, Macy, and Sebastian have 234 stamps in all. Naomi gives 16 stamps to Macy and 24 stamps to Sebastian. Naomi then has 3 times as many stamps as Macy, and Macy has twice as many stamps as Sebastian. How many stamps does Naomi have at first?

8. A group of people pays $720 for admission tickets to an amusement park. The price of an adult ticket is $15, and a child ticket is $8. There are 25 more adults than children. How many children are in the group?

9. A tank and a pail contain a total of 5,136 milliliters of water. Jacob pours 314 milliliters of water from the pail into the tank. The amount of water in the tank is now 7 times what is left in the pail. How much water was in the pail at first?

ON YOUR OWN

Go to Workbook A:
Practice 8, pages 69–74

CRITICAL THINKING SKILLS

Put On Your Thinking Cap!

PROBLEM SOLVING

The [9] key on the calculator is not working.

Explain how you can still use the calculator to find 1,234 × 79 in two ways.

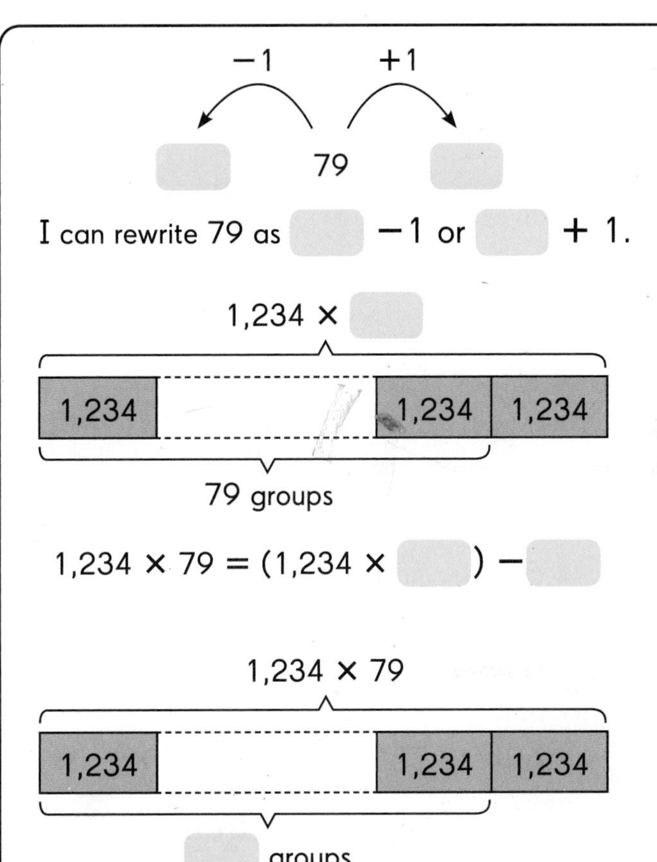

ON YOUR OWN

Go to Workbook A: Put on Your Thinking Cap, pages 75–78

Chapter Wrap Up

Study Guide

You have learned...

Whole Numbers

Using a calculator

- Add
- Subtract
- Multiply
- Divide

Multiplication

Use a rule to multiply a number by 10, 100, or 1,000.

Write one, two, or three zeros after the number to find the product.

1,234 × 1**0** = 12,34**0**
1,234 × 1**00** = 123,4**00**
1,234 × 1,**000** = 1,234,**000**

Use strategies to multiply a 2-digit, 3-digit, or 4-digit number by a 2-digit number.

Estimate the product by rounding or front-end estimation.

By rounding:	By front-end estimation:
4,694 × 58	1,259 × 26
5,000 × 60 = 300,000	1,000 × 20 = 20,000
4,694 × 58 is about 300,000.	1,259 × 26 is about 20,000.

- Patterns can be used to help multiply and divide numbers.
- Numeric expressions can be simplified using the order of operations.
- Multiplication and division can be used to solve real-world problems.

Division

Use a rule to divide a number by 10, 100, or 1,000.

Drop one, two, or three zeros after the number to find the quotient.

5,678,00**0** ÷ 1**0** = 567,800
5,678,0**00** ÷ 1**00** = 56,780
5,678,**000** ÷ 1**000** = 5,678

Use strategies to divide a 2-digit, 3-digit, or 4-digit number by a 2-digit number.

Order of operations

1. Work inside the parentheses.
2. Multiply and divide from left to right.
3. Add and subtract from left to right.

Estimate the quotient by rounding the divisor. Then find the multiple of the divisor that is nearest to the dividend.

3,310 ÷ 42

40 × 80 = 3,200
40 × 90 = 3,600
3,310 is nearer to 3,200 than to 3,600.

3,200 ÷ 40 = 80
So, 3,310 ÷ 42 is about 80.

Use multiplication and division to solve real-world problems.

Chapter Review/Test

Vocabulary

Fill in the blanks.

product
factors
dividend
divisor
quotient
remainder
numeric expressions
order of operations

1. In 5,280 × 63 = 332,640,

   5,280 and 63 are the ___ and 332,640 is the ___.

2. In 9,472 ÷ 15 = 631 R 7,

   9,472 is the ___, 15 is the ___,

   631 is the ___ and 7 is the ___.

3. 8,167 + 929, and 1,597 × 16 are examples of ___.

4. A numeric expression with more than two operations is simplified using the ___.

Concepts and Skills

Multiply.

5. 718 × 10
6. 502 × 100
7. 863 × 1,000
8. 548 × 60
9. 659 × 300
10. 935 × 8,000

Estimate each product.

11. 4,734 × 28
12. 7,651 × 46
13. 9,470 × 32

Multiply. Estimate to check if your answers are reasonable.

14. 2,757 × 14
15. 3,648 × 27
16. 8,359 × 55

Divide.

17. 680 ÷ 10
18. 7,000 ÷ 100
19. 241,000 ÷ 1,000
20. 1,200 ÷ 40
21. 6,900 ÷ 300
22. 64,000 ÷ 8,000

Estimate each quotient.

23. 4,232 ÷ 18
24. 8,267 ÷ 93
25. 1,135 ÷ 84

Divide. Give the quotient and remainder.

26. 295 ÷ 31
27. 4,135 ÷ 14
28. 6,397 ÷ 28

Simplify.

29. 51 − 17 + 37
30. 81 ÷ 9 × 24
31. 66 − 16 ÷ 8
32. 28 × (69 + 50)

Problem Solving

Solve.

33. 

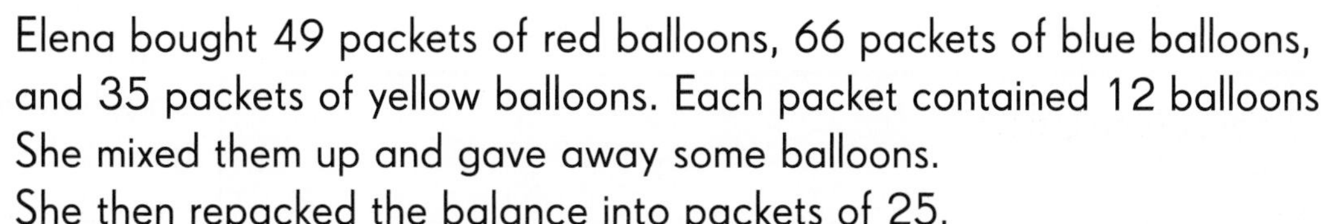

Elena bought 49 packets of red balloons, 66 packets of blue balloons, and 35 packets of yellow balloons. Each packet contained 12 balloons. She mixed them up and gave away some balloons. She then repacked the balance into packets of 25.

a. How many balloons were there altogether?

b. She gave away 225 balloons. How many large packets of 25 balloons were there?

a. She paid $3 for each packet of a dozen balloons. She sold each new packet of 25 balloons at $10 each. How much money did she make?

Chapter 3

Fractions and Mixed Numbers

Share the granola bars among the 3 of you. How many granola bars will you each get?
If I eat 1 granola bar, and ask the 3 of you to share the remaining granola bars, how many granola bars will you each get?

Lessons

- **3.1** Adding Unlike Fractions
- **3.2** Subtracting Unlike Fractions
- **3.3** Fractions, Mixed Numbers, and Division Expressions
- **3.4** Expressing Fractions, Division Expressions, and Mixed Numbers as Decimals
- **3.5** Adding Mixed Numbers
- **3.6** Subtracting Mixed Numbers
- **3.7** Real-World Problems: Fractions and Mixed Numbers

▶ Add and subtract unlike fractions and mixed numbers by rewriting them with like denominators.

Recall Prior Knowledge

Like fractions have the same denominator.

Liam had $\frac{2}{5}$ of a cracker.

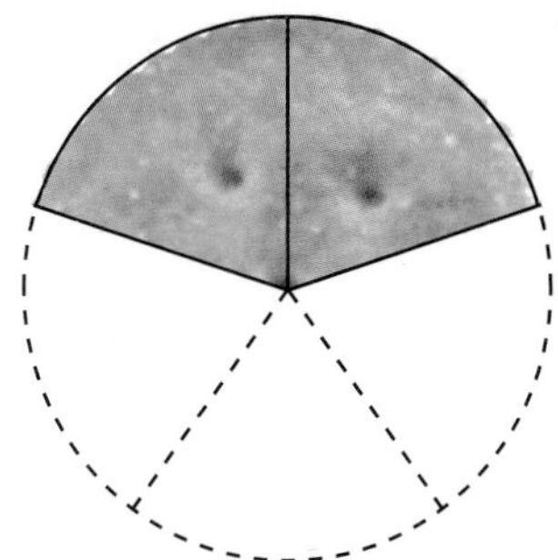

Walt had $\frac{3}{5}$ of a cracker.

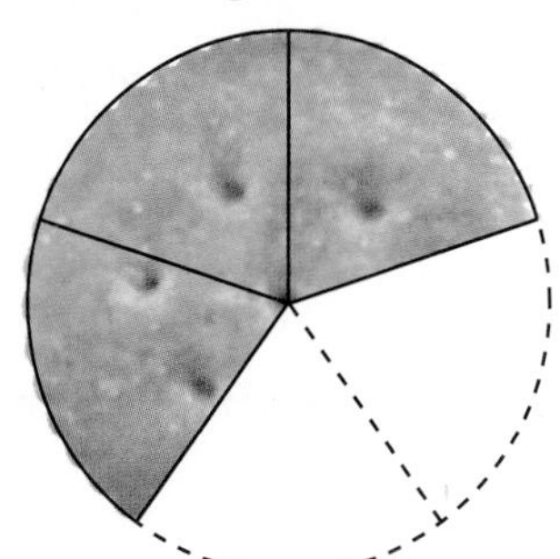

$\frac{2}{5}$ and $\frac{3}{5}$ are like fractions.

They have the same denominator, 5.

Unlike fractions have different denominators.

In one box, $\frac{3}{4}$ of a pizza was left.

In another box, $\frac{2}{5}$ of a pizza was left.

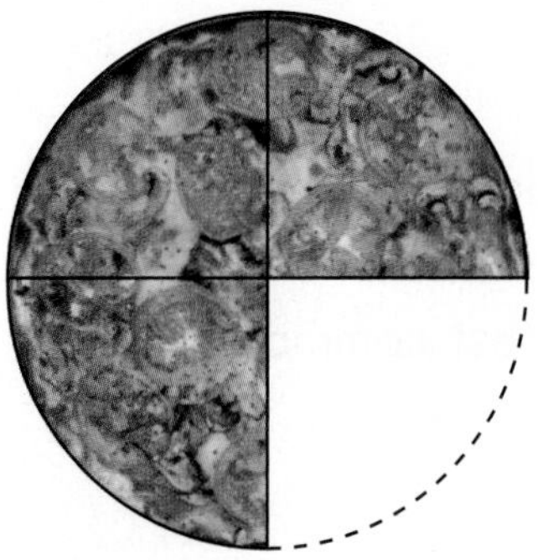

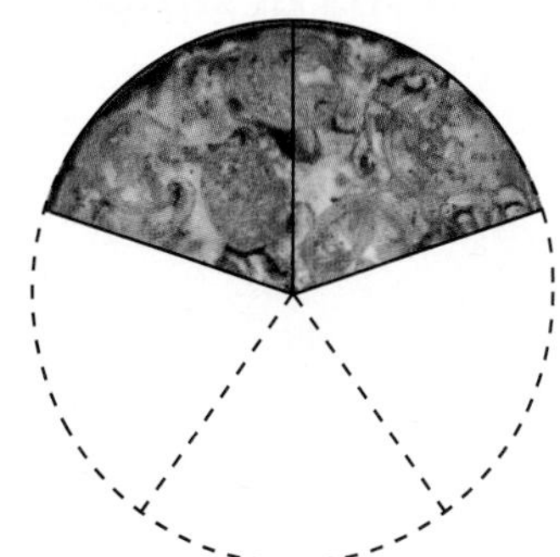

$\frac{3}{4}$ and $\frac{2}{5}$ are unlike fractions.

They have different denominators, 4 and 5.

A mixed number consists of a whole number and a fraction.

1 whole

1 whole

1 half

$$2 + \frac{1}{2} = 2\frac{1}{2}$$

whole number (2), fraction ($\frac{1}{2}$), mixed number ($2\frac{1}{2}$)

Finding equivalent fractions

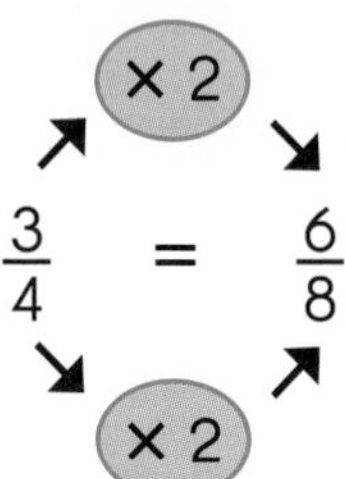

$$\frac{3}{4} = \frac{6}{8} \quad (\times 2)$$

$$\frac{8}{12} = \frac{4}{6} \quad (\div 2)$$

Expressing fractions in simplest form

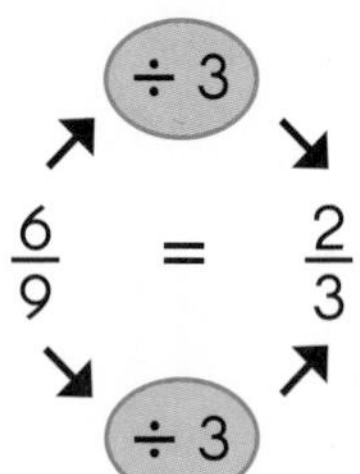

$$\frac{6}{9} = \frac{2}{3} \quad (\div 3)$$

$$\frac{8}{12} = \frac{2}{3} \quad (\div 4)$$

Divide the numerator and denominator by their greatest common factor.

Representing fractions on a number line

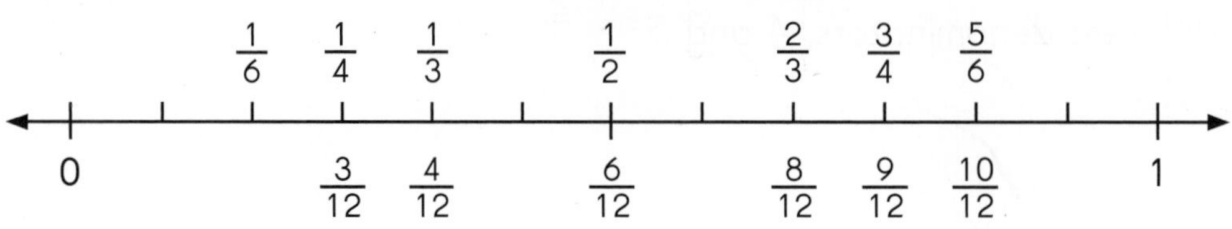

Identifying prime and composite numbers

2 and 5 are prime numbers. They have no factors other than 1 and themselves.

$2 = 2 \times 1$ $\qquad\qquad$ $5 = 5 \times 1$

8 and 24 are composite numbers. They have factors other than 1 and themselves.

$$\begin{aligned} 8 &= 1 \times 8 \\ &= 2 \times 4 \end{aligned}$$

$$\begin{aligned} 24 &= 1 \times 24 \\ &= 2 \times 12 \\ &= 3 \times 8 \\ &= 4 \times 6 \end{aligned}$$

Expressing improper fractions as mixed numbers

Express $\frac{5}{3}$ as a mixed number.

Using models:

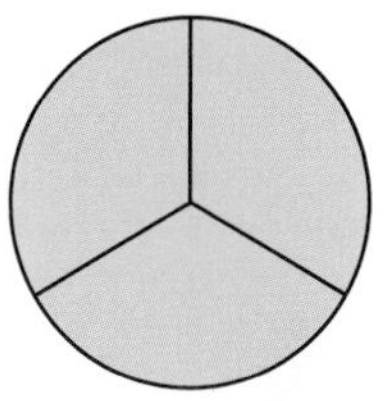

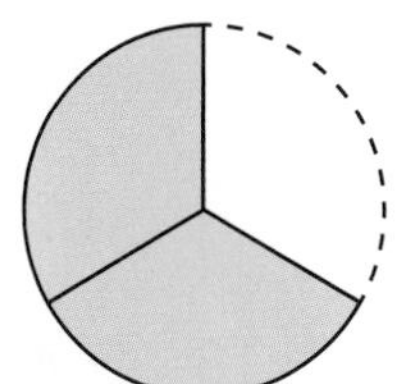

$$\begin{aligned} \frac{5}{3} &= 5 \text{ thirds} \\ &= 3 \text{ thirds} + 2 \text{ thirds} \\ &= \frac{3}{3} + \frac{2}{3} \\ &= 1 + \frac{2}{3} \\ &= 1\frac{2}{3} \end{aligned}$$

Using division:

$\frac{5}{3}$ means 5 divided by 3.

number of wholes → 1

$$\begin{array}{r} 1 \\ 3\overline{)5} \\ \underline{3} \\ 2 \end{array}$$

2 ← number of thirds

> Divide the numerator by the denominator.
> $5 \div 3 = 1$ R 2
> This is the division rule.

There is 1 whole and 2 thirds in $\frac{5}{3}$.

$\frac{5}{3} = 1\frac{2}{3}$

Adding and subtracting like fractions

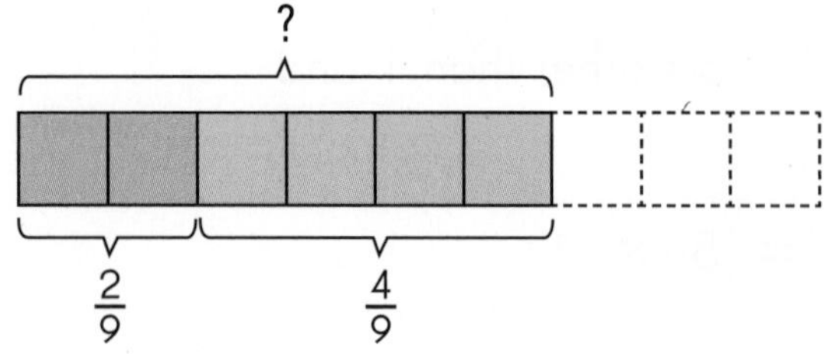

$$\frac{2}{9} + \frac{4}{9} = \frac{6}{9}$$
$$= \frac{2}{3}$$

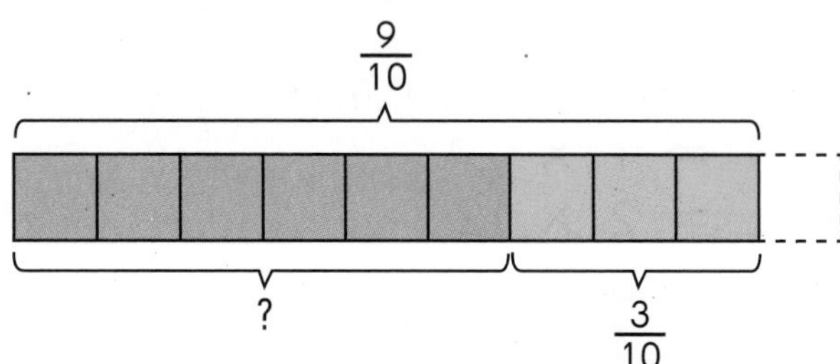

$$\frac{9}{10} - \frac{3}{10} = \frac{6}{10}$$
$$= \frac{3}{5}$$

Adding and subtracting unlike fractions

$$\frac{2}{3} + \frac{1}{6} = \frac{4}{6} + \frac{1}{6}$$
$$= \frac{5}{6}$$

$$\frac{1}{3} + \frac{4}{9} + \frac{2}{3} = \frac{3}{9} + \frac{4}{9} + \frac{6}{9}$$
$$= \frac{13}{9}$$
$$= 1\frac{4}{9}$$

$$\frac{3}{4} - \frac{5}{12} = \frac{9}{12} - \frac{5}{12}$$
$$= \frac{4}{12}$$
$$= \frac{1}{3}$$

$$1 - \frac{2}{9} - \frac{7}{18} = \frac{18}{18} - \frac{4}{18} - \frac{7}{18}$$
$$= \frac{7}{18}$$

$$2 - \frac{4}{5} - \frac{9}{10} = \frac{20}{10} - \frac{8}{10} - \frac{9}{10}$$
$$= \frac{3}{10}$$

Reading and writing tenths and hundredths in decimal and fractional forms

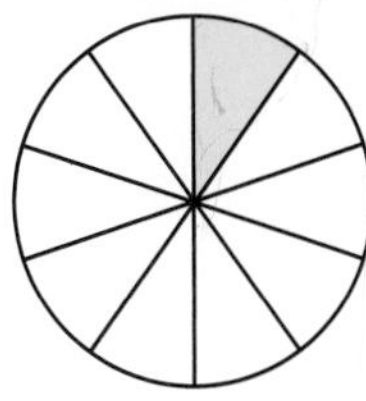

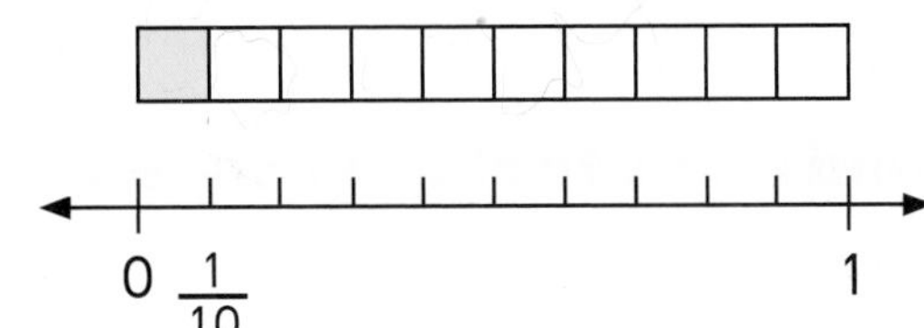

$\frac{1}{10}$ (one tenth) is 0.1 in decimal form. You read 0.1 as one tenth.

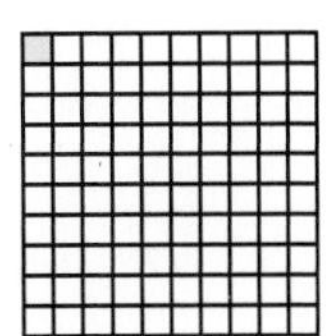

$\frac{1}{100}$

0 0.1 0.2 0.3 0.4 0.5 0.6 0.7 0.8 0.9 1

$\frac{1}{100}$ (one hundredth) is 0.01 in decimal form. You read 0.01 as one hundredth.

Expressing fractions as decimals

Express $\frac{9}{10}$ as a decimal.

$\frac{1}{10}$ = 1 tenth

= 0.1

$\frac{9}{10}$ = 9 tenths

= 0.9

Express $\frac{17}{100}$ as a decimal.

10 hundredths = 1 tenth

$\frac{17}{100}$ = 17 hundredths

1 tenth 7 hundredths

$\frac{17}{100}$ = 1 tenth 7 hundredths

= 0.17

✔ Quick Check

Find the like fractions in each set.

1. $\frac{3}{4}$, $\frac{1}{2}$, $\frac{2}{5}$, $\frac{1}{4}$

2. $\frac{5}{6}$, $\frac{5}{9}$, $\frac{9}{10}$, $\frac{7}{9}$

Find the unlike fractions in each set.

3. $\frac{1}{8}$, $\frac{2}{7}$, $\frac{3}{8}$, $\frac{1}{2}$

4. $\frac{5}{9}$, $\frac{5}{12}$, $\frac{1}{10}$, $\frac{7}{9}$

Find the number of wholes and parts that are shaded. Then write the mixed number.

   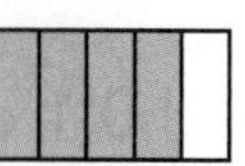

☐ wholes ☐ parts = ☐ $\frac{☐}{☐}$

Complete to show the equivalent fractions.

6. $\frac{3}{5} = \frac{☐}{10}$

7. $\frac{15}{20} = \frac{☐}{4}$

Express each fraction in simplest form.

8. $\frac{8}{10}$ = ☐

9. $\frac{12}{16}$ = ☐

Find the equivalent fractions which are missing from the number line. Give your answers in simplest form.

10.

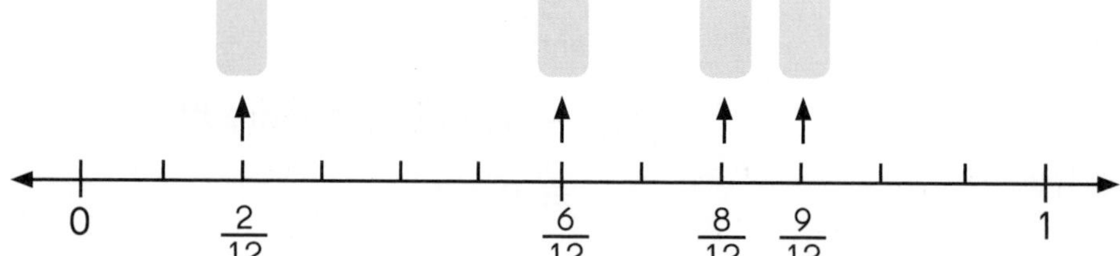

Find the prime numbers.

11. 12, 2, 8, 3, 7, 15

Find the composite numbers.

12. 2, 14, 18, 13, 5, 10

Express the improper fraction as a mixed number.

13. $\frac{8}{3}$ = ☐ thirds

= ☐ thirds + ☐ thirds

= ☐ + ☐

= ☐ + ☐

= ☐

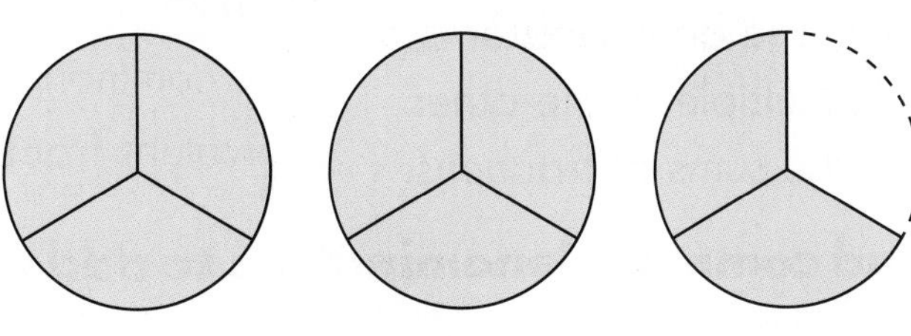

Express each improper fraction as a mixed number.
Use the division rule.

14. $\frac{13}{4} =$ ☐

15. $\frac{19}{5} =$ ☐

Add or subtract. Express the sum or difference in simplest form.

16. $\frac{5}{8} + \frac{1}{8} =$ ☐

17. $\frac{3}{10} - \frac{1}{10} =$ ☐

18. $\frac{1}{2} + \frac{3}{8} =$ ☐

19. $\frac{2}{3} + \frac{3}{4} + \frac{10}{12} =$ ☐

20. $\frac{4}{5} - \frac{3}{10} =$ ☐

21. $\frac{6}{7} - \frac{11}{14} =$ ☐

22. $1 - \frac{1}{6} - \frac{11}{18} =$ ☐

23. $3 - \frac{1}{3} - \frac{2}{9} =$ ☐

Express each fraction as a decimal.

24. $\frac{7}{10}$

25. $\frac{3}{100}$

26. $\frac{89}{100}$

Lesson 3.1 Adding Unlike Fractions

Lesson Objectives

- Add two unlike fractions where one denominator is not a multiple of the other.
- Estimate sums of fractions.

Vocabulary

multiple
least common multiple
equivalent fractions
least common denominator
benchmarks

Learn Find common denominators to add unlike fractions.

A plank is painted $\frac{1}{2}$ red and $\frac{1}{3}$ green. The rest is painted yellow. What fraction of the plank is painted red and green?

$\frac{1}{2} + \frac{1}{3} = ?$

$\frac{1}{2}$ and $\frac{1}{3}$ are unlike fractions. To add, rewrite $\frac{1}{2}$ and $\frac{1}{3}$ as like fractions.

List the **multiples** of the denominators, 2 and 3.

Multiples of 2: 2, 4, 6, 8, ... Multiples of 3: 3, 6, 9, 12, ...

The **least common multiple** of 2 and 3 is 6.

So, 6 is the **least common denominator** of $\frac{1}{2}$ and $\frac{1}{3}$. Use it to rewrite $\frac{1}{2}$ and $\frac{1}{3}$ as like fractions.

$\frac{1 \times 3}{2 \times 3} = \frac{3}{6}$ $\frac{1 \times 2}{3 \times 2} = \frac{2}{6}$

$\frac{1}{2}$ and $\frac{3}{6}$, and $\frac{1}{3}$ and $\frac{2}{6}$ are **equivalent fractions**.

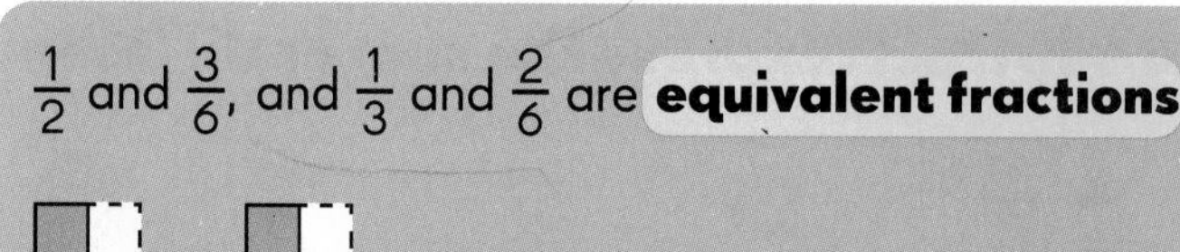

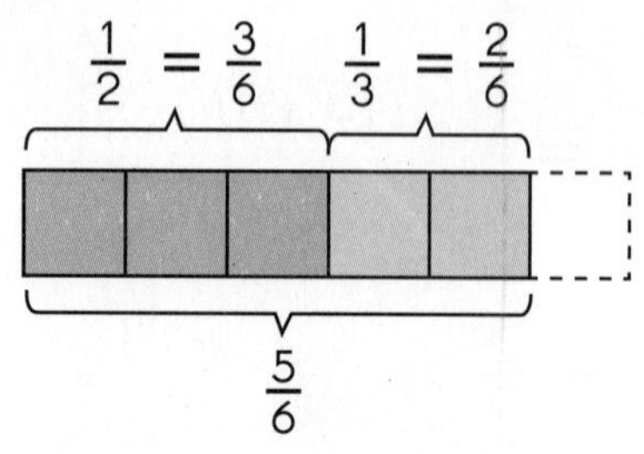

Since 6 is the least common multiple, I draw a model with 6 units.

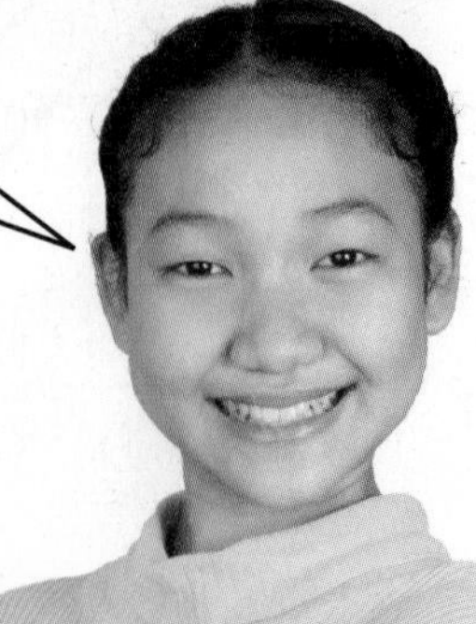

$$\frac{1}{2} + \frac{1}{3} = \frac{3}{6} + \frac{2}{6} = \frac{5}{6}$$

$\frac{5}{6}$ of the plank is painted red and green.

Guided Practice

Add the fractions.

1 $\frac{1}{2} + \frac{2}{7}$

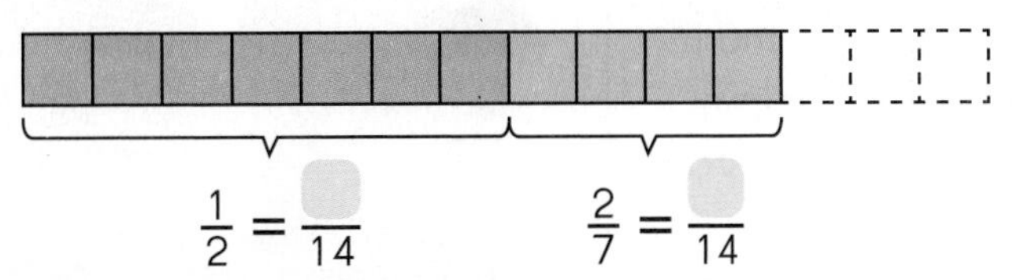

The least common multiple of 2 and 7 is 14.
$\frac{1}{2} = \frac{\square}{14}$
$\frac{2}{7} = \frac{\square}{14}$

$\frac{1}{2} \xrightarrow{\times 7} = \frac{7}{14}$ $\qquad$ $\frac{2}{7} \xrightarrow{\times 2} = \frac{4}{14}$

$\frac{1}{2} + \frac{2}{7} = \frac{\square}{14} + \frac{\square}{14}$

$= \frac{\square}{\square}$

2 $\frac{3}{4} + \frac{2}{3} = \frac{\square}{\square} + \frac{\square}{\square}$

$= \frac{\square}{\square}$

$= \frac{\square}{\square} + \frac{\square}{\square}$

$= \square$

$\frac{3}{4} \xrightarrow{\times 3} = \frac{\square}{\square}$ $\qquad$ $\frac{2}{3} \xrightarrow{\times 4} = \frac{\square}{\square}$

Hands-On Activity

Use a computer drawing tool. Draw models that show the sum for each pair of fractions. Then find the sum.

1 $\frac{1}{2} + \frac{1}{4}$ $\qquad$ **2** $\frac{1}{5} + \frac{3}{4}$ $\qquad$ **3** $\frac{1}{4} + \frac{2}{3}$

Learn Use benchmarks to estimate sums of fractions.

Benchmarks are numbers that are easier to work with and to picture than others. They help compare numbers and estimate answers.

In estimating with fractions, you approximate each fraction to the closest benchmark. Common benchmarks for estimating with fractions are 0, $\frac{1}{2}$ and 1.

Estimate the sum of $\frac{11}{12}$, $\frac{2}{3}$ and $\frac{1}{6}$.

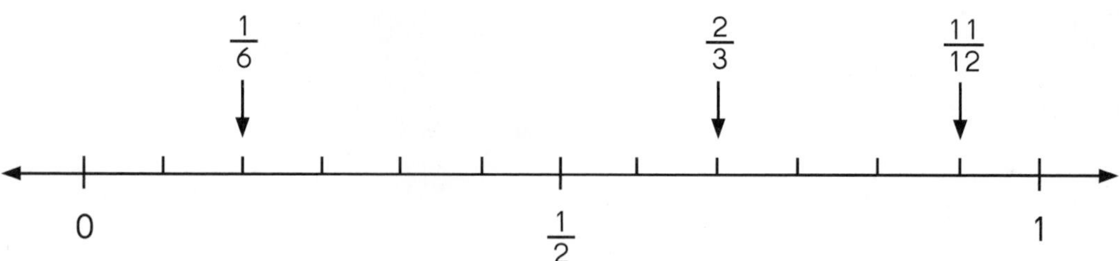

$\frac{11}{12}$ is about 1.

$\frac{2}{3}$ is about $\frac{1}{2}$.

$\frac{1}{6}$ is about 0.

$$\frac{11}{12} + \frac{2}{3} + \frac{1}{6}$$

$$1 + \frac{1}{2} + 0 = 1\frac{1}{2}$$

The sum of $\frac{11}{12}$, $\frac{2}{3}$ and $\frac{1}{6}$ is about $1\frac{1}{2}$.

Guided Practice

Use benchmarks to estimate each sum.

3 $\frac{1}{10} + \frac{2}{5}$

4 $\frac{8}{9} + \frac{9}{10}$

5 $\frac{1}{6} + \frac{7}{12} + \frac{5}{6}$

Let's Explore!

1. Without solving, do you think the sum of $\frac{1}{3}$ and $\frac{3}{8}$ is less than 1? Explain your reasoning.
2. Do you think the sum of $\frac{5}{9}$ and $\frac{6}{11}$ is greater than 1? Why do you think so?
3. Can you tell if the sum of $\frac{5}{11}$ and $\frac{4}{7}$ is greater than or less than 1? Why or why not?

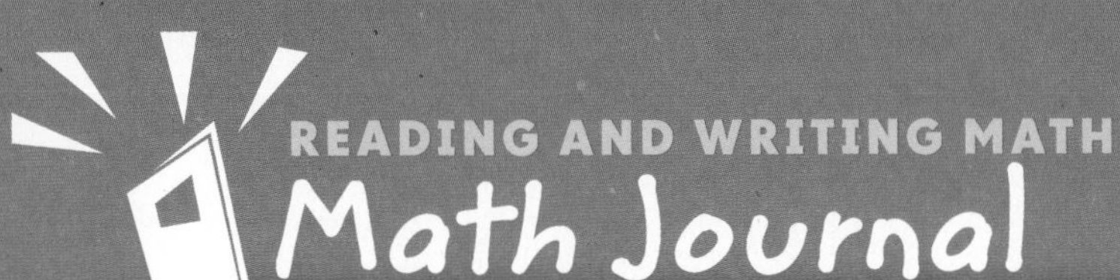

One of the three models shows the sum of $\frac{1}{2}$ and $\frac{1}{7}$. The other two models are incorrect.

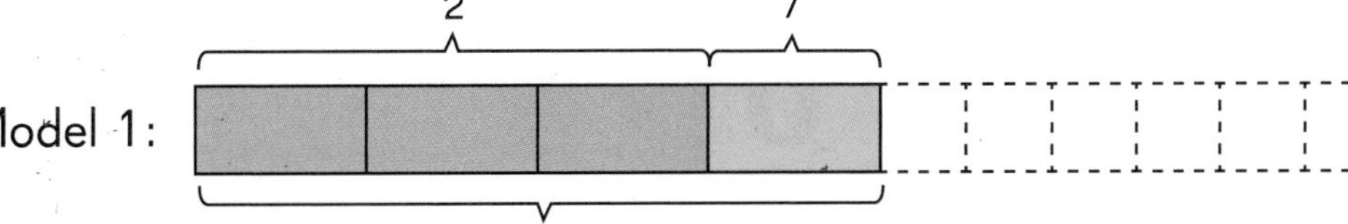

$\frac{1}{2}$ $\frac{1}{7}$

Model 2:

?

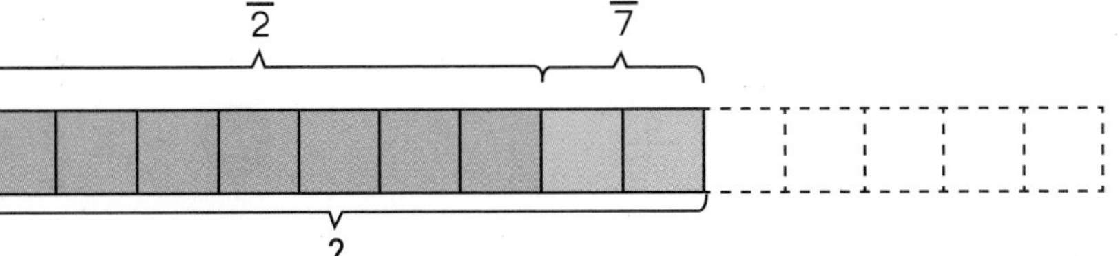

a. Identify the correct one of the three.

b. Explain why the other two are incorrect.

Let's Practice

Find the part of the model that shows the fractions $\frac{1}{2}$, $\frac{2}{5}$ and $\frac{9}{10}$. Then write two addition sentences using the fractions.

1

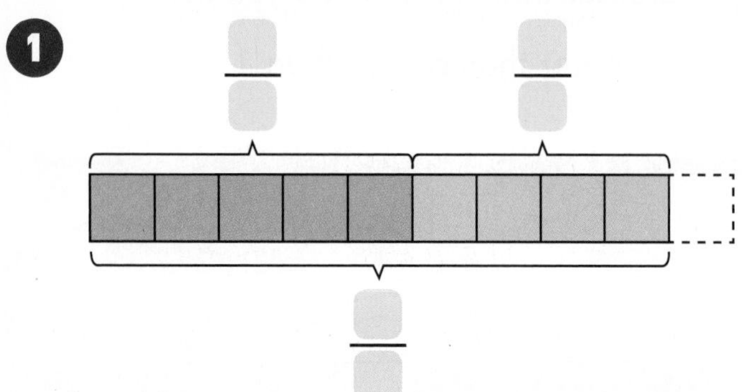

Draw a model to find each sum.

2 $\frac{1}{3}$ and $\frac{1}{4}$

3 $\frac{3}{5}$ and $\frac{1}{3}$

Add. Express each sum in simplest form.

4 $\frac{2}{3} + \frac{1}{8}$

5 $\frac{2}{3} + \frac{1}{12}$

6 $\frac{1}{5} + \frac{3}{10}$

7 $\frac{1}{4} + \frac{1}{6}$

8 $\frac{5}{9} + \frac{1}{2}$

9 $\frac{2}{5} + \frac{5}{6}$

10 $\frac{3}{4} + \frac{5}{12}$

11 $\frac{1}{6} + \frac{5}{8}$

Use benchmarks to estimate each sum.

12 $\frac{2}{5} + \frac{6}{7}$

13 $\frac{4}{9} + \frac{4}{10}$

14 $\frac{1}{8} + \frac{3}{5} + \frac{9}{10}$

ON YOUR OWN

Go to Workbook A:
Practice 1, pages 93–98

Lesson 3.2 Subtracting Unlike Fractions

Lesson Objectives

- Subtract two unlike fractions where one denominator is not a multiple of the other.
- Estimate differences between fractions.

Learn Find common denominators to subtract unlike fractions.

A carton contains $\frac{3}{4}$ quart of milk. Larry pours $\frac{1}{3}$ quart of the milk into a mug. How much milk is left in the carton?

$\frac{3}{4} - \frac{1}{3} = ?$

$\frac{1}{3}$ and $\frac{3}{4}$ are unlike fractions. To subtract, rewrite $\frac{1}{3}$ and $\frac{3}{4}$ as like fractions.

List the multiples of the denominators, 3 and 4.

Multiples of 3: 3, 6, 9, 12, ... Multiples of 4: 4, 8, 12, 16, ...

The least common multiple of 3 and 4 is 12.

So, 12 is the least common denominator of $\frac{1}{3}$ and $\frac{3}{4}$. Use it to rewrite $\frac{3}{4}$ and $\frac{1}{3}$ as like fractions.

$\frac{3}{4} = \frac{3 \times 3}{4 \times 3} = \frac{9}{12}$ $\frac{1}{3} = \frac{1 \times 4}{3 \times 4} = \frac{4}{12}$

$\frac{3}{4}$ and $\frac{9}{12}$, and $\frac{1}{3}$ and $\frac{4}{12}$ are equivalent fractions.

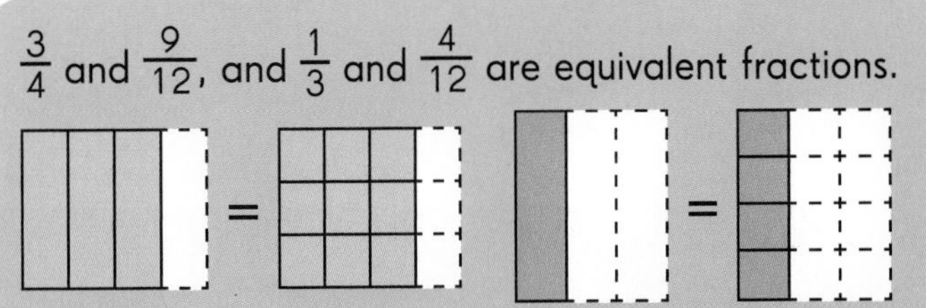

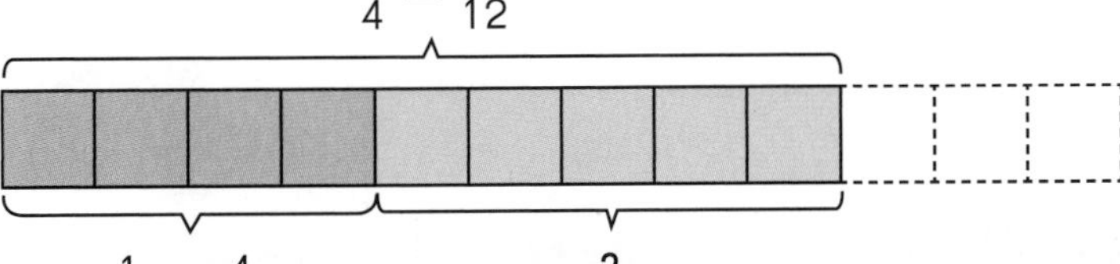

$$\frac{3}{4} - \frac{1}{3} = \frac{9}{12} - \frac{4}{12}$$
$$= \frac{5}{12}$$

Since 12 is the least common multiple, I draw a model with 12 units.

$\frac{5}{12}$ quart of milk is left in the carton.

Guided Practice

Subtract the fractions.

1 $\frac{2}{3} - \frac{1}{5}$

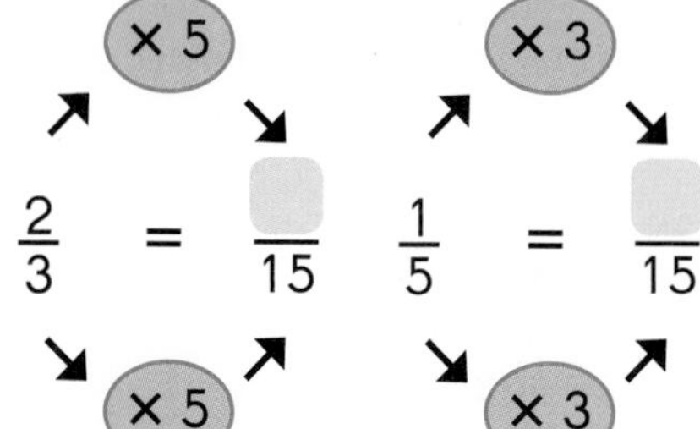

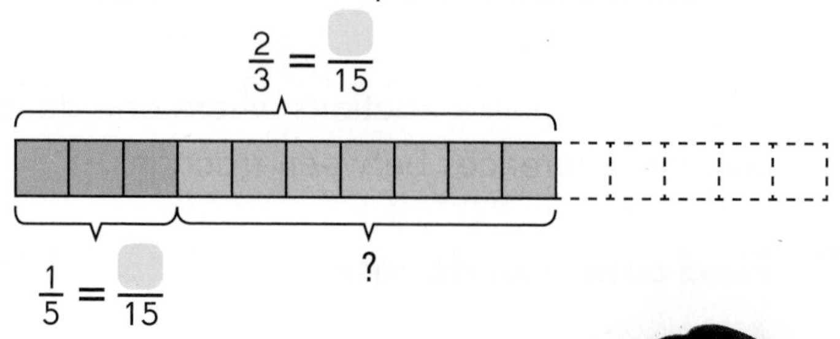
The least common multiple of 3 and 5 is 15.
2/3 = ?/15
1/5 = ?/15
?

$\frac{2}{3} - \frac{1}{5} = \frac{\square}{15} - \frac{\square}{15}$

$= \frac{\square}{15}$

2 $1 - \frac{1}{4} - \frac{1}{6} = 1 - \frac{\square}{\square} - \frac{\square}{\square}$

$= \frac{\square}{\square} - \frac{\square}{\square} - \frac{\square}{\square}$

$= \frac{\square}{\square}$

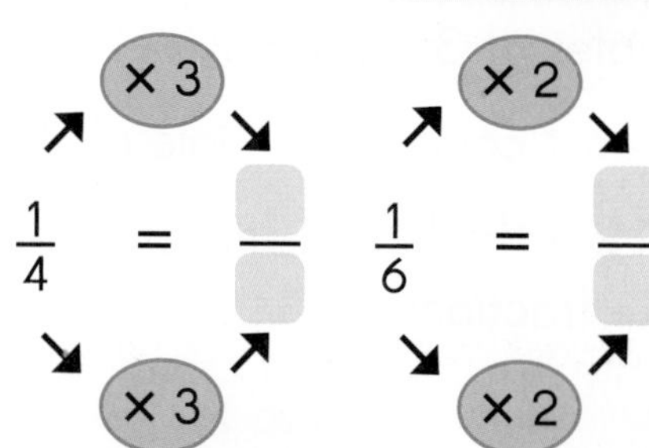

Hands-On Activity

Tech Connection

Use a computer drawing tool. Draw models that show the difference for each pair of fractions. Then find the difference.

1 $\frac{1}{2} - \frac{2}{7}$ **2** $\frac{5}{6} - \frac{4}{9}$ **3** $\frac{3}{4} - \frac{3}{5}$

Learn Use benchmarks to estimate differences between fractions.

Estimate the difference between $\frac{8}{9}$ and $\frac{4}{10}$.

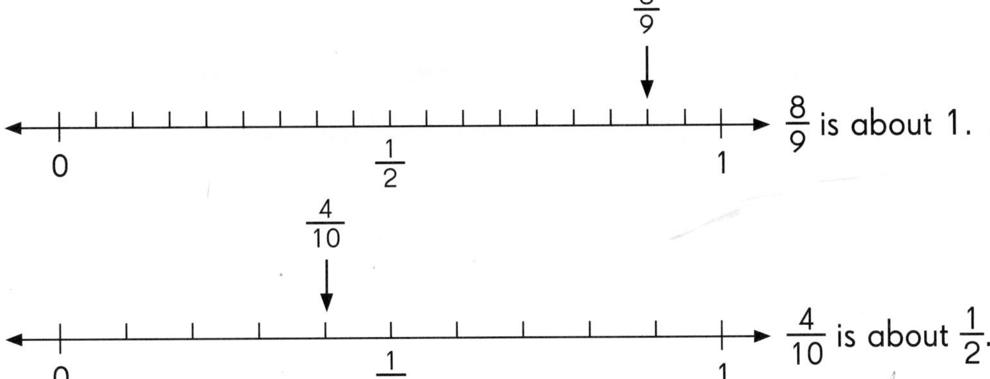

$$\begin{array}{ccccc} \frac{8}{9} & - & \frac{4}{10} & & \\ \downarrow & & \downarrow & & \\ 1 & - & \frac{1}{2} & = & \frac{1}{2} \end{array}$$

The difference between $\frac{8}{9}$ and $\frac{4}{10}$ is about $\frac{1}{2}$.

Guided Practice

Use benchmarks to estimate each difference.

3. $\frac{5}{6} - \frac{2}{5}$

4. $\frac{9}{10} - \frac{1}{8}$

5. $\frac{7}{12} - \frac{4}{9}$

Let's Explore!

1. Without solving, do you think the difference between 1 and $\frac{3}{7}$ is greater than $\frac{1}{2}$? Explain your reasoning.
2. Do you think the difference between 1 and $\frac{7}{12}$ is less than $\frac{1}{2}$? Explain your reasoning.
3. Can you tell if the difference between $\frac{11}{12}$ and $\frac{1}{4}$ is greater than or less than $\frac{1}{2}$? Explain your reasoning.

Let's Practice

Find the part of the model that shows the fractions $\frac{1}{2}$, $\frac{3}{10}$ and $\frac{4}{5}$. Then write two subtraction sentences using the fractions.

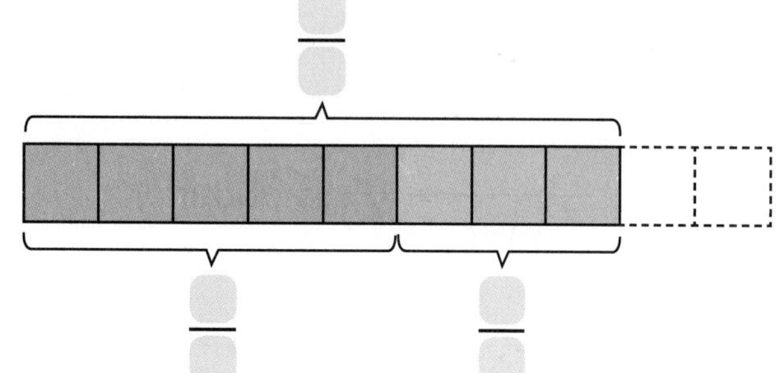

Draw a model to find each difference.

2. $\frac{5}{8} - \frac{1}{2}$

3. $\frac{4}{5} - \frac{1}{4}$

Subtract. Express each difference in simplest form.

4. $\frac{8}{9} - \frac{5}{6}$

5. $\frac{11}{12} - \frac{7}{8}$

6. $\frac{4}{5} - \frac{2}{7}$

7. $\frac{7}{9} - \frac{3}{4}$

8. $\frac{4}{7} - \frac{1}{6}$

9. $\frac{2}{3} - \frac{3}{8}$

10. $2 - \frac{1}{3} - \frac{9}{10}$

11. $4 - \frac{5}{6} - \frac{3}{8}$

Use benchmarks to estimate each difference.

12. $\frac{4}{5} - \frac{3}{7}$

13. $\frac{5}{8} - \frac{1}{9}$

14. $\frac{11}{12} - \frac{5}{6}$

ON YOUR OWN

Go to Workbook A: Practice 2, pages 99–102

Lesson

3.3 Fractions, Mixed Numbers, and Division Expressions

Lesson Objective

- Understand and apply the relationships between fractions, mixed numbers, and division expressions.

Vocabulary
division expression
mixed number

Learn

Rewrite division expressions as fractions.

Three friends share 2 pizzas equally.
What fraction of a pizza does each friend get?

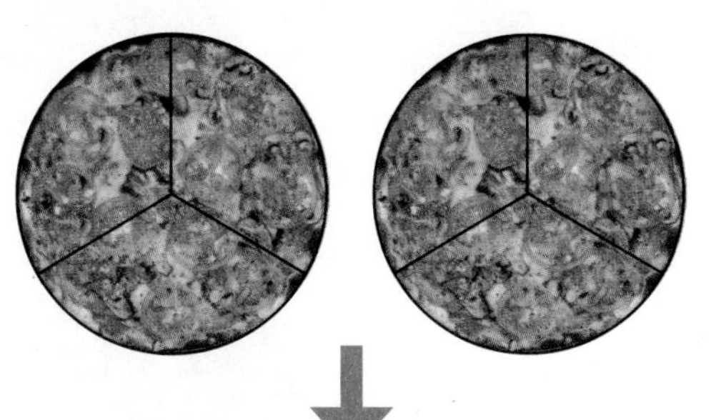

Each pizza is divided into 3 equal parts. Each part is $\frac{1}{3}$ of a pizza.

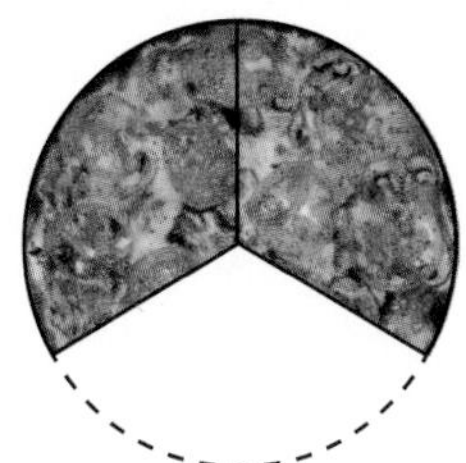

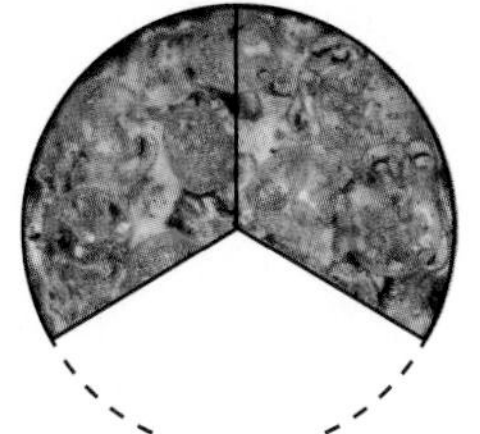

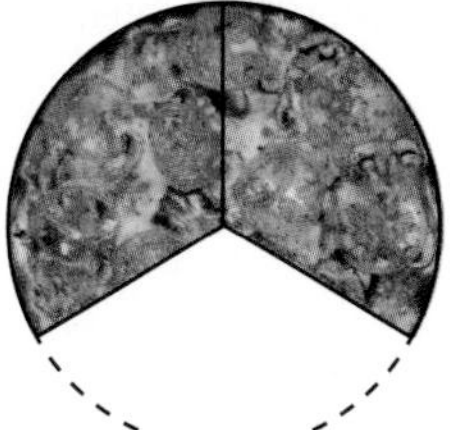

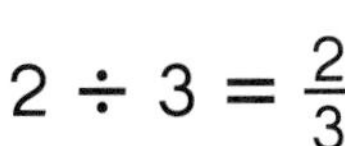

$2 \div 3 = \frac{2}{3}$

Each friend will get $\frac{2}{3}$ of a pizza.

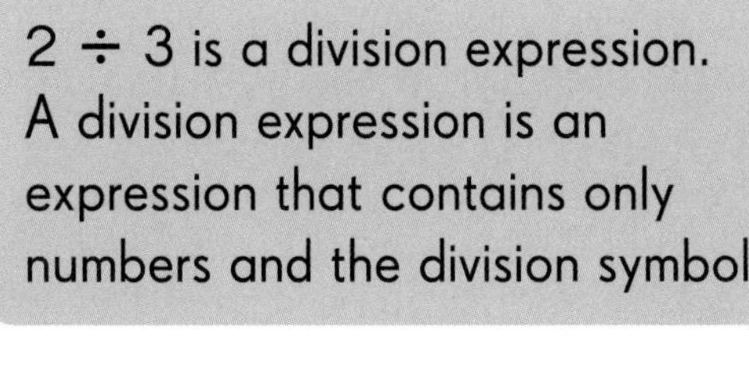

$2 \div 3$ is a division expression. A division expression is an expression that contains only numbers and the division symbol.

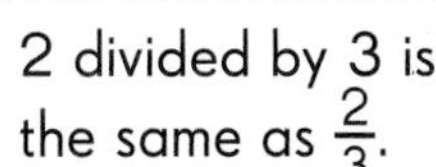

2 divided by 3 is the same as $\frac{2}{3}$.

Guided Practice

Solve.

1 Mr. Sheldon cuts 3 strawberry pies to share equally among 4 children. What fraction of a strawberry pie does each child get?

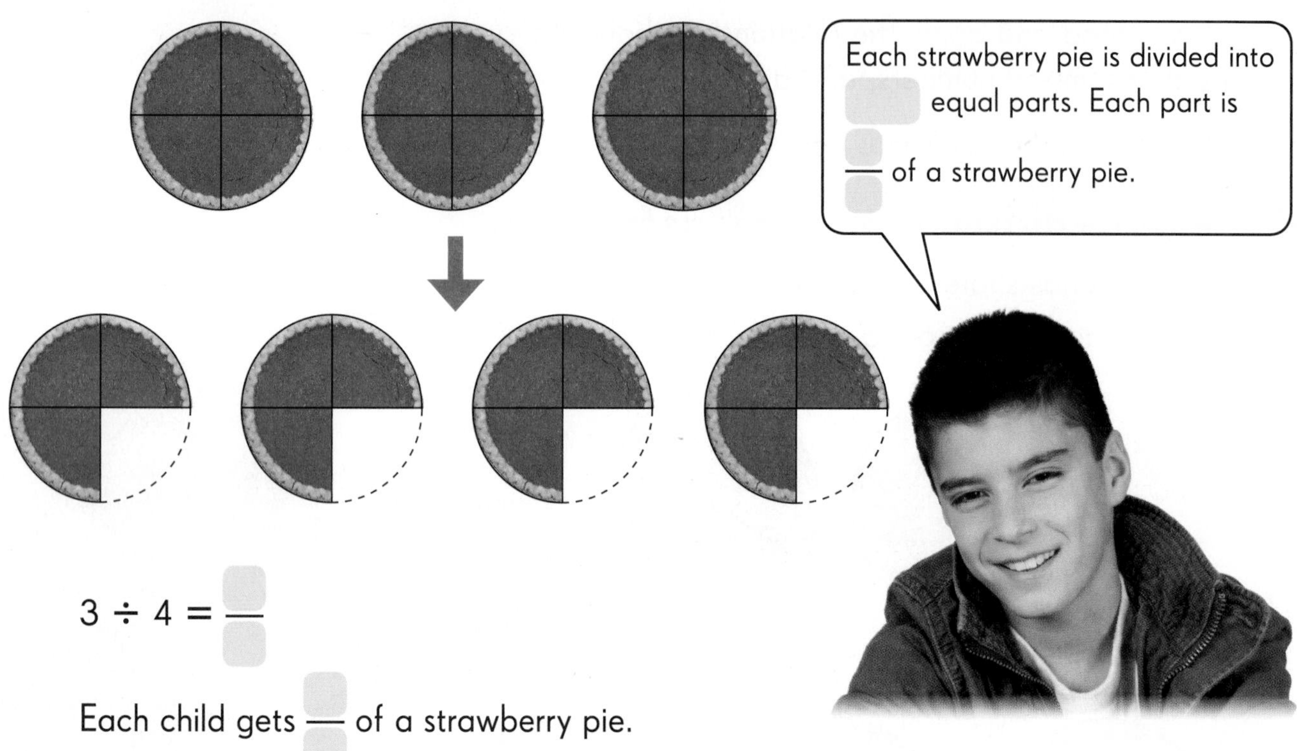
Each strawberry pie is divided into $\square$ equal parts. Each part is $\frac{\square}{\square}$ of a strawberry pie.

$3 \div 4 = \frac{\square}{\square}$

Each child gets $\frac{\square}{\square}$ of a strawberry pie.

3 divided by 4 is the same as $\frac{\square}{\square}$.

Hands-On Activity

WORKING TOGETHER

Use paper strips of the same size and length. Use fewer paper strips than the number of students in your group.

Cut the strips into equal pieces so that each student gets the same number of pieces.

Example

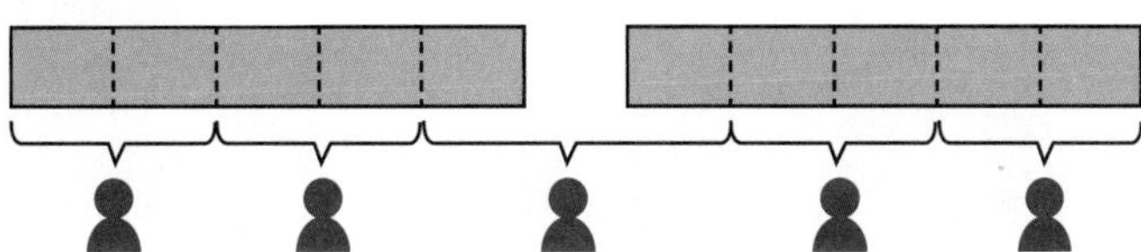

Write a division expression to show the fraction of a strip that each person gets. For example in STEP 1, write $2 \div 5 = \frac{2}{5}$.

Guided Practice

Rewrite each division expression as a fraction.

2. $4 \div 5 = \frac{\square}{\square}$

3. $7 \div 9 = \frac{\square}{\square}$

4. $5 \div 8 = \frac{\square}{\square}$

5. $7 \div 11 = \frac{\square}{\square}$

Rewrite each fraction as a division expression.

6. $\frac{3}{7} = \square \div \square$

7. $\frac{8}{12} = \square \div \square$

8. $\frac{3}{10} = \square \div \square$

9. $\frac{5}{6} = \square \div \square$

Learn Rewrite division expressions as **mixed numbers.**

Katie uses a mold to make 5 equal-sized pies. She then divides the 5 pies equally among 4 people. How many pies does each person get?

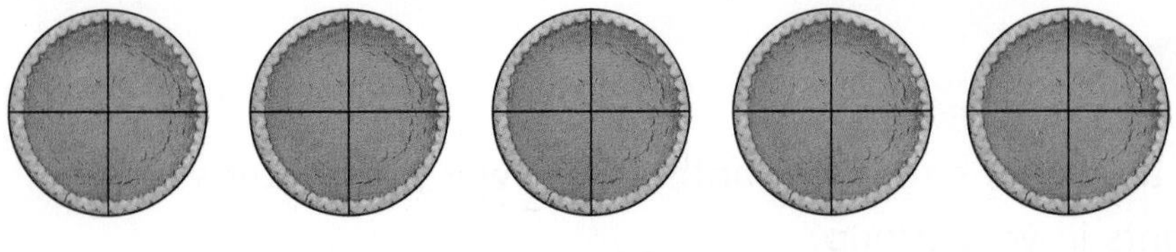

Each pie is divided into 4 equal parts.

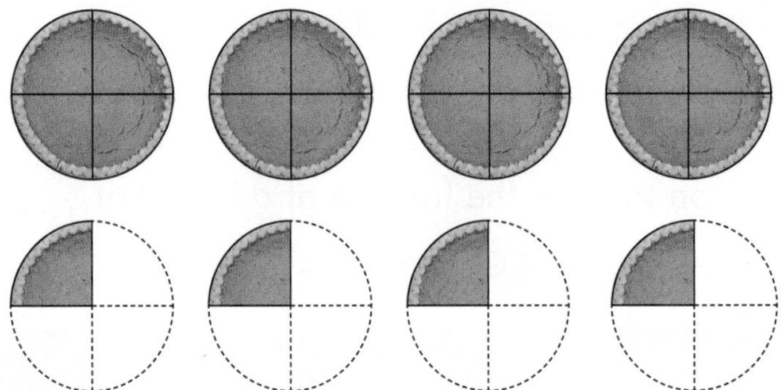

Method 1

$$\begin{aligned} 5 \div 4 &= \frac{5}{4} \\ &= \frac{4}{4} + \frac{1}{4} \\ &= 1\frac{1}{4} \end{aligned}$$

5 divided by 4 is the same as $\frac{5}{4}$ or $1\frac{1}{4}$.

Method 2

$$\begin{array}{r} 1 \\ 4\overline{)5} \\ \underline{4} \\ 1 \end{array}$$

1 ← number of wholes

1 ← number of fourths

$5 \div 4 = 1\frac{1}{4}$

Each person gets $1\frac{1}{4}$ pies.

Use paper strips of the same size and length. Use a greater number of paper strips than the number of students in your group.

STEP 1 Cut the strips into equal pieces so that each person gets the same number of pieces.

Example

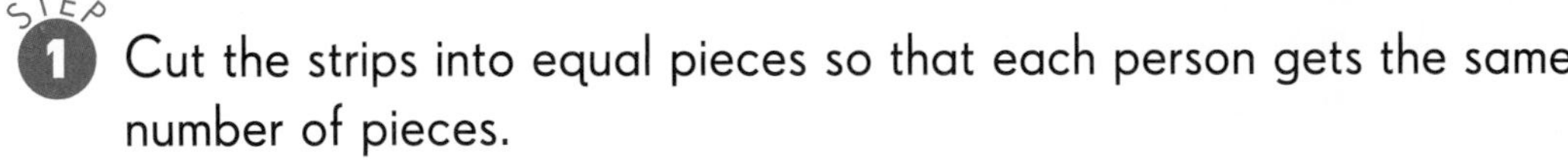

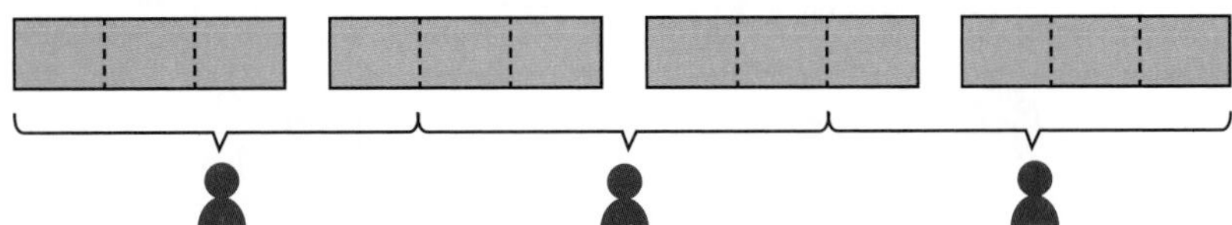

STEP 2 Write a division expression to show the number of strips each person gets. Then, express it as a fraction and a mixed number.

For example in STEP 1, write $4 \div 3 = \frac{4}{3} = 1\frac{1}{3}$.

Guided Practice

Express 14 ÷ 4 as a fraction in simplest form. Then rewrite the fraction as a mixed number.

10 $14 \div 4 = \frac{\square \div \square}{\square \div \square}$

$= \frac{\square}{\square}$

$= \square\frac{\square}{\square}$

Express each division expression as a fraction in simplest form. Then rewrite the fraction as a mixed number.

11. 19 ÷ 2
12. 43 ÷ 4
13. 49 ÷ 5
14. 20 ÷ 8

Let's Practice

Rewrite each fraction as a division expression.

1. $\frac{4}{7}$ = ☐ ÷ ☐
2. $\frac{5}{11}$ = ☐ ÷ ☐
3. $\frac{9}{13}$ = ☐ ÷ ☐

Express each division expression as a fraction or mixed number in simplest form.

4. $10 \div 12 = \frac{☐}{☐}$

   $= \frac{☐}{☐}$

5. $3 \div 2 = \frac{3}{2}$

   $= \frac{☐}{☐} + \frac{☐}{☐}$

   $= ☐\frac{☐}{☐}$

   2) 3 (quotient ☐; ☐ subtracted; remainder ☐)

6. 7 ÷ 3
7. 11 ÷ 4
8. 25 ÷ 7

Express each division expression as a fraction in simplest form. Then rewrite the fraction as a mixed number.

9. 22 ÷ 4
10. 32 ÷ 12

ON YOUR OWN

Go to Workbook A: Practice 3, pages 103–106

Expressing Fractions, Division Expressions, and Mixed Numbers as Decimals

Lesson Objective

- Express fractions, division expressions, and mixed numbers as decimals.

Learn Express a fraction as a decimal by finding an equivalent fraction.

Express $\frac{2}{5}$ as a decimal.

Use a denominator of 10.

$$\frac{2}{5} = \frac{2 \times 2}{5 \times 2}$$
$$= \frac{4}{10}$$
$$= 0.4$$

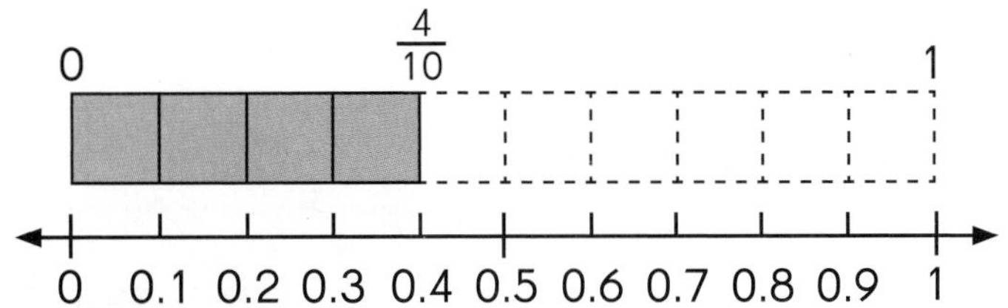

Read 0.4 as four tenths.

Express $\frac{9}{20}$ as a decimal.

Use a denominator of 100.

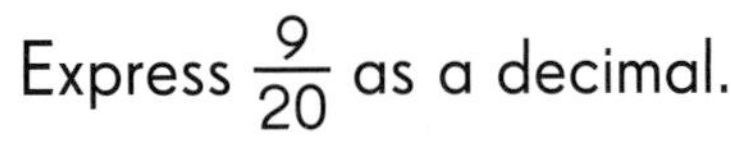

$$\frac{9}{20} = \frac{9 \times 5}{20 \times 5}$$
$$= \frac{45}{100}$$
$$= 0.45$$

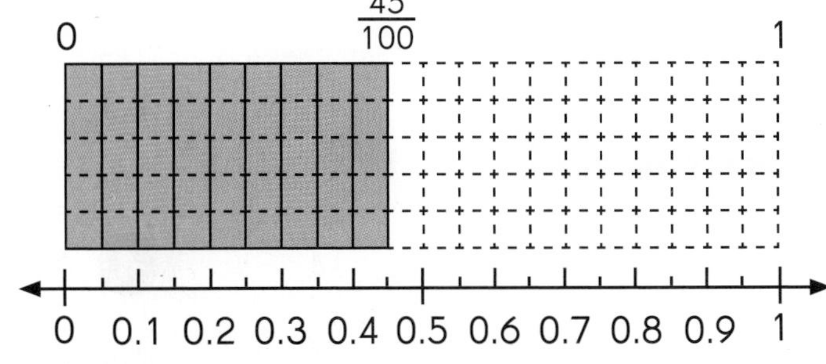

Read 0.45 as forty-five hundredths.

Guided Practice

Express each fraction as a decimal.

1. $\frac{4}{5} = \frac{\square}{10} = \square$

2. $\frac{7}{20} = \frac{\square}{100} = \square$

Learn Express division expressions as decimals.

Express $9 \div 6$ as a decimal.

$$9 \div 6 = \frac{9}{6}$$
$$= 1 + \frac{3}{6}$$
$$= 1 + \frac{1}{2}$$
$$= 1 + 0.5$$
$$= 1.5$$

$$\frac{1}{2} \overset{\times 5}{=} \frac{5}{10} = 0.5$$

Learn Express mixed numbers as decimals.

Express $2\frac{1}{4}$ as a decimal.

$$2\frac{1}{4} = 2 + \frac{1}{4}$$
$$= 2 + 0.25$$
$$= 2.25$$

$$\frac{1}{4} \overset{\times 25}{=} \frac{25}{100} = 0.25$$

Guided Practice

Express as a decimal.

3. $12 \div 5$

4. $67 \div 25$

5. $3\frac{3}{5}$

6. $5\frac{7}{20}$

Write a division expression for the problem. Then solve.

7. Mr. Jones has a bolt of cloth that is 6 yards long. He wants to divide it into 5 equal pieces. How long must each piece be?
Give your answer as

a. a mixed number,

b. a decimal.

Let's Practice

Express each fraction as a decimal.

1. $\frac{3}{5}$
2. $\frac{17}{20}$
3. $\frac{9}{25}$
4. $\frac{16}{25}$

Write a division expression for the problem. Then solve.

5. Jeff makes 16 quarts of lemonade. He then divides the lemonade equally among 5 jugs. How many quarts of lemonade are in each jug?

   Give your answer as

   a. a mixed number,
   b. a decimal.

6. The perimeter of a square court is 39 yards. What is the length of each of its sides?

   Give your answer as

   a. a mixed number,
   b. a decimal.

Express as a mixed number and as a decimal.

7. $7 \div 4$
8. $13 \div 10$
9. $36 \div 30$
10. $\frac{14}{5}$
11. $\frac{45}{20}$
12. $\frac{37}{25}$

ON YOUR OWN

Go to Workbook A:
Practice 4, pages 107–108

Lesson 3.5 Adding Mixed Numbers

Lesson Objectives

- Add mixed numbers with or without renaming.
- Estimate sums of mixed numbers.

Learn Add mixed numbers without renaming.

Maia bought $2\frac{1}{5}$ pounds of oranges. She also bought $1\frac{1}{2}$ pounds of grapes. What is the total weight of fruit that she bought?

$2\frac{1}{5} + 1\frac{1}{2} = ?$

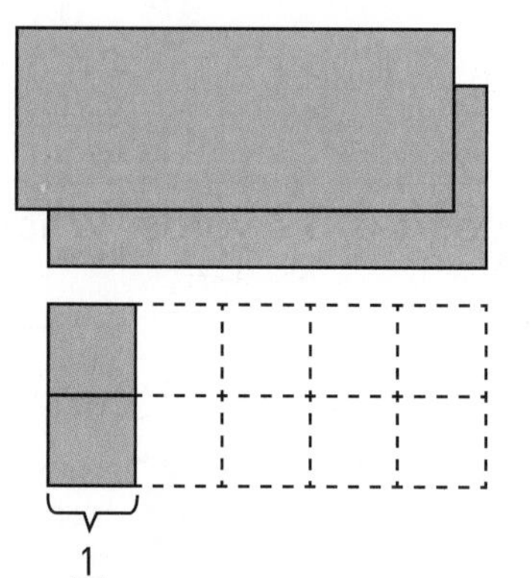

+

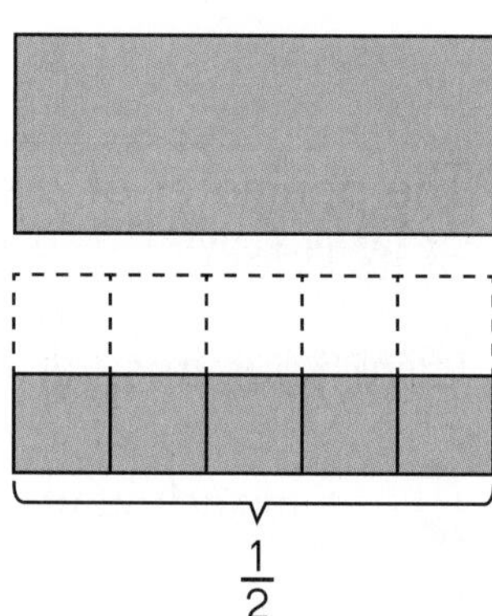

To add, rewrite the fractional parts as like fractions first. Then, add the fractional parts before adding the whole numbers.

$$\frac{1}{5} \xrightarrow{\times 2} = \frac{2}{10}$$

$$\frac{1}{2} \xrightarrow{\times 5} = \frac{5}{10}$$

$$2\frac{1}{5} + 1\frac{1}{2} = 2\frac{2}{10} + 1\frac{5}{10}$$
$$= 3\frac{7}{10}$$

Maia bought $3\frac{7}{10}$ pounds of fruit.

Guided Practice

Add.

1 $3\frac{1}{2} + 2\frac{4}{9}$

$= 3\frac{?}{?} + 2\frac{?}{?}$

$= ?\frac{?}{?}$

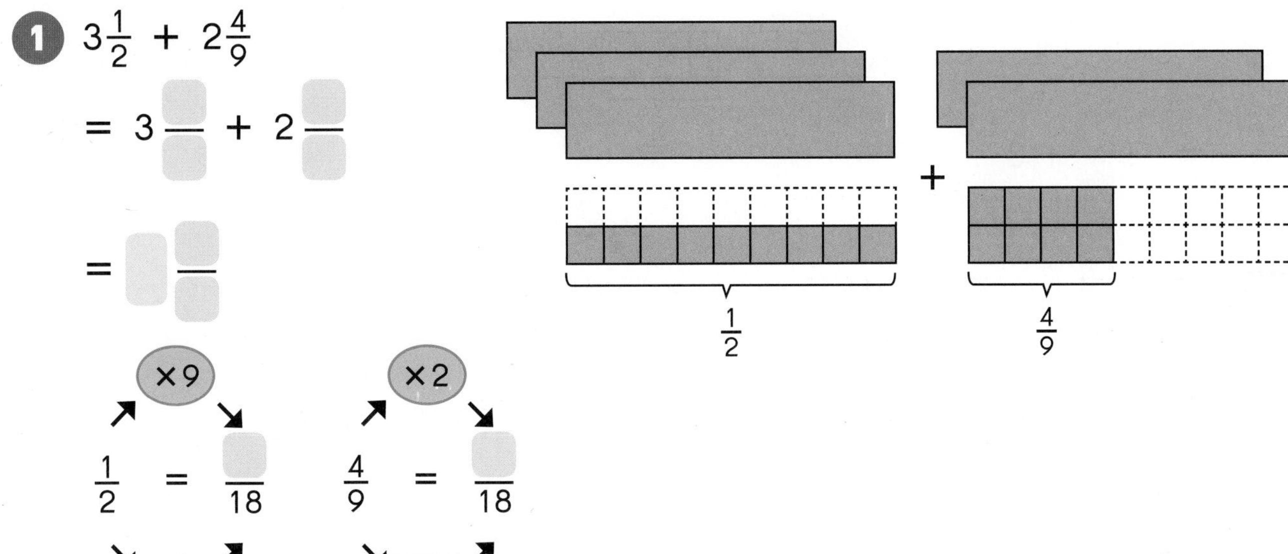

Learn

Add mixed numbers with renaming.

Serena jogged $2\frac{3}{4}$ miles and walked $1\frac{1}{2}$ miles. How many miles did she jog and walk altogether?

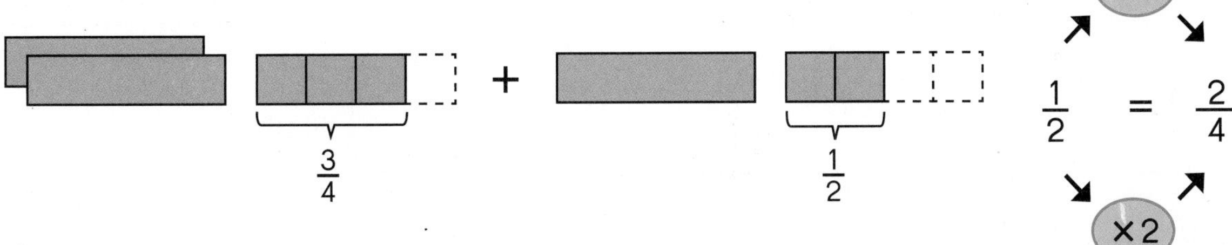

$2\frac{3}{4} + 1\frac{1}{2} = 2\frac{3}{4} + 1\frac{2}{4}$
$= 3\frac{5}{4}$
$= 4\frac{1}{4}$

$3\frac{5}{4} = 3 + \frac{4}{4} + \frac{1}{4}$
$= 3 + 1 + \frac{1}{4}$
$= 4\frac{1}{4}$

$4\overline{)5}$ quotient 1, -4, remainder 1

I can also rename $3\frac{5}{4}$ this way:
$\frac{5}{4} = 1\frac{1}{4}$
$3\frac{5}{4} = 3 + 1\frac{1}{4}$
$= 4\frac{1}{4}$

Serena jogged and walked $4\frac{1}{4}$ miles altogether.

Guided Practice

Find the sum of the mixed numbers.

2 $2\frac{2}{3} + 3\frac{1}{2}$

$= 2\frac{\square}{\square} + 3\frac{\square}{\square}$

$= 5\frac{\square}{\square}$

$= \square\frac{\square}{\square}$

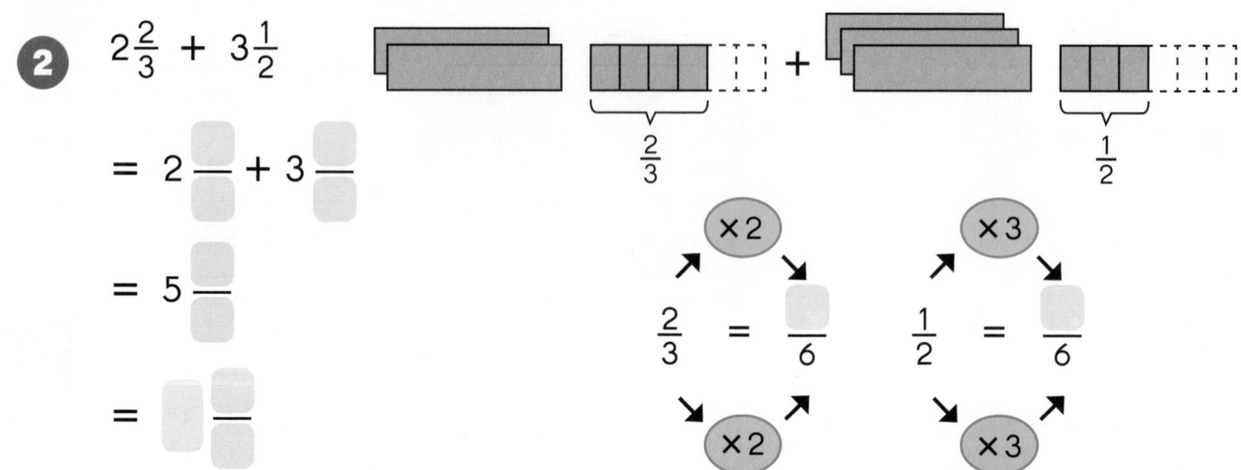

Learn: Use benchmarks to estimate sums of mixed numbers.

Estimate the sum of $2\frac{1}{3}$ and $3\frac{2}{5}$.

Compare the fractional part in each mixed number to the benchmarks,

$0, \frac{1}{2}$ and 1.

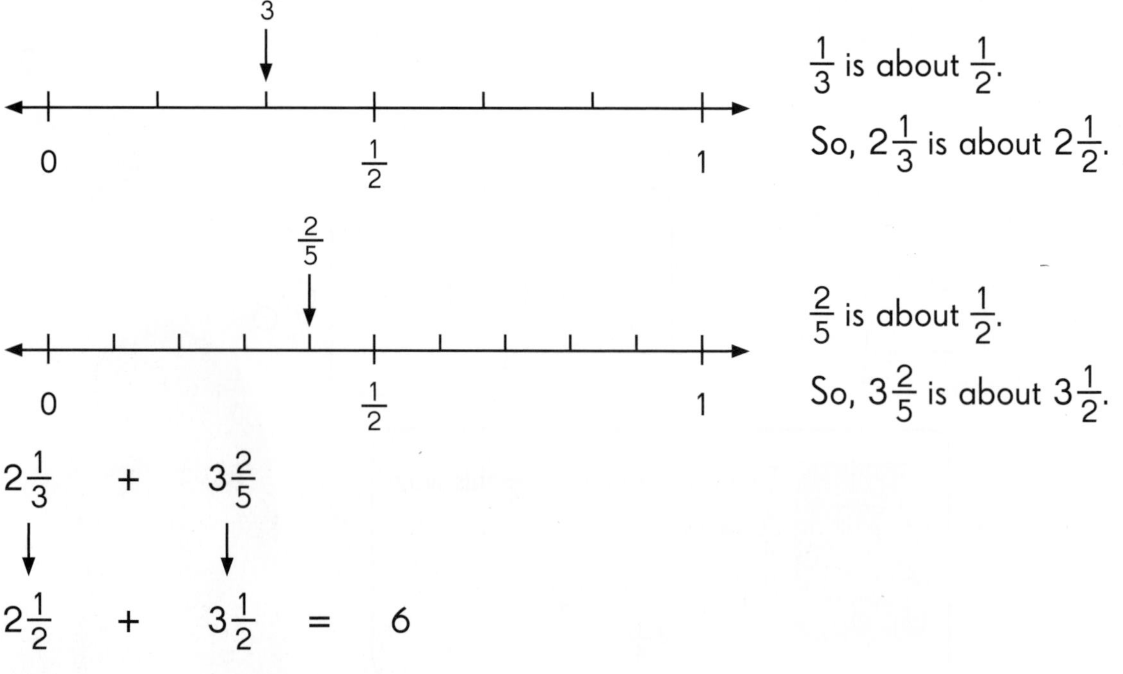

$\frac{1}{3}$ is about $\frac{1}{2}$.

So, $2\frac{1}{3}$ is about $2\frac{1}{2}$.

$\frac{2}{5}$ is about $\frac{1}{2}$.

So, $3\frac{2}{5}$ is about $3\frac{1}{2}$.

$2\frac{1}{3} + 3\frac{2}{5}$

$2\frac{1}{2} + 3\frac{1}{2} = 6$

The sum of $2\frac{1}{3}$ and $3\frac{2}{5}$ is about 6.

Guided Practice

Use benchmarks to estimate each sum.

3. $6\frac{7}{12} + 9\frac{3}{8}$

4. $11\frac{5}{6} + 5\frac{5}{9}$

5. $8\frac{3}{7} + 10\frac{1}{9}$

6. $32\frac{1}{5} + 14\frac{9}{10}$

7. $16\frac{9}{11} + 37\frac{2}{5}$

Let's Explore!

1. Without solving, do you think the sum of $1\frac{1}{4}$ and $3\frac{4}{9}$ is less than 5? Explain your reasoning.

2. Do you think the sum of $3\frac{5}{9}$ and $2\frac{7}{12}$ is greater than 6? Explain your reasoning.

3. Can you tell whether the sum of $3\frac{3}{8}$ and $5\frac{3}{5}$ is greater than or less than 9 by estimating? Explain your reasoning.

Let's Practice

Add. Express each sum in simplest form.

1. $1\frac{1}{4} + 2\frac{2}{5}$

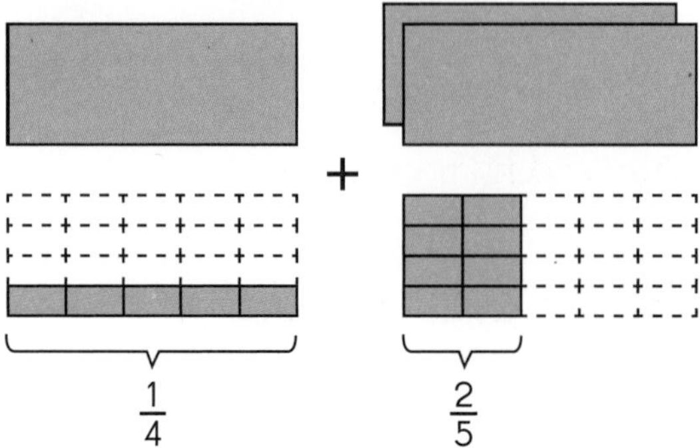

2. $3\frac{3}{8} + 4\frac{1}{3}$

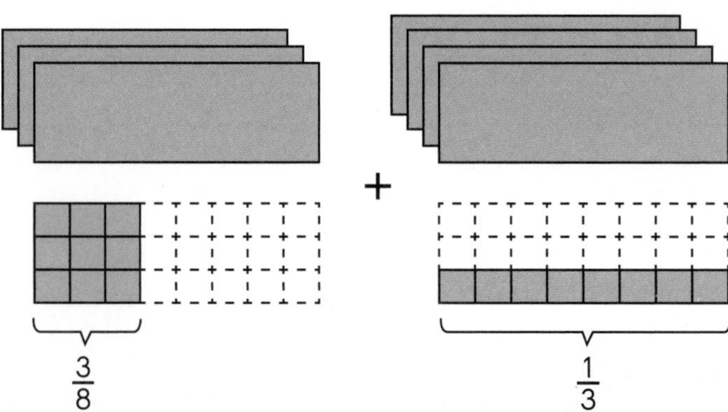

3. $5\frac{5}{6} + 3\frac{5}{12}$

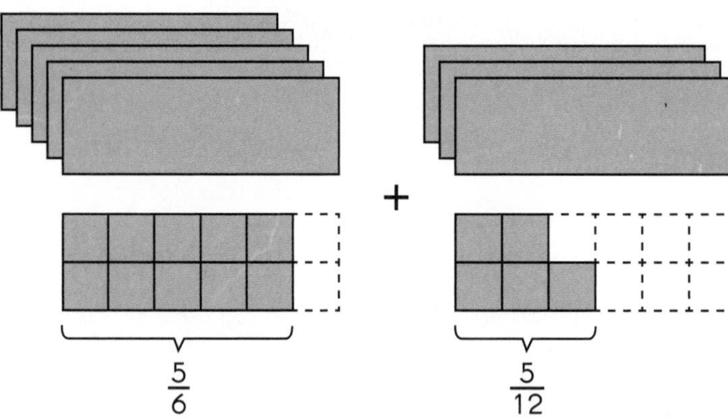

4. $1\frac{3}{5} + 2\frac{3}{8}$
5. $3\frac{3}{4} + 5\frac{2}{7}$
6. $5\frac{1}{6} + 2\frac{8}{9}$

Use benchmarks to estimate each sum.

7. $1\frac{3}{5} + 3\frac{4}{7}$
8. $5\frac{1}{8} + 7\frac{1}{12}$
9. $43\frac{5}{6} + 69\frac{5}{12}$

ON YOUR OWN

Go to Workbook A:
Practice 5, pages 109–112

Lesson 3.6 Subtracting Mixed Numbers

Lesson Objectives

- Subtract mixed numbers with or without renaming.
- Estimate differences between mixed numbers.

Learn Subtract mixed numbers without renaming.

Kim buys $2\frac{3}{4}$ yards of fabric. She cuts $1\frac{1}{8}$ yards to make a dress. How much fabric does she have left?

$2\frac{3}{4} - 1\frac{1}{8} = ?$

To subtract, rewrite the fractional parts as like fractions first. Then subtract the fractional parts before subtracting the whole numbers.

$$2\frac{3}{4} - 1\frac{1}{8} = 2\frac{6}{8} - 1\frac{1}{8}$$
$$= 1\frac{5}{8}$$

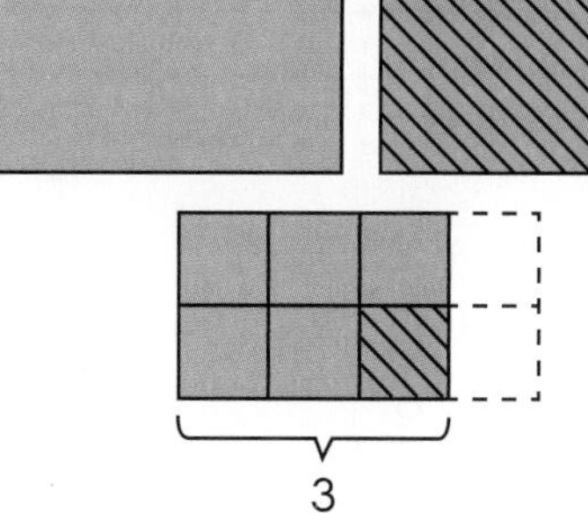

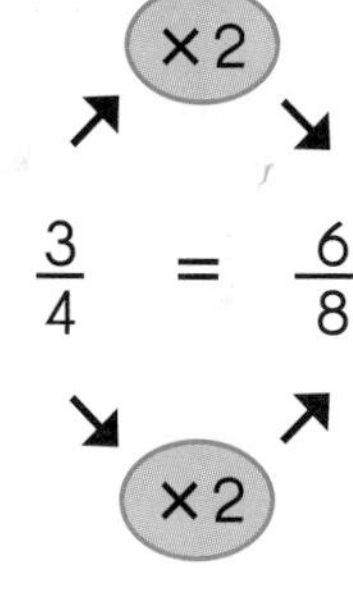

Kim has $1\frac{5}{8}$ yards of fabric left.

Guided Practice

Subtract.

1 $5\frac{5}{9} - 2\frac{1}{3} = 5\frac{\square}{9} - 2\frac{\square}{\square}$

$= \square\frac{\square}{\square}$

$\frac{1}{3} = \frac{\square}{9}$ (×3)

2 $3\frac{4}{5} - 2\frac{1}{2} = \square\frac{\square}{\square} - \square\frac{\square}{\square}$

$= \square\frac{\square}{\square}$

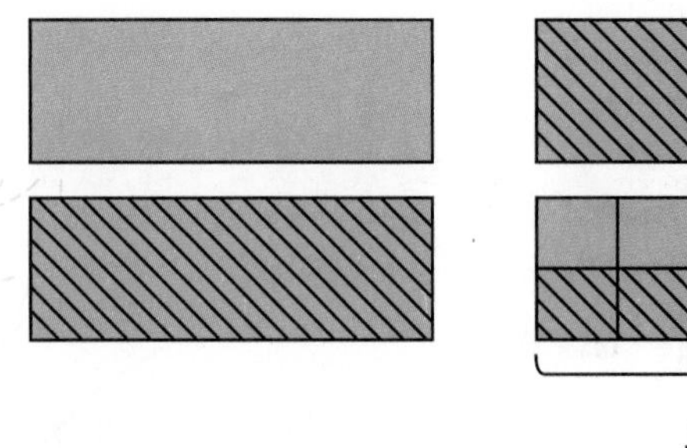

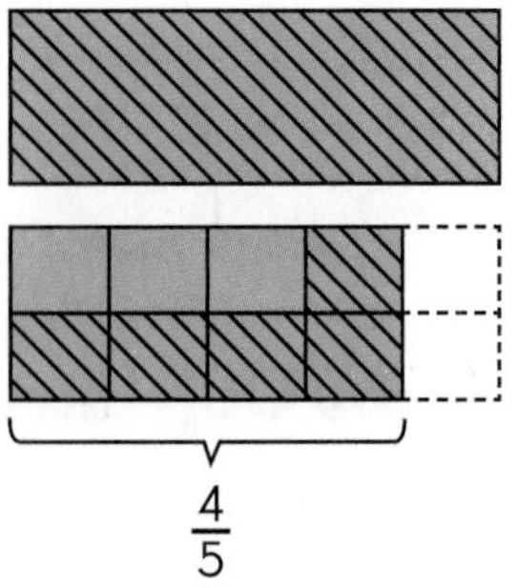

Learn **Subtract mixed numbers with renaming.**

A bottle contains $3\frac{1}{3}$ quarts of juice. Margaret uses $1\frac{3}{8}$ quarts of juice to make a fruit punch. How much juice is left in the bottle?

$3\frac{1}{3} - 1\frac{3}{8} = ?$

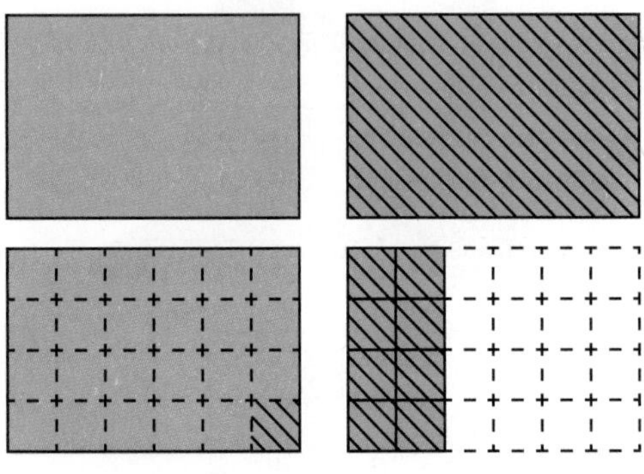

$\frac{1}{3} = \frac{8}{24}$ (×8) $\quad \frac{3}{8} = \frac{9}{24}$ (×3)

$$3\frac{1}{3} - 1\frac{3}{8} = 3\frac{8}{24} - 1\frac{9}{24}$$
$$= 2\frac{32}{24} - 1\frac{9}{24}$$
$$= 1\frac{23}{24}$$

$1\frac{23}{24}$ quarts of juice is left in the bottle.

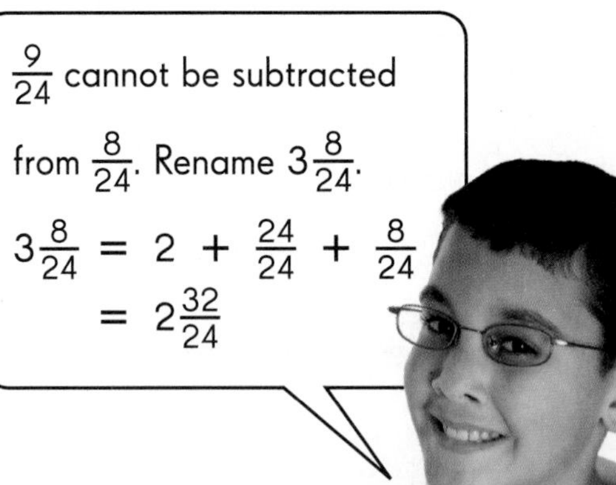

$\frac{9}{24}$ cannot be subtracted from $\frac{8}{24}$. Rename $3\frac{8}{24}$.
$3\frac{8}{24} = 2 + \frac{24}{24} + \frac{8}{24}$
$= 2\frac{32}{24}$

Guided Practice

Find the difference between the mixed numbers.

3 $4\frac{5}{9} - 3\frac{5}{6}$

$= 4\frac{\square}{\square} - 3\frac{\square}{\square}$

$= \square\frac{\square}{\square} - \square\frac{\square}{\square}$

$= \frac{\square}{\square}$

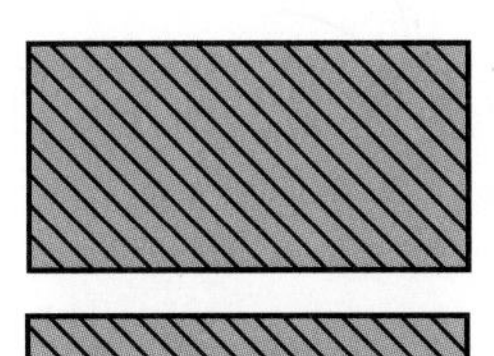

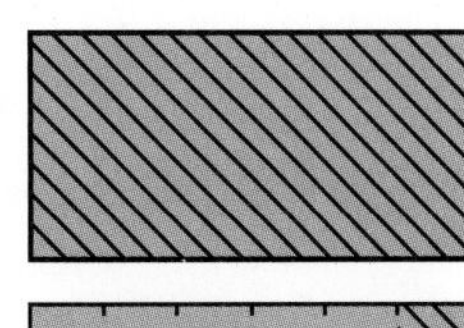

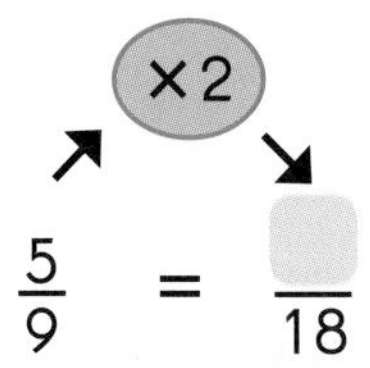

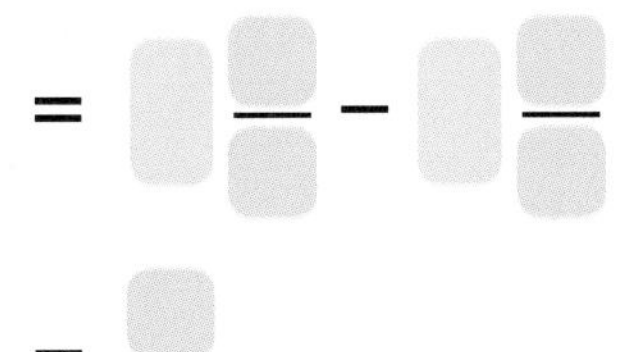

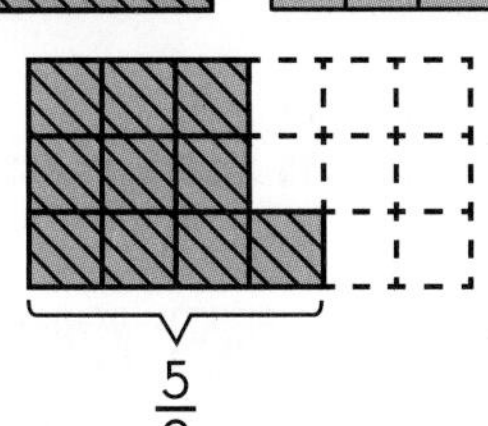

Learn: Use benchmarks to estimate differences between mixed numbers.

Estimate the difference between $4\frac{7}{8}$ and $3\frac{5}{12}$.

Compare the fractional part in each mixed number to the benchmarks,

$0, \frac{1}{2}$ and 1.

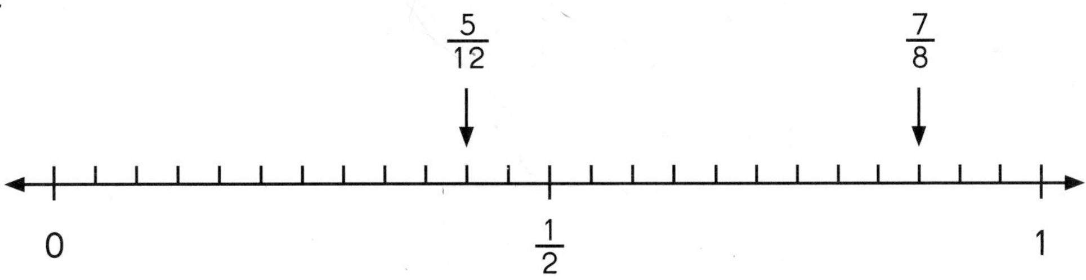

$\frac{7}{8}$ is about 1. So, $4\frac{7}{8}$ is about 5.

$\frac{5}{12}$ is about $\frac{1}{2}$. So, $3\frac{5}{12}$ is about $3\frac{1}{2}$.

$$4\frac{7}{8} - 3\frac{5}{12}$$

$$\downarrow \qquad \downarrow$$

$$5 - 3\frac{1}{2} = 1\frac{1}{2}$$

The difference between $4\frac{7}{8}$ and $3\frac{5}{12}$ is about $1\frac{1}{2}$.

Guided Practice

Use benchmarks to estimate each difference.

4. $7\frac{7}{9} - 3\frac{4}{7}$

5. $23\frac{2}{5} - 17\frac{1}{6}$

Let's Practice

Subtract. Express each difference in simplest form.

1. $3\frac{3}{4} - 1\frac{1}{2}$

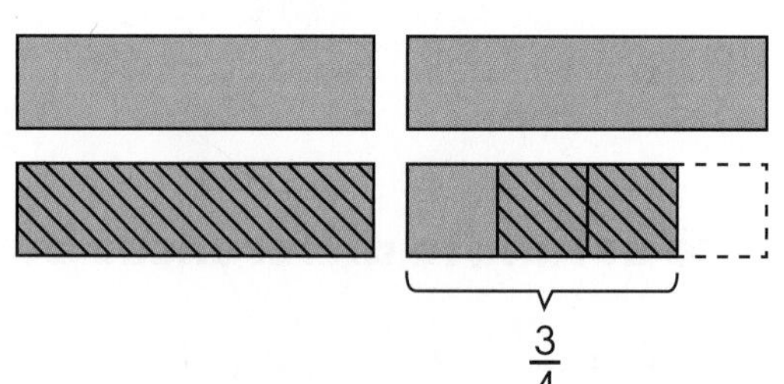

2. $5\frac{5}{6} - 2\frac{2}{3}$

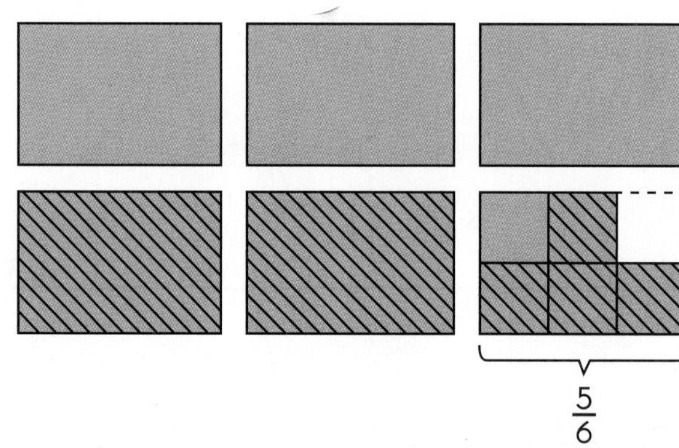

3. $4\frac{3}{8} - 1\frac{3}{4}$

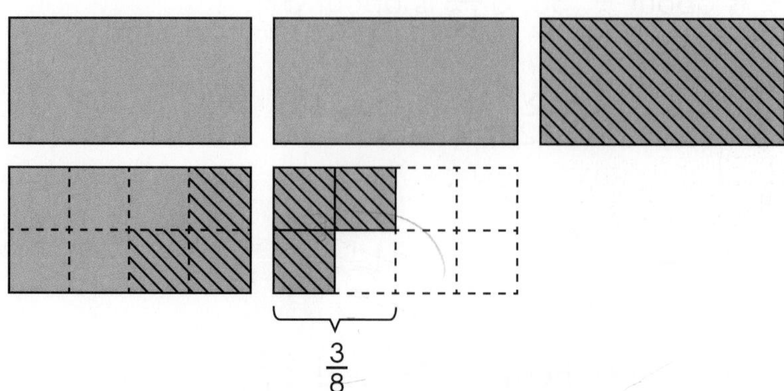

4 $3\frac{1}{4} - 1\frac{1}{3}$

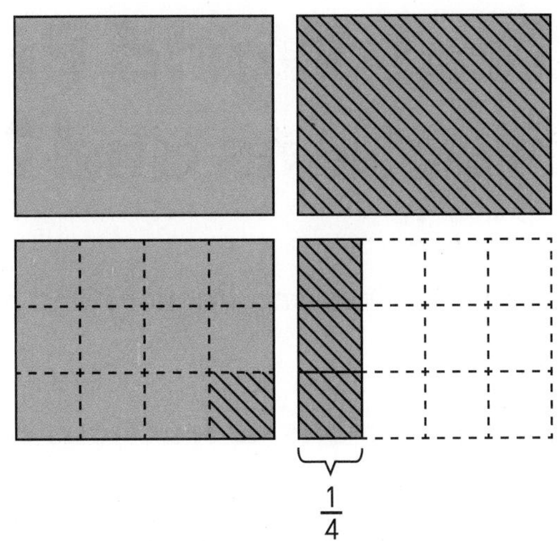

5 $4\frac{1}{6} - 3\frac{5}{8}$

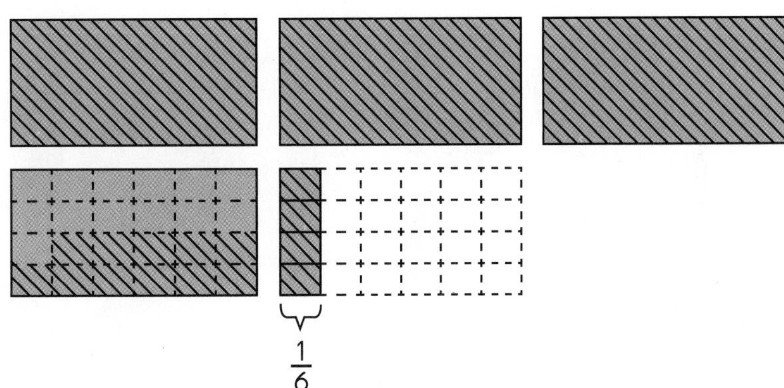

6 $7\frac{2}{3} - 4\frac{1}{2}$

7 $9\frac{4}{7} - 2\frac{1}{3}$

8 $6\frac{1}{10} - 3\frac{1}{5}$

9 $4\frac{1}{2} - 1\frac{7}{8}$

10 $5\frac{1}{4} - 2\frac{1}{3}$

11 $12\frac{7}{12} - 5\frac{8}{9}$

Use benchmarks to estimate each difference.

12 $6\frac{7}{10} - 4\frac{3}{5}$

13 $39\frac{4}{5} - 13\frac{5}{9}$

ON YOUR OWN

Go to Workbook A: Practice 6, pages 113–116

Lesson

3.7 Real-World Problems: Fractions and Mixed Numbers

Lesson Objective

- Solve real-world problems involving fractions and mixed numbers.

Learn

Write division expressions as fractions and mixed numbers.

Sheena bakes 5 pans of lasagna. She divides each of the 5 pans into 3 equal shares. How many pans are in each share?

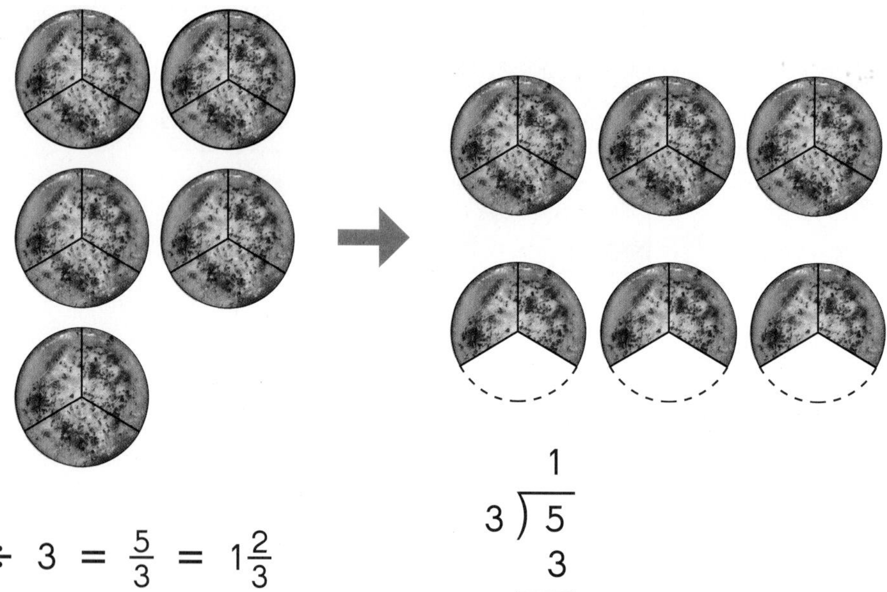

$$5 \div 3 = \frac{5}{3} = 1\frac{2}{3}$$

$$\begin{array}{r} 1 \\ 3\overline{)\,5} \\ \underline{3} \\ 2 \end{array}$$

There are $1\frac{2}{3}$ pans in each share.

Guided Practice

Solve.

1. Jerry pours 12 quarts of spring water equally among 5 bottles. How much water is in each bottle?

$\square \div \square = \frac{\square}{\square} = \square\frac{\square}{\square}$

There are $\square\frac{\square}{\square}$ quarts of water in each bottle.

Learn Draw a model to solve a one-step problem.

Adam expected his homework to take $\frac{4}{5}$ hour. He completed it in $\frac{3}{4}$ hour. How much faster did Adam complete his homework than he expected?

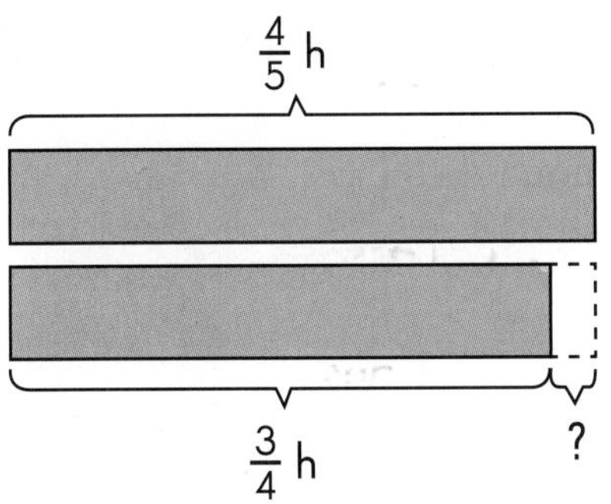

$$\frac{4}{5} - \frac{3}{4} = \frac{16}{20} - \frac{15}{20}$$
$$= \frac{1}{20}$$

Adam completed his homework $\frac{1}{20}$ hour faster.

Guided Practice

Solve.

2 Lisa has $1\frac{2}{9}$ pounds of peaches. She buys another $2\frac{1}{6}$ pounds of peaches. How many pounds of peaches does Lisa have now?

[ ] $\frac{[\ ]}{[\ ]}$ lb [ ] $\frac{[\ ]}{[\ ]}$ lb

?

[ ] $\frac{[\ ]}{[\ ]}$ + [ ] $\frac{[\ ]}{[\ ]}$ = [ ] $\frac{[\ ]}{[\ ]}$ + [ ] $\frac{[\ ]}{[\ ]}$

= [ ] $\frac{[\ ]}{[\ ]}$

Lisa has [ ] $\frac{[\ ]}{[\ ]}$ pounds of peaches now.

Learn Draw a model to solve a two-step problem.

Megan spent $\frac{1}{6}$ of her money on food and $\frac{5}{8}$ of her money on a new outfit. What fraction of Megan's money is left?

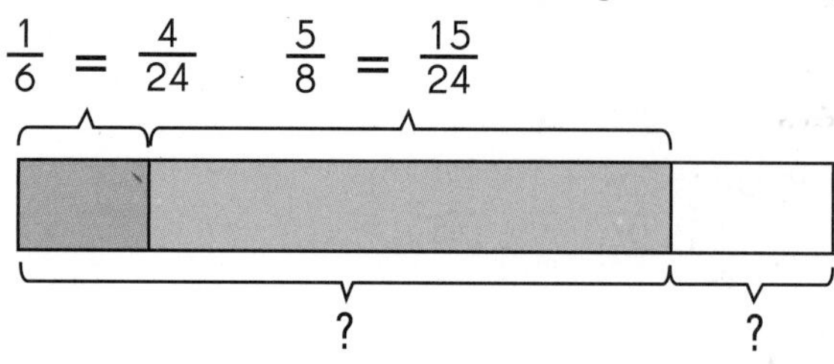

First, find the amount of money Megan spent on food and the new outfit.

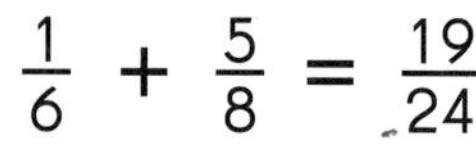

Megan spent $\frac{19}{24}$ of her money on food and the new outfit.

$$1 - \frac{19}{24} = \frac{5}{24}$$

$\frac{5}{24}$ of Megan's money is left.

Guided Practice

Solve.

3 Claire took $2\frac{3}{4}$ hours to read a book. Her brother, Dan, took $\frac{2}{3}$ hour less to read his book. How much time did they spend altogether reading their books?

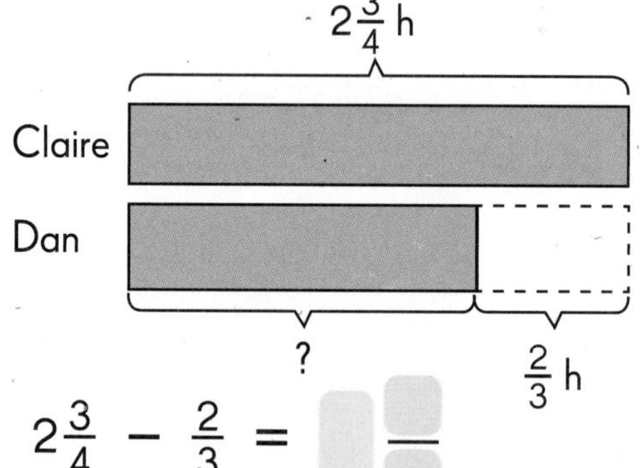

First, find the time Dan took to read the book.

$2\frac{3}{4} - \frac{2}{3} = \square\frac{\square}{\square}$

Dan read his book in $\square\frac{\square}{\square}$ hours.

$2\frac{3}{4} + \square\frac{\square}{\square} = \square\frac{\square}{\square}$

Claire and Dan spent  hours altogether reading their books.

Let's Practice

Solve. Show your work.

1. The produce manager receives 5 containers of green beans, each weighing 7 pounds. She divides the total amount of green beans into 3 equal-weight portions. What is the weight of the beans in each portion?

2. Nisha spent $\frac{1}{4}$ of her money on Monday and $\frac{7}{10}$ of it on Tuesday. What fraction of her money did Nisha spend during the two days?

3. Lee drank $1\frac{2}{3}$ quarts of water today. He drank $\frac{2}{5}$ quart less water than Sarita. How many quarts of water did Sarita drink today?

4. Kathy uses $2\frac{5}{9}$ pounds of flour to make baked goods. She uses $\frac{5}{6}$ pounds more flour than Diana. How many pounds of flour does Diana use?

5. The Lido family has $2\frac{1}{2}$ pints of apple juice. They drink $\frac{7}{8}$ pint of the juice on Monday and $\frac{5}{12}$ pint on Tuesday. How many pints of apple juice are left?

6. A market sells $5\frac{2}{3}$ pounds of blueberries in the morning. In the afternoon, the market sells $\frac{11}{12}$ pound less blueberries. How many pounds of blueberries are sold in the morning and afternoon altogether?

ON YOUR OWN

Go to Workbook A:
Practice 7 and 8, pages 117–128

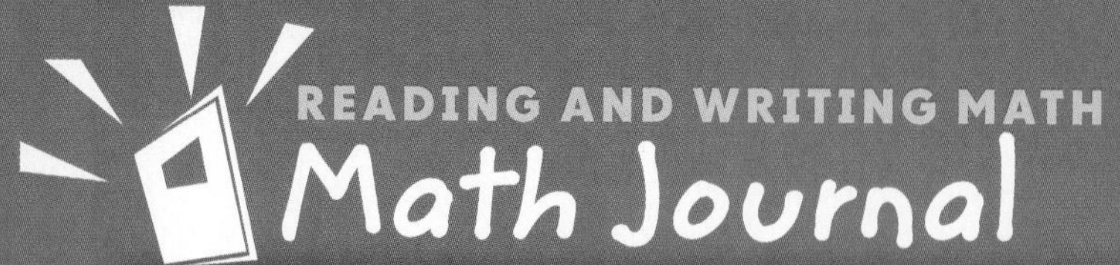

Leah, Marta and Noah each added these fractions.

$$\frac{5}{6} + \frac{7}{9} = ?$$

Leah's answer: $\frac{12}{15}$ Marta's answer: $2\frac{9}{18}$ Noah's answer: $1\frac{11}{18}$

Two of the three answers are incorrect.

a Whose answers are incorrect?

b Explain why.

To add $\frac{5}{6}$ and $\frac{7}{9}$, I will have to rewrite them as like fractions.

6, 12, 18, 24, 30, ...
9, 18, 27, 36, 45, ...

The least common multiple of 6 and 9 is ▢.

The least common denominator of $\frac{5}{6}$ and $\frac{7}{9}$ is ▢.

$\frac{5}{6} + \frac{7}{9} = \frac{▢}{▢} + \frac{▢}{▢}$

$= \frac{▢}{▢}$

$= ▢\frac{▢}{▢}$

The correct answer should be $▢\frac{▢}{▢}$.

I can check Leah's, Marta's and Noah's answers against $▢\frac{▢}{▢}$ to spot the incorrect answers.

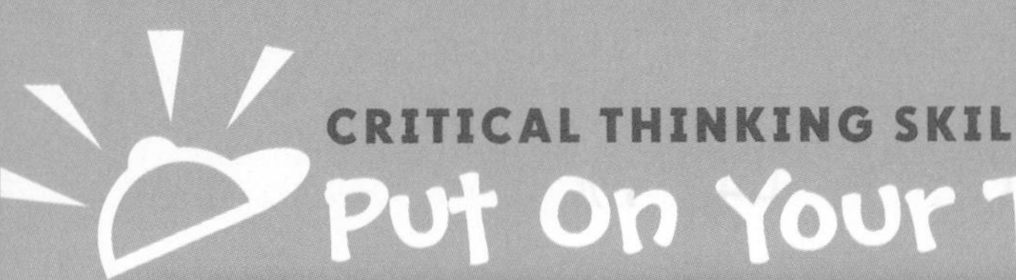

CRITICAL THINKING SKILLS

Put On Your Thinking Cap!

PROBLEM SOLVING

Jackie has two equal-sized bottles. The first bottle contains 1 quart of water. The second bottle has $\frac{5}{9}$ quart of water. What amount of water must Jackie pour from the first bottle into the second bottle so that both bottles contain the same amount of water? Express your answer as a fraction. Explain your answer using bar models.

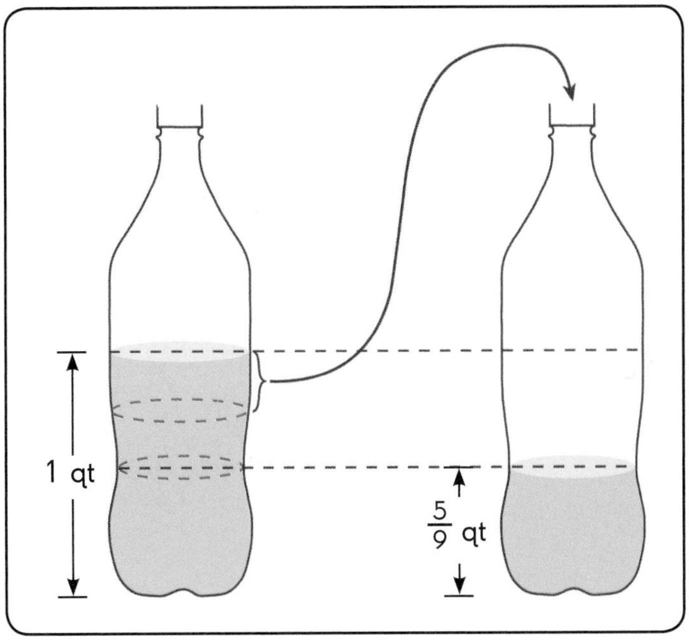

1 qt

$\frac{5}{9}$ qt

ON YOUR OWN

Go to Workbook A: Put on Your Thinking Cap! pages 129–130

Chapter Wrap Up

Study Guide

You have learned...

Fractions and Mixed Numbers

Adding and Subtracting Unlike Fractions

Find the least common multiple of their denominators. Use it to rewrite the fractions as like fractions. Then add or subtract.

$\frac{1}{4} + \frac{1}{6} = ?$

Multiples of 4: 4, 8, 12, ...
Multiples of 6: 6, 12, ...
12 is the least common multiple of 4 and 6.

$$\frac{1}{4} + \frac{1}{6} = \frac{3}{12} + \frac{2}{12}$$
$$= \frac{5}{12}$$

Adding and Subtracting Mixed Numbers

First rewrite the fractional parts as like fractions. Then add or subtract the fractional parts before adding or subtracting the whole numbers.

Without Renaming	With Renaming
$3\frac{1}{2} - 1\frac{1}{3}$ $= 3\frac{3}{6} - 1\frac{2}{6}$ $= 2\frac{1}{6}$	$3\frac{1}{2} - 1\frac{2}{3}$ $= 3\frac{3}{6} - 1\frac{4}{6}$ $= 2\frac{9}{6} - 1\frac{4}{6}$ $= 1\frac{5}{6}$

Use Benchmarks to Estimate Sums and Differences

$\frac{4}{9} - \frac{7}{12}$ ↓ ↓ $\frac{1}{2} - \frac{1}{2} = 0$	$2\frac{7}{8} + 2\frac{3}{5}$ ↓ ↓ $3 + 2\frac{1}{2} = 5\frac{1}{2}$

▶ Add and subtract unlike fractions and mixed numbers by rewriting them with like denominators.

Fractions, Mixed Numbers and Division Expressions

Express division expressions as fractions or mixed numbers.

$$10 \div 6 = \frac{10 \div 2}{6 \div 2} = \frac{5}{3} = 1\frac{2}{3}$$

Express fractions as division expressions.

$$\frac{4}{5} = 4 \div 5$$

Expressing Fractions, Division Expressions and Mixed Numbers as Decimals

Express a fraction as a decimal by finding an equivalent fraction with a denominator of 10 or 100.

$$\frac{20}{25} = \frac{20 \times 4}{25 \times 4} = \frac{80}{100} = 0.8$$

Express division expressions and mixed numbers as decimals.

$$5 \div 4 = \frac{5}{4} = 1 + \frac{1}{4} = 1 + 0.25 = 1.25$$

Solve Real-World Problems

Chapter Review/Test

Vocabulary

Choose the correct word.

multiple	least common multiple
least common denominator	equivalent fractions
benchmark	division expression
mixed number	

1. The first multiple that is the same for two numbers is called the ___.

2. $\frac{3}{4}$ and $\frac{6}{8}$ are ___. $2\frac{2}{3}$ is a ___.

3. In estimating with fractions, you approximate each fraction to the closest ___.

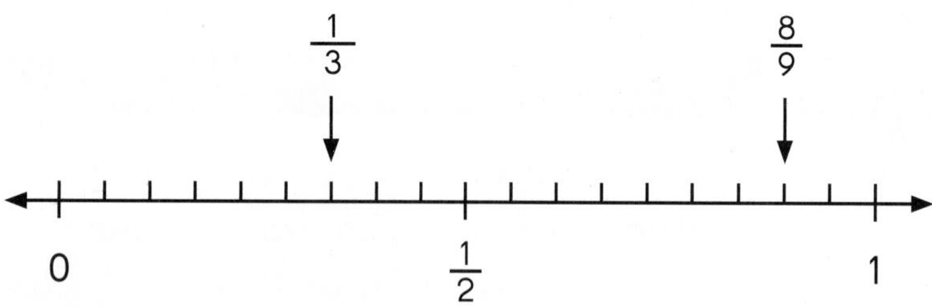

$\frac{1}{3}$ is about $\frac{1}{2}$. $\frac{8}{9}$ is about 1.

$\frac{1}{3} + \frac{8}{9}$

$\rightarrow \frac{1}{2} + 1$

$= 1\frac{1}{2}$

The sum of $\frac{1}{3}$ and $\frac{8}{9}$ is about $1\frac{1}{2}$.

4. $7 \div 6$ is a ___.

Concepts and Skills

Add or subtract. Express each sum or difference in simplest form.

5. $\frac{1}{2} + \frac{3}{7}$

6. $\frac{1}{6} + \frac{3}{10}$

7. $\frac{7}{8} - \frac{1}{2}$

8. $\frac{7}{9} - \frac{1}{4}$

Use benchmarks to estimate each sum or difference.

9. $\frac{4}{9} - \frac{3}{7}$

10. $\frac{7}{9} + \frac{4}{7} + \frac{1}{6}$

Express each division expression as a fraction or mixed number in simplest form.

11. $6 \div 8$

12. $10 \div 3$

Express each fraction as a decimal.

13. $\frac{1}{4}$

14. $\frac{18}{25}$

Express as a mixed number and as a decimal.

15. $21 \div 5$

16. $\frac{42}{8}$

Add or subtract. Express each sum or difference in simplest form.

17. $1\frac{2}{9} + 1\frac{1}{6}$

18. $3\frac{4}{5} + 2\frac{1}{2}$

19. $6\frac{3}{4} - 1\frac{1}{2}$

20. $5\frac{2}{9} - 3\frac{1}{3}$

Use benchmarks to estimate each sum or difference.

21. $4\frac{3}{5} + 2\frac{3}{8}$

22. $8\frac{11}{12} - 2\frac{11}{20}$

Problem Solving

Solve. Show your work.

23. Audrey bought 7 pounds of diced apples and shared them equally among 4 friends.

    a. How many pounds of apples did each person receive?

    b. Two of the friends put the portions they received together and then gave them to the food pantry. How many pounds of apples did they give to the food pantry?

    c. Audrey used $1\frac{2}{3}$ pounds of the apples the two friends gave to the food pantry to make apple sauce and the remaining to make apple pies. How many pounds of apples did Audrey use to make apple pies?

Multiplying and Dividing Fractions and Mixed Numbers

Lessons

- **4.1** Multiplying Proper Fractions
- **4.2** Real-World Problems: Multiplying with Proper Fractions
- **4.3** Multiplying Improper Fractions by Fractions
- **4.4** Multiplying Mixed Numbers and Whole Numbers
- **4.5** Real-World Problems: Multiplying with Mixed Numbers
- **4.6** Dividing a Fraction by a Whole Number
- **4.7** Real-World Problems: Multiplying and Dividing with Fractions

- Whole numbers, fractions, and mixed numbers can be multiplied or divided in any combination.

Recall Prior Knowledge

Finding equivalent fractions

$\frac{3}{4}$ is the same as $\frac{6}{8}$.

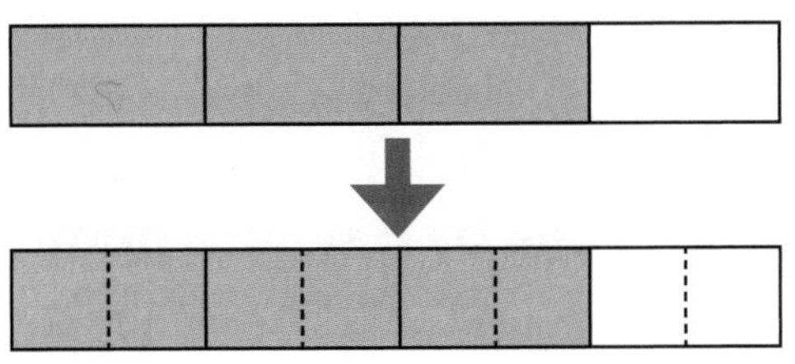

$$\frac{3}{4} = \frac{3 \times 2}{4 \times 2}$$
$$= \frac{6}{8}$$

Simplifying fractions

$$\frac{6}{8} = \frac{6 \div 2}{8 \div 2}$$ ← Divide the numerator and denominator by their greatest common factor.

$$= \frac{3}{4}$$

Adding and subtracting fractions

$$\frac{1}{4} + \frac{2}{4} = \frac{3}{4}$$

$$\frac{2}{5} + \frac{3}{10} = \frac{4}{10} + \frac{3}{10}$$
$$= \frac{7}{10}$$

$$\frac{4}{5} - \frac{3}{5} = \frac{1}{5}$$

$$\frac{7}{9} - \frac{2}{3} = \frac{7}{9} - \frac{6}{9}$$
$$= \frac{1}{9}$$

$$1 - \frac{3}{8} = \frac{8}{8} - \frac{3}{8}$$
$$= \frac{5}{8}$$

Expressing improper fractions as mixed numbers and mixed numbers as improper fractions

$$\frac{10}{3} = \frac{9}{3} + \frac{1}{3}$$
$$= 3 + \frac{1}{3}$$
$$= 3\frac{1}{3}$$

$$3\frac{1}{2} = 3 + \frac{1}{2}$$
$$= \frac{6}{2} + \frac{1}{2}$$
$$= \frac{7}{2}$$

Expressing fractions as decimals

$$\frac{1}{4} = \frac{1 \times 25}{4 \times 25}$$
$$= \frac{25}{100}$$
$$= 0.25$$

Multiplying fractions by a whole number

$$\frac{2}{5} \times 7 = \frac{2 \times 7}{5}$$
$$= \frac{14}{5}$$
$$= 2\frac{4}{5}$$

Finding the number of units to solve a problem

7 tickets cost \$49. How much do 6 tickets cost?

7 units $\longrightarrow$ \$49
1 unit $\longrightarrow$ \$49 ÷ 7 = \$7
6 units $\longrightarrow$ 6 × \$7 = \$42

6 tickets cost \$42.

Drawing a model to show what is stated

Three friends share a foot-long turkey sandwich. Jeff eats $\frac{1}{2}$ of the sandwich. Anne eats $\frac{1}{3}$ of the sandwich. Andy eats the rest.

Least common multiple: 2 × 3 = 6

$\frac{1}{2} = \frac{3}{6}$ $\quad$ $\frac{1}{3} = \frac{2}{6}$ $\quad$ $1 - \frac{3}{6} - \frac{2}{6} = \frac{1}{6}$

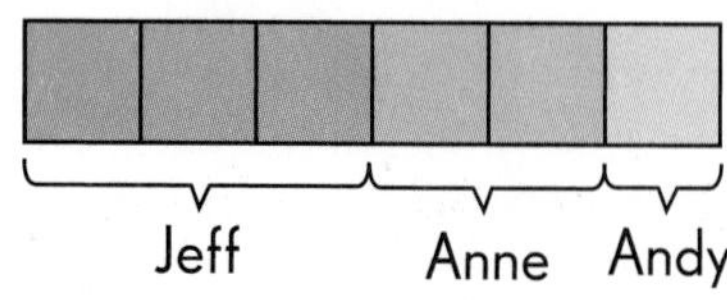

Using order of operations to simplify expressions

Simplify $(32 + 40) - 8 \times 6$.

First expression $(32 + 40) - 8 \times 6$ ← Perform all operations in the parentheses first.

Second expression $72 - 8 \times 6$ ← Then multiply.

Third expression $72 - 48$ ← Finally subtract.

24

✔ Quick Check

Find an equivalent fraction.

1. $\frac{2}{3}$
2. $\frac{3}{4}$
3. $\frac{5}{6}$

Simplify.

4. $\frac{5}{10}$
5. $\frac{15}{25}$
6. $\frac{18}{32}$

Subtract.

7. $\frac{2}{3} - \frac{8}{15}$
8. $3 - \frac{5}{7}$
9. $4 - \frac{8}{11}$

Express each improper fraction as a mixed number in simplest form.

10. $\frac{17}{4}$
11. $\frac{22}{6}$
12. $\frac{40}{9}$

Express each mixed number as an improper fraction.

13 $3\frac{3}{7}$ 14 $6\frac{5}{9}$ 15 $8\frac{2}{5}$

Express each fraction as a decimal.

16 $\frac{3}{4}$ 17 $\frac{13}{20}$ 18 $\frac{21}{25}$

Find the product.

19 $\frac{1}{4} \times 12$ 20 $\frac{3}{8} \times 10$ 21 $\frac{5}{9} \times 24$

Solve.

22 A store sells 5 CDs for \$15. How much do 3 CDs cost?

5 CDs → \$15

1 CD → \$15 ÷ ___ = \$___

3 CDs → ___ × \$___ = \$___

3 CDs cost \$___.

Draw a model to show what is stated.

23 Miguel has some trading cards. $\frac{1}{2}$ of the cards are baseball cards, $\frac{2}{5}$ are soccer cards, and the rest are basketball cards.

Simplify.

24 $(60 + 6 \times 80) \div 20$

25 $27 \div (1 + 2) \times 5 - 9$

Lesson 4.1 Multiplying Proper Fractions

Lesson Objective

- Multiply proper fractions.

Vocabulary
product
common factor

Learn Use models to multiply fractions.

Find $\frac{1}{2} \times \frac{2}{3}$.

Margie drew a rectangle and colored $\frac{2}{3}$ of it blue.

She then drew stripes over $\frac{1}{2}$ of the colored parts.

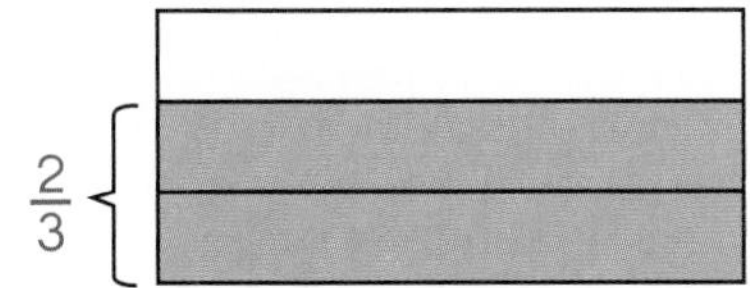

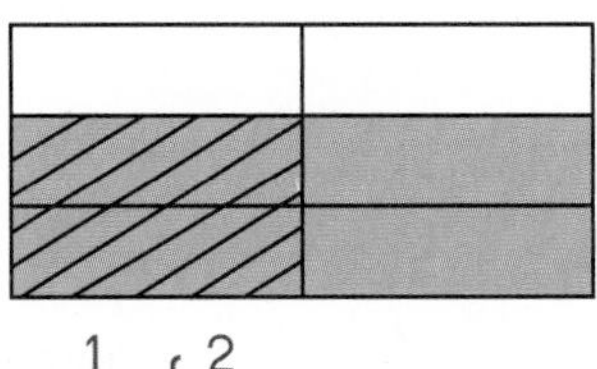

$\frac{1}{2}$ of $\frac{2}{3}$

$$\frac{1}{2} \times \frac{2}{3} = \frac{1}{2} \text{ of } \frac{2}{3}$$

$$= \frac{2}{6} \begin{array}{l} \leftarrow \text{Number of parts with stripes} \\ \leftarrow \text{Total number of parts} \end{array}$$

$$= \frac{1}{3}$$

Paul drew an identical rectangle and colored $\frac{1}{2}$ of it blue.

He then drew stripes over $\frac{2}{3}$ of the colored part.

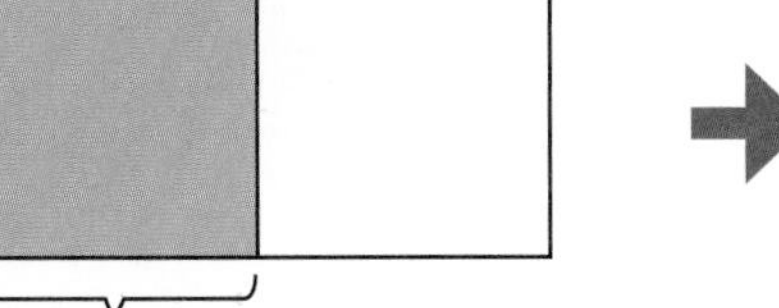

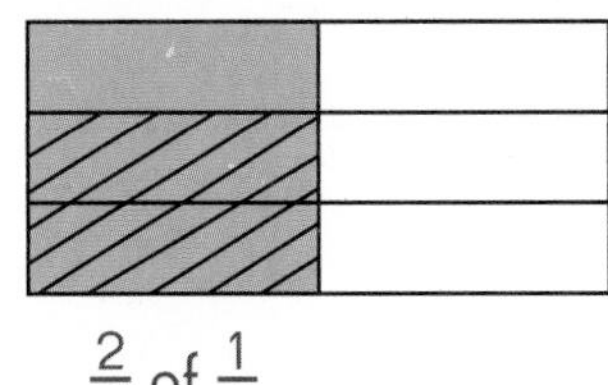

$\frac{2}{3}$ of $\frac{1}{2}$

$$\frac{2}{3} \times \frac{1}{2} = \frac{2}{3} \text{ of } \frac{1}{2}$$

$$= \frac{2}{6} \begin{array}{l} \leftarrow \text{Number of parts with stripes} \\ \leftarrow \text{Total number of parts} \end{array}$$

$$= \frac{1}{3}$$

Margie and Paul get the same **product** : $\frac{1}{3}$.

So, $\frac{1}{2} \times \frac{2}{3} = \frac{2}{3} \times \frac{1}{2}$.

Learn Multiply fractions without models.

Find $\frac{3}{4} \times \frac{8}{9}$.

Method 1

$\frac{3}{4} \times \frac{8}{9} = \frac{3 \times 8}{4 \times 9}$ ← Multiply the numerators. Multiply the denominators.

$= \frac{24}{36}$ ← Simplify the product.

$= \frac{2}{3}$

Method 2

$\frac{3}{4} \times \frac{8}{9} = \frac{3 \div 3}{4} \times \frac{8}{9 \div 3}$ ← Divide both the numerator and denominator by the **common factor**, 3.

$= \frac{1}{4 \div 4} \times \frac{8 \div 4}{3}$ ← Divide both the numerator and denominator by the common factor, 4.

$= \frac{1 \times 2}{1 \times 3}$ ← Multiply the numerators. Multiply the denominators.

$= \frac{2}{3}$

Division Rule
Other than zero, any number when divided by itself will give a quotient of 1.

So, $3 \div 3 = 1$
$4 \div 4 = 1$

Multiplication Property of 1
Any number multiplied by 1 will give a product that is equal to itself.

So, $1 \times 2 = 2$
$1 \times 3 = 3$

Guided Practice

Use models to find each product. Write each product in simplest form.

1. $\frac{1}{3} \times \frac{3}{4} = \frac{?}{?}$

2. $\frac{2}{5} \times \frac{5}{8} = \frac{?}{?}$

Find each product in simplest form.

3. $\frac{4}{10} \times \frac{5}{12} = \frac{?}{?}$

4. $\frac{3}{10} \times \frac{5}{9} = \frac{?}{?}$

Hands-On Activity

Materials:
- grid paper
- 1 yellow crayon
- 1 blue crayon

Draw a 4 × 4 square on the grid paper.

Divide the square into four equal parts using horizontal lines. Color $\frac{3}{4}$ of it yellow.

Divide the square into four equal parts using vertical lines. Draw stripes on $\frac{1}{4}$ of the yellow parts with a blue crayon.

Refer to your model.

Complete: $\frac{1}{4} \times \frac{3}{4} = \frac{\square}{\square}$

Draw another 4 × 4 square.

Divide the square into four equal parts using horizontal lines. Color $\frac{1}{4}$ of it blue.

Divide the square into four equal parts using vertical lines. Draw stripes on $\frac{3}{4}$ of the blue parts with a yellow crayon.

Refer to your model.

Complete: $\frac{3}{4} \times \frac{1}{4} = \frac{\square}{\square}$

Do you get the same answer in both cases?

What can you say about $\frac{1}{4} \times \frac{3}{4}$ and $\frac{3}{4} \times \frac{1}{4}$?

Let's Explore!

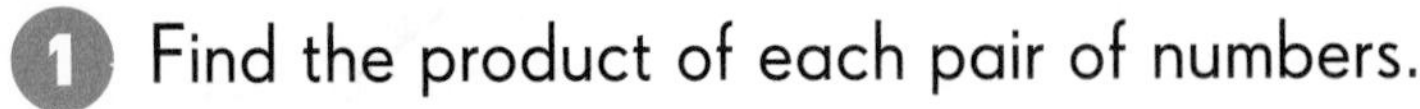

1 Find the product of each pair of numbers.

$3 \times 4 = \square$ $\qquad$ $5 \times 17 = \square$

$9 \times 8 = \square$ $\qquad$ $12 \times 7 = \square$

Notice that each product is greater than each of its factors. Explain why.

2 Find the product of each pair of fractions.

$\frac{1}{2} \times \frac{3}{4} = \frac{\square}{\square}$ $\qquad$ $\frac{3}{4} \times \frac{4}{5} = \frac{\square}{\square}$

$\frac{2}{7} \times \frac{3}{4} = \frac{\square}{\square}$ $\qquad$ $\frac{1}{6} \times \frac{5}{9} = \frac{\square}{\square}$

Notice that each product is less than each of its factors. Explain why.

Let's Practice

Find each product in simplest form.

1 $\frac{1}{3} \times \frac{6}{7}$

2 $\frac{6}{8} \times \frac{4}{9}$

3 $\frac{10}{15} \times \frac{3}{4}$

4 $\frac{7}{10}$ of $\frac{5}{10}$

5 $\frac{3}{8}$ of $\frac{4}{6}$

6 $\frac{7}{12}$ of $\frac{9}{14}$

ON YOUR OWN

Go to Workbook A: Practice 1, pages 131–132

Lesson

4.2 Real-World Problems: Multiplying with Proper Fractions

Lesson Objective

- Solve real-world problems involving multiplication of proper fractions.

Learn

Multiply fractions to solve real-world problems.

Maurice has $\frac{3}{4}$ quart of chicken stock. He uses $\frac{2}{3}$ of it to make some soup.

a) How much chicken stock does he use to make the soup?

b) How much chicken stock does he have left?

Method 1

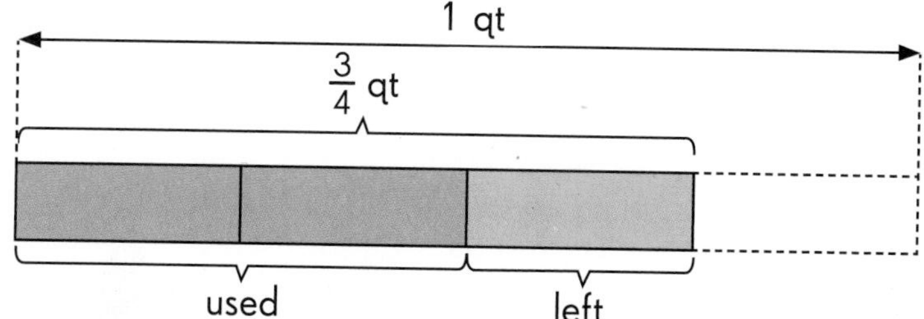

The model shows that:

4 units → 1 qt

1 unit → $\frac{1}{4}$ qt

2 units → $\frac{1}{2}$ qt

a) Maurice uses $\frac{1}{2}$ quart of chicken stock to make the soup.

b) He has $\frac{1}{4}$ quart of chicken stock left.

Method 2

a) $\frac{2}{3} \times \frac{3}{4} = \frac{6}{12} = \frac{1}{2}$

Maurice uses $\frac{1}{2}$ quart of chicken stock to make the soup.

b) $\frac{3}{4} - \frac{1}{2} = \frac{3}{4} - \frac{2}{4}$

$= \frac{1}{4}$

He has $\frac{1}{4}$ quart of chicken stock left.

Guided Practice

Solve.

1 Michelle has $\frac{4}{5}$ gallon of paint. She uses $\frac{3}{4}$ of it to paint a door.

a How much paint does she use?

b How much paint is left?

Method 1

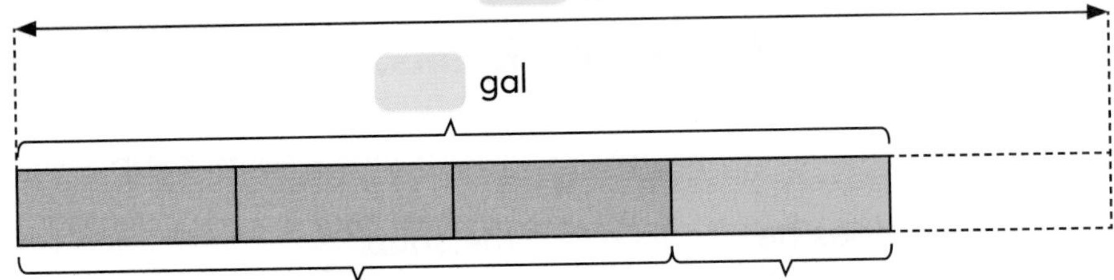

The model shows that:

___ units → ___ gal

___ unit → $\frac{\square}{\square}$ gal

___ units → $\frac{\square}{\square}$ gal

a Michelle uses $\frac{\square}{\square}$ gallon of paint.

b There is $\frac{\square}{\square}$ gallon of paint left.

Method 2

a $\frac{3}{4} \times \frac{\square}{\square} = \frac{12}{20}$

$= \frac{\square}{\square}$

Michelle uses $\frac{\square}{\square}$ gallon of paint.

b $\frac{4}{5} - \frac{\square}{\square} = \frac{\square}{\square}$

There is $\frac{\square}{\square}$ gallon of paint left.

Learn Give the answer as a fractional remainder.

Len received some money for a vacation job. He saved $\frac{1}{4}$ of the money, spent $\frac{4}{9}$ of the remainder on a DVD, and spent the rest on a T-shirt.

a What fraction of his money was spent on the DVD?

b What fraction of his money was spent on the T-shirt?

Method 1

$1 - \frac{1}{4} = \frac{3}{4}$

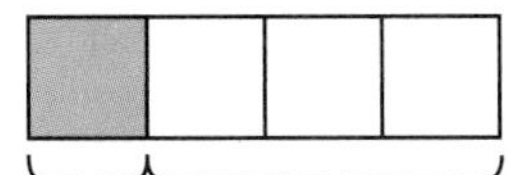

Remainder → 3 parts

To show $\frac{4}{9}$ of the remainder is spent on the DVD, I have to further divide the remainder into 9 parts.

Least common multiple of 3 and 9 = 9

By equivalent fractions:

$\frac{3}{4} = \frac{9}{12}$ (× 3, × 3)

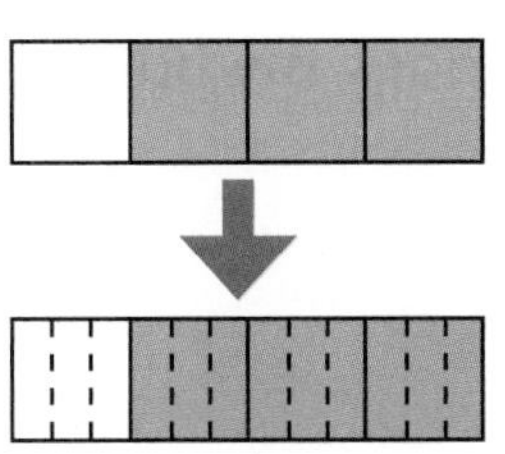

I need to draw a model with 12 equal units to show the problem.

saved | spent on DVD | spent on T-shirt

$\frac{1}{4}$ of 12 units = 3 units

$\frac{4}{9}$ of 9 units = 4 units

The model shows that:

Number of units spent on DVD = 4

Number of units spent on T-shirt = 5

Total number of units in 1 whole = 12

a $\frac{4}{12} = \frac{1}{3}$

Len spent $\frac{1}{3}$ of his money on the DVD.

b Len spent $\frac{5}{12}$ of his money on the T-shirt.

Method 2

a $1 - \frac{1}{4} = \frac{3}{4}$

$\frac{3}{4}$ of Len's money is left after he saves $\frac{1}{4}$ of it.

$\frac{4}{9} \times \frac{3}{4} = \frac{12}{36} = \frac{1}{3}$

Len spent $\frac{1}{3}$ of his money on the DVD.

b $\frac{3}{4} - \frac{1}{3} = \frac{9}{12} - \frac{4}{12}$

$= \frac{5}{12}$

Len spent $\frac{5}{12}$ of his money on the T-shirt.

Guided Practice

Solve.

2 Janice picks some strawberries. She uses $\frac{3}{5}$ of the strawberries to make jam. She gives $\frac{3}{4}$ of the remainder to her neighbor.

a What fraction of the strawberries does she give to her neighbor?

b What fraction of the strawberries does she have left?

Method 1

$1 - \frac{3}{5} = \frac{2}{5}$

Remainder → 2 parts

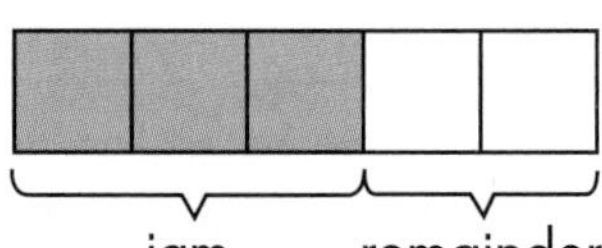

To show $\frac{3}{4}$ of the remainder is given to Janice's neighbor, I have to further divide the remainder into 4 parts.

Least common multiple of 2 and 4 = 4

By equivalent fractions:

$\frac{2}{5} \overset{\times 2}{=} \frac{4}{10}$

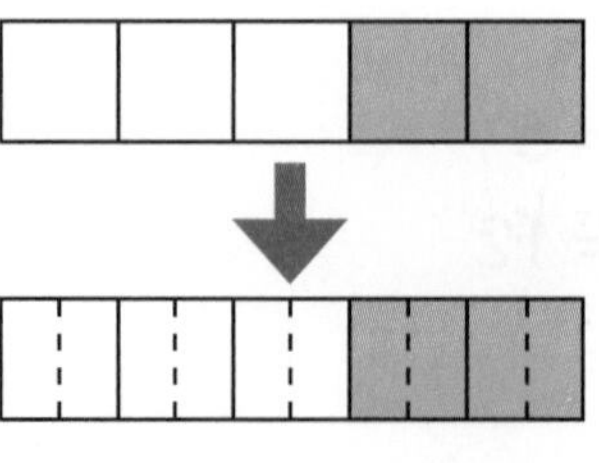

I need to draw a model with 10 equal units to show the problem.

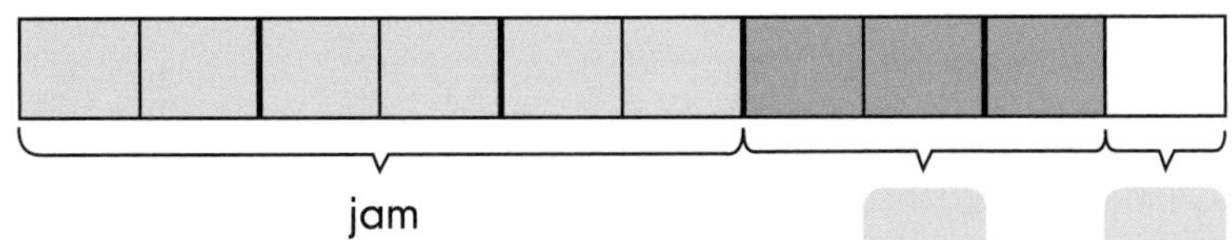

$\frac{3}{5}$ of 10 units = 6 units

$\frac{3}{4}$ of 4 units = 3 units

The model shows that:
Number of units given to the neighbor = ___

Total number of units in 1 whole = ___

a She gives $\frac{\square}{\square}$ of the strawberries to her neighbor.

b She has $\frac{\square}{\square}$ of the strawberries left.

Method 2

a $1 - \frac{\square}{\square} = \frac{\square}{\square}$

$\frac{\square}{\square}$ of Janice's strawberries is left after she makes jam with $\frac{3}{5}$ of them.

$\frac{3}{4} \times \frac{\square}{\square} = \frac{6}{20}$

$= \frac{\square}{\square}$

She gives $\frac{\square}{\square}$ of the strawberries to her neighbor.

b $\frac{\square}{\square} - \frac{\square}{\square} = \frac{\square}{\square} - \frac{\square}{\square}$

$= \frac{\square}{\square}$

She has $\frac{\square}{\square}$ of the strawberries left.

Let's Practice

Solve. Show your work.

1. Mrs. Smith has a plot of land. She plants flowers on $\frac{3}{4}$ of the land. $\frac{2}{3}$ of the flowers are sunflowers. What fraction of the land is planted with sunflowers?

2. Justin spends $\frac{7}{9}$ of his homework time on math and social studies. He spends $\frac{4}{7}$ of this time on math. What fraction of the total time does he spend on social studies?

3. Priya has a piece of string $\frac{5}{6}$ yard long. She cuts $\frac{3}{5}$ of the piece of string for a craft. What is the length of the string left?

4. Jeff spends $\frac{1}{2}$ of his paycheck. He then gives $\frac{1}{3}$ of the remainder to charity and puts the rest in the bank. What fraction of his paycheck does he put in the bank?

5. Mrs. Kong uses $\frac{1}{3}$ of a stick of butter in a sauce. She then uses $\frac{5}{8}$ of the remaining butter to make garlic bread. What fraction of the stick of butter is left?

6. Gia spends $\frac{2}{5}$ of her money on a shirt. She then spends $\frac{4}{9}$ of her remaining money on a pair of shoes. What fraction of her money is left?

7. Ben sells $\frac{7}{12}$ of the pottery he made. Of the remaining pottery, $\frac{3}{5}$ are vases and the rest are bowls. What fraction of all the pottery is the unsold bowls?

ON YOUR OWN

Go to Workbook A: Practice 2, pages 133–138

Lesson

4.3 Multiplying Improper Fractions by Fractions

Lesson Objective

- Multiply improper fractions by proper or improper fractions.

Vocabulary
proper fraction
improper fraction

Learn **Multiply improper fractions by proper fractions.**

Find the product of $\frac{6}{5}$ and $\frac{3}{4}$.

Method 1

$\frac{6}{5} \times \frac{3}{4}$

$= \frac{3}{4} \times \frac{6}{5}$

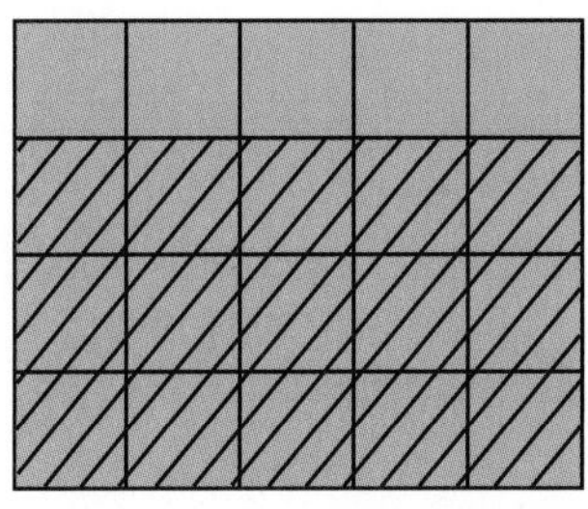

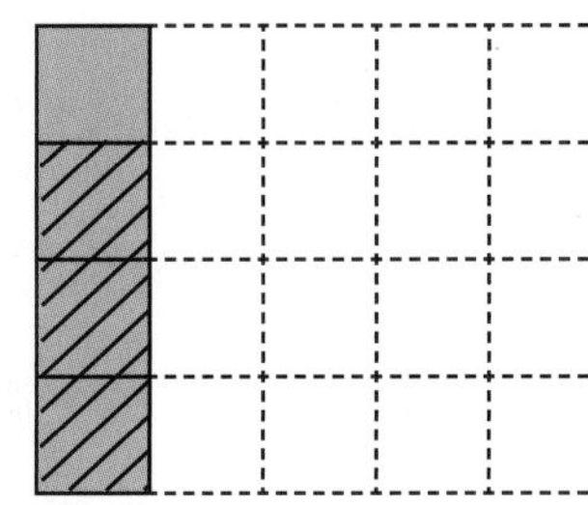

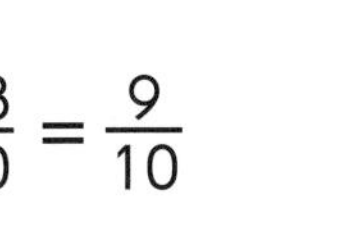

$\frac{18}{20} = \frac{9}{10}$

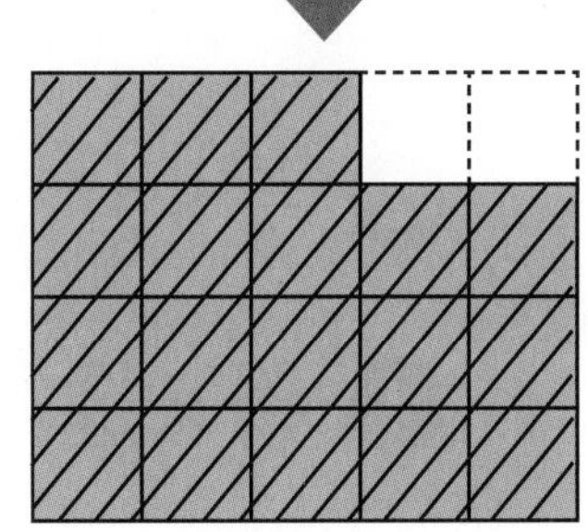

In $\frac{3}{4}$, the numerator is less than the denominator. $\frac{3}{4}$ is a **proper fraction**.

In $\frac{6}{5}$, the numerator is greater than the denominator. $\frac{6}{5}$ is an **improper fraction**.

Method 2

$\frac{6}{5} \times \frac{3}{4} = \frac{6 \div 2}{5} \times \frac{3}{4 \div 2}$

$= \frac{3 \times 3}{5 \times 2}$

$= \frac{9}{10}$

Divide both the numerator and denominator by the common factor, 2.

Guided Practice

Multiply. Express the product in simplest form.

1. $\frac{1}{3} \times \frac{7}{5}$
2. $\frac{2}{7} \times \frac{21}{12}$

Multiply. Express the product as a whole number or a mixed number in simplest form.

3. $\frac{3}{7} \times \frac{14}{5}$
4. $\frac{5}{9} \times \frac{24}{7}$
5. $\frac{9}{4} \times \frac{10}{3}$
6. $\frac{7}{5} \times \frac{9}{2}$
7. $\frac{27}{6} \times \frac{15}{8}$
8. $\frac{16}{3} \times \frac{9}{4}$

Let's Practice

Multiply. Express the product as a whole number or a mixed number in simplest form.

1. $\frac{22}{6} \times \frac{3}{11}$
2. $\frac{15}{6} \times \frac{4}{5}$
3. $\frac{21}{8} \times \frac{10}{7}$
4. $\frac{32}{12} \times \frac{15}{4}$
5. $\frac{17}{3} \times \frac{21}{5}$
6. $\frac{15}{9} \times \frac{11}{3}$
7. $\frac{28}{11} \times \frac{44}{12}$
8. $\frac{23}{10} \times \frac{11}{3}$

ON YOUR OWN

Go to Workbook A: Practice 3, pages 139–142

Multiplying Mixed Numbers and Whole Numbers

Lesson Objective

- Multiply a mixed number by a whole number.

Vocabulary
mixed number

Multiply mixed numbers by whole numbers.

There are 6 students in a group. Each student works $1\frac{1}{2}$ hours on a group project. What is the total amount of time they spend working on the project?

Method 1

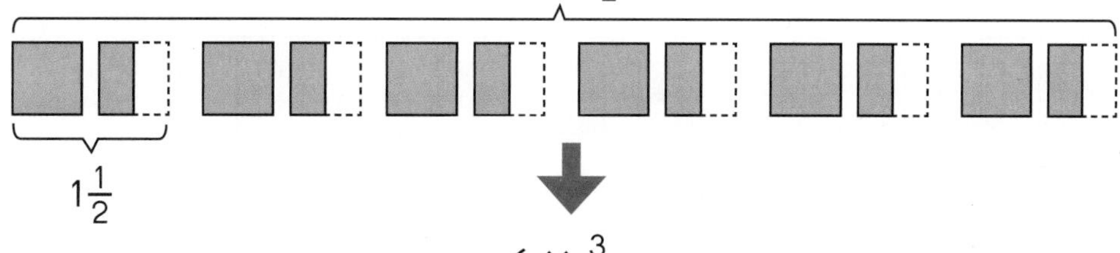

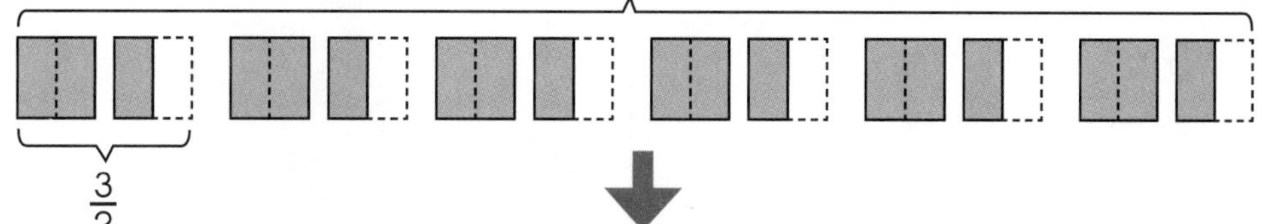

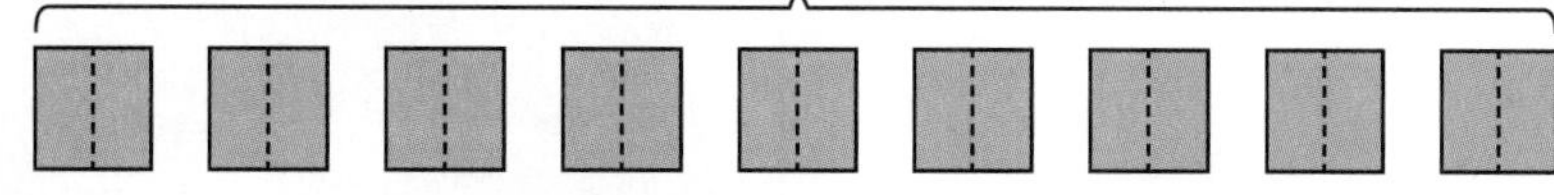

The group works on the project for a total of 9 hours.

Method 2

$$1\frac{1}{2} \times 6 = \frac{3}{2} \times 6$$
$$= \frac{18}{2}$$
$$= 9$$

$1\frac{1}{2} = \frac{3}{2}$
So, $1\frac{1}{2} \times 6$ is the same as 6 groups of $\frac{3}{2}$.

The group works on the project for a total of 9 hours.

Guided Practice

Find the product of $2\frac{1}{3}$ and 5.

1 ***Method 1***

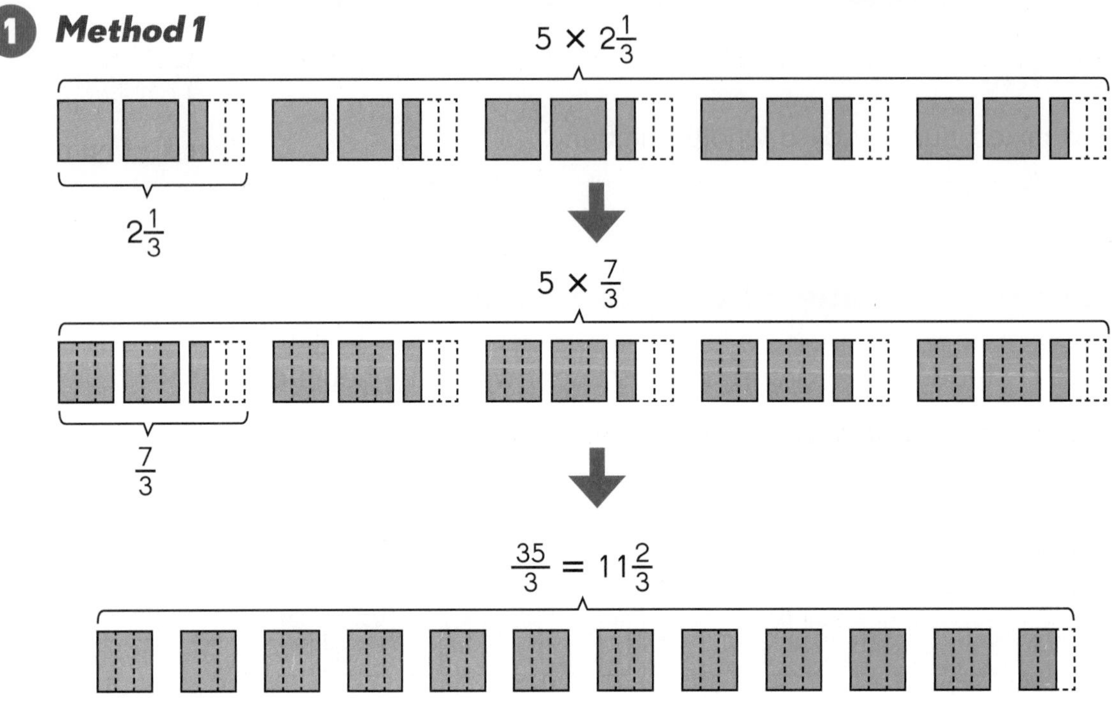

Method 2

$2\frac{1}{3} \times 5 = \frac{\square}{\square} \times 5$

$= \frac{\square}{\square}$

$= \frac{33}{3} + \frac{\square}{\square}$

$= 11 + \frac{\square}{\square}$

$= \square\frac{\square}{\square}$

$2\frac{1}{3} = \frac{\square}{\square}$

So, $2\frac{1}{3} \times 5$ is the same as $\square$ groups of $\frac{\square}{\square}$.

Hands-On Activity

STEP 1 Use a sheet of paper to represent 1 whole. Next, fold another sheet of paper into half and cut it into two equal pieces. Use one of these pieces to represent $\frac{1}{2}$. Do this with several pieces.

1 whole $\quad \frac{1}{2}$

STEP 2 Use the pieces of paper to show each of the following.

a) $3\frac{1}{2}$ b) $4 \times 3\frac{1}{2}$ c) $3\frac{1}{2} \times 5$

d) Rearrange the pieces of paper representing $4 \times 3\frac{1}{2}$. How many wholes are in $4 \times 3\frac{1}{2}$?

Let's Explore!

The model shows $4\frac{1}{2}$.  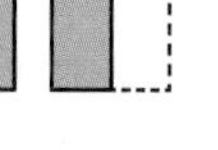

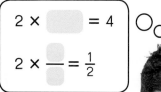

1. Express this product as a product of another mixed number and a whole number.

$4\frac{1}{2} = \square\frac{\square}{\square} \times 2$

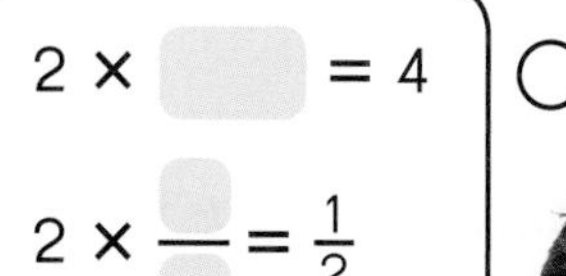

2. Use the same method to find the missing number below.

$8\frac{1}{4} = \square\frac{\square}{\square} \times 2$

Let's Practice

Complete. Express the product as a mixed number.

1. $1\frac{1}{2} \times 3 = \square\frac{\square}{\square}$

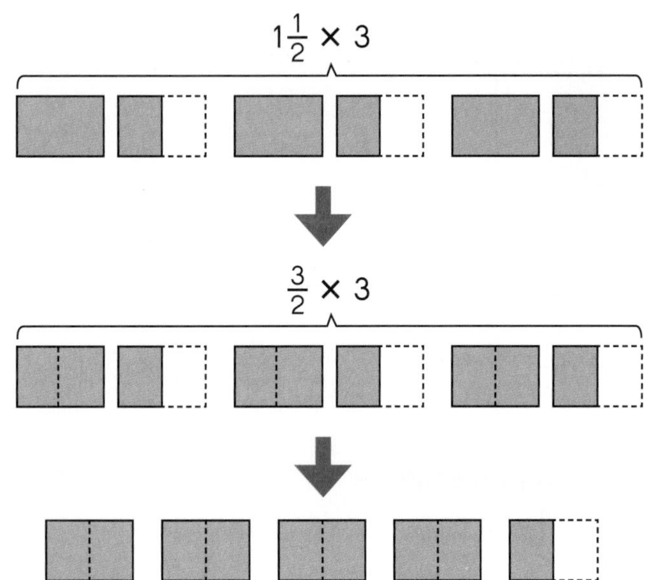

2. $2\frac{1}{3} \times 2 = \square\frac{\square}{\square}$

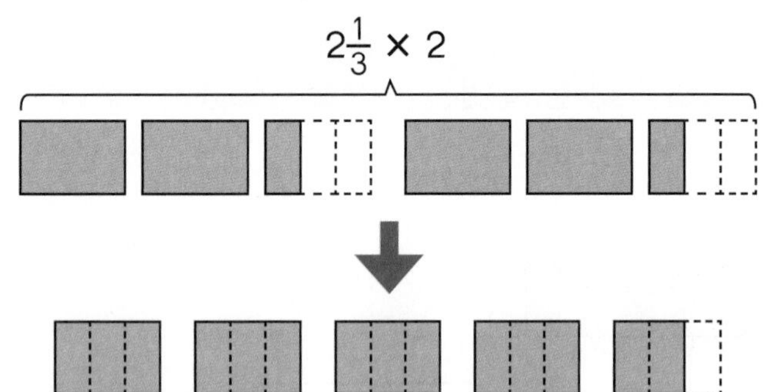

Multiply. Express the product as a whole number or a mixed number in simplest form.

3. $3\frac{9}{11} \times 33$

4. $14 \times 2\frac{3}{5}$

5. $38 \times 5\frac{2}{7}$

ON YOUR OWN

Go to Workbook A: Practice 4, pages 143–146

Real-World Problems: Multiplying with Mixed Numbers

Lesson Objective

- Solve real-world problems involving multiplication of whole numbers and mixed numbers.

Learn **Multiply mixed numbers by whole numbers to solve real-world problems.**

There are 40 guests at a party. Each guest eats $2\frac{3}{4}$ mini pizzas. How many mini pizzas do the guests eat altogether?

1 guest → $2\frac{3}{4}$ mini pizzas

40 guests → $40 \times 2\frac{3}{4}$ mini pizzas

$= 40 \times \frac{11}{4}$

$= \frac{440}{4}$

$= 110$

The guests eat 110 mini pizzas.

Guided Practice

Solve.

1. Ken uses $2\frac{1}{4}$ feet of tape to wrap a package. How many feet of tape does he use to wrap 20 of these packages?

1 package → $2\frac{1}{4}$ ft

20 packages → ___ $\times 2\frac{1}{4}$

$=$ ___ $\times \frac{\_\_}{\_\_}$

$= \frac{\_\_}{\_\_}$

$=$ ___ ft

He uses ___ feet of tape.

Learn Express the product of a mixed number and a whole number as a decimal.

Justina has 5 ribbons, each $2\frac{1}{4}$ feet long. What is the total length of the ribbons? Express your answer as a decimal.

$$2\frac{1}{4} \times 5 = \frac{9}{4} \times 5$$
$$= \frac{45}{4}$$
$$= 11\frac{1}{4}$$
$$= 11\frac{25}{100}$$
$$= 11.25$$

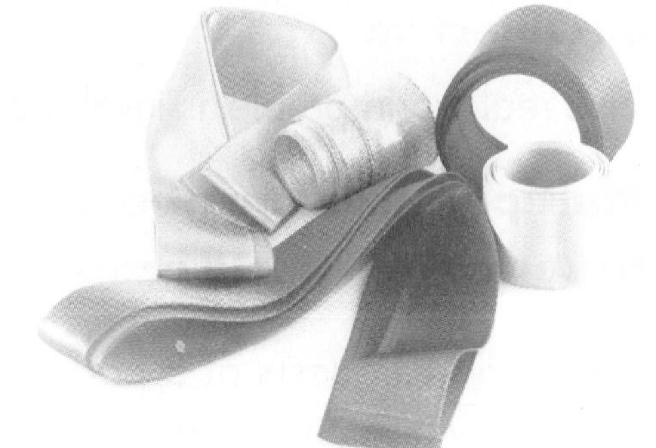

The total length of the ribbons is 11.25 feet.

Guided Practice

Solve.

2 Andrew's rectangular garden has a length of $12\frac{3}{4}$ yards and a width of 7 yards. Find the area of Andrew's garden. Express your answer as a decimal.

Area of Andrew's rectangular garden = length × width

$$= \square\frac{\square}{\square} \times \square$$
$$= \frac{\square}{\square} \times \square$$
$$= \frac{\square}{\square}$$
$$= \square\frac{\square}{\square}$$
$$= \square\frac{\square}{100}$$
$$= \square \text{ yd}^2$$

The area of Andrew's garden is ▢ square yards.

Learn: Solve two-step problems involving multiplication with mixed numbers.

Liza buys 4 packages of chicken. Each package weighs $2\frac{3}{5}$ pounds. The price of the chicken is \$2 per pound. How much does Liza pay for the 4 packages of chicken?

1 package of chicken → $2\frac{3}{5}$ lb

4 packages of chicken → $4 \times 2\frac{3}{5}$

$= 10\frac{2}{5}$ lb

$$4 \times 2\frac{3}{5} = 4 \times \frac{13}{5} = \frac{52}{5} = 10\frac{2}{5}$$

The weight of the 4 packages of chicken is $10\frac{2}{5}$ pounds.

1 pound of chicken → \$2

$10\frac{2}{5}$ pounds of chicken → $10\frac{2}{5} \times \$2$

$= \$20\frac{4}{5}$

$= \$20\frac{8}{10}$

$= \$20.80$

$$10\frac{2}{5} \times 2 = \frac{52}{5} \times 2 = \frac{104}{5} = 20\frac{4}{5}$$

Liza pays \$20.80 for the 4 packages of chicken.

Guided Practice

Solve.

3 A chef uses 3 bottles of olive oil to make salad dressing. Each bottle contains $1\frac{1}{2}$ quarts of oil. The cost of 1 quart of olive oil is \$5. Find the total cost of the oil she uses.

1 bottle → ___ $\frac{?}{?}$ qt

3 bottles → $3 \times$ ___ $\frac{?}{?}$

= ___ $\frac{?}{?}$ qt

3 bottles contain ___ $\frac{?}{?}$ quarts of olive oil.

1 qt of olive oil → \$5

___ $\frac{?}{?}$ qt of olive oil → ___ $\frac{?}{?} \times \$5$

$= \frac{?}{?} \times \$5$

= ___

The total cost of the olive oil is \$___.

Let's Practice

Solve.

1. There are 6 children at a birthday party. Each child gets $2\frac{1}{3}$ cups of fruit punch. How many cups of fruit punch are needed for all 6 children?

2. Amin cuts a ball of string into 14 equal pieces. The length of each piece of string is $2\frac{1}{4}$ yards. What is the original length of the ball of string?

3. Regan uses $4\frac{1}{8}$ ounces of paint to paint a chair. How many ounces of paint will he need to paint 9 such chairs?

4. At a zoo, each adult elephant gets $70\frac{1}{4}$ pounds of bananas every day. The zoo keeps 5 adult elephants. How many pounds of bananas will the zoo need for all 5 adult elephants on a day?

5. Mr. Richards bought 3 packages of meat for a neighborhood barbecue. Each package weighs $7\frac{1}{2}$ pounds. The price of the meat is \$3 per pound. How much did he pay for all the meat he bought?

6. Ms. Scutter is tiling a bathroom with a length of 9 feet and a width of $8\frac{1}{2}$ feet. The tile that she chose sells at \$4 per square foot. How much will Ms. Scutter need to pay for the tiles she needs?

ON YOUR OWN

Go to Workbook A: Practice 5, pages 147–148

Lesson

4.6 Dividing a Fraction by a Whole Number

Lesson Objective

- Divide a fraction by a whole number.

Vocabulary
reciprocal

Learn

Divide a fraction by a whole number.

Maura cuts a piece of rectangular clay in half. She then divides one half into 3 equal parts. What fraction of the whole piece of clay is each of the 3 parts?

Method 1

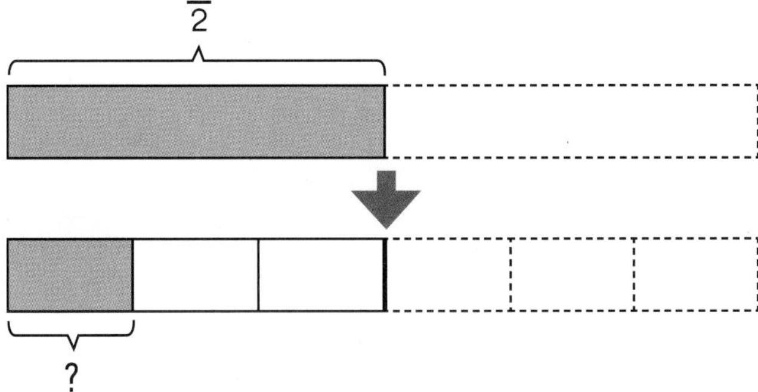

$\frac{1}{2} \div 3 = \frac{1}{6}$

The model shows that each part is $\frac{1}{6}$ of the whole piece of clay.

Method 2

$$\begin{aligned}\frac{1}{2} \div 3 &= \frac{1}{3} \text{ of } \frac{1}{2} \\ &= \frac{1}{3} \times \frac{1}{2} \\ &= \frac{1}{6}\end{aligned}$$

Each part is $\frac{1}{3}$ of $\frac{1}{2}$ the piece of clay.

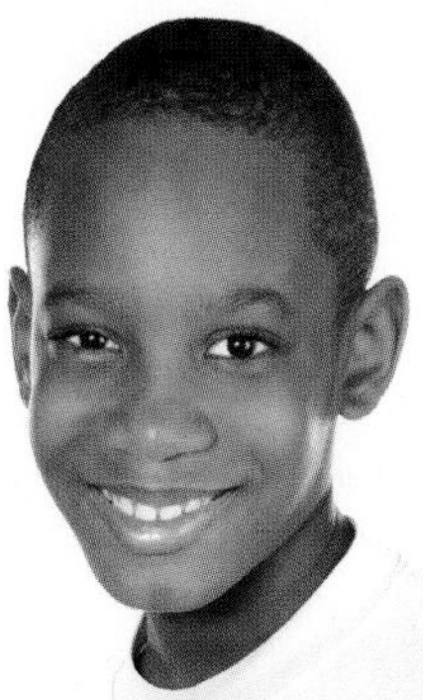

Each part is $\frac{1}{6}$ of the whole piece of clay.

Method 3

$$\begin{aligned}\frac{1}{2} \div 3 &= \frac{1}{2} \div \frac{3}{1} \\ &= \frac{1}{2} \times \frac{1}{3} \\ &= \frac{1}{6}\end{aligned}$$

$\frac{1}{3}$ is the **reciprocal** of $\frac{3}{1}$ or 3. Dividing by a number is the same as multiplying by the reciprocal of the number.

Each part is $\frac{1}{6}$ of the whole piece of clay.

Guided Practice

Solve.

1 A roll of wire, $\frac{3}{5}$ feet long, is cut into 6 equal pieces. How long is each piece?

Method 1

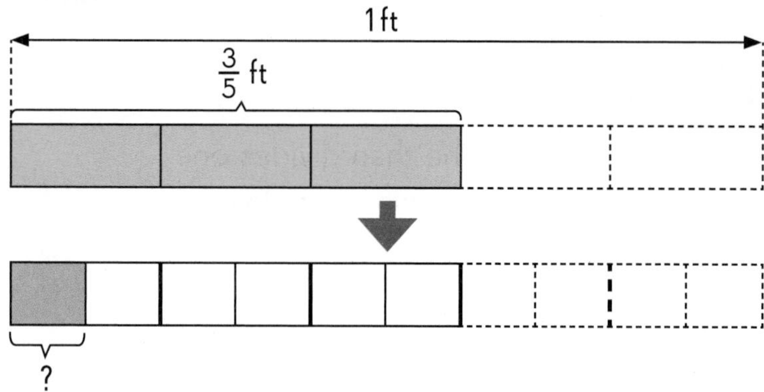

$\frac{3}{5} \div 6 = \frac{\square}{\square}$

The model shows that each piece is $\frac{\square}{\square}$ feet long.

Method 2

$\frac{3}{5} \div 6 = \frac{1}{6}$ of $\frac{3}{5}$

$= \frac{\square}{\square} \times \frac{\square}{\square}$

$= \frac{\square}{\square}$

$= \frac{\square}{\square}$

Each piece is $\frac{\square}{\square}$ feet long.

Method 3

$\frac{3}{5} \div 6 = \frac{3}{5} \div \frac{6}{1}$

$= \frac{3}{5} \times \frac{\square}{\square}$

$= \frac{\square}{\square}$

$= \frac{\square}{\square}$

Each piece is $\frac{\square}{\square}$ feet long.

Learn Divide a fraction by a whole number.

A $\frac{4}{5}$-pound cantaloupe is cut into 2 equal pieces. What is the weight of each piece of cantaloupe?

Method 1

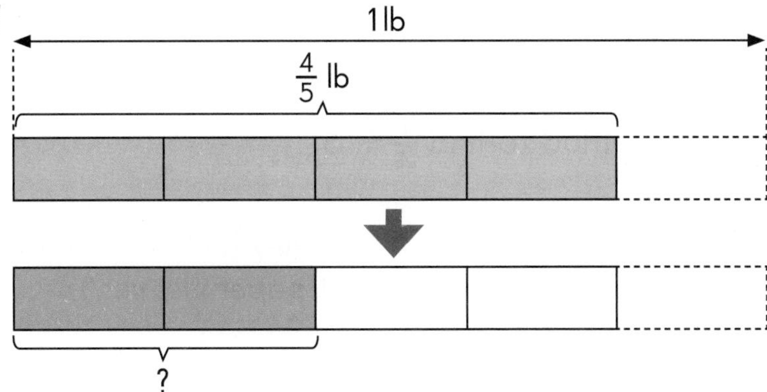

The model shows that the weight of each piece of cantaloupe is $\frac{2}{5}$ pound.

Method 2

$$\frac{4}{5} \div 2 = \frac{4}{5} \times \frac{1}{2}$$
$$= \frac{2}{5}$$

The weight of each piece of cantaloupe is $\frac{2}{5}$ pound.

Guided Practice

Solve.

2 Find $\frac{9}{11} \div 3$.

Method 1

The model shows that

$\frac{9}{11} \div 3 = \frac{?}{?}$.

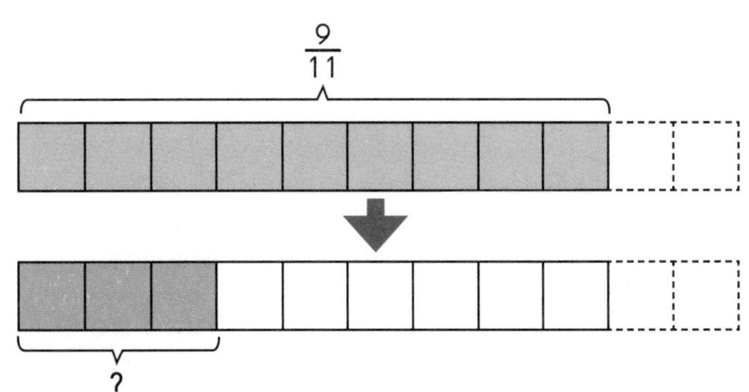

Method 2

$$\frac{9}{11} \div 3 = \frac{9}{11} \times \frac{?}{?}$$
$$= \frac{?}{?}$$

Hands-On Activity

Materials:
- paper
- colored pencil

1 Use the following method to find $\frac{1}{4} \div 3$.

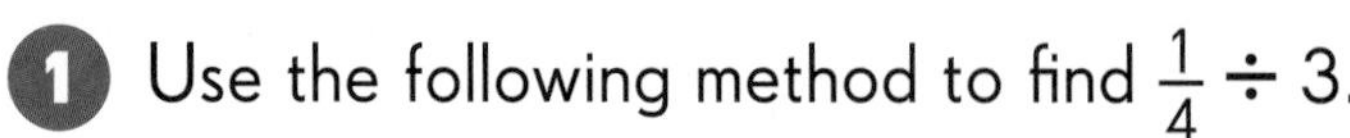

STEP 1 Use a piece of paper to represent one whole. Fold it into fourths. (Do not unfold the piece of paper just yet.)

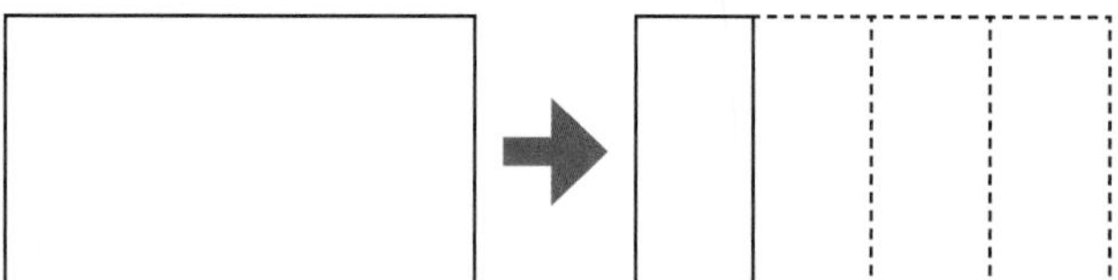

STEP 2 Continue to fold the paper further into thirds. Color any one side.

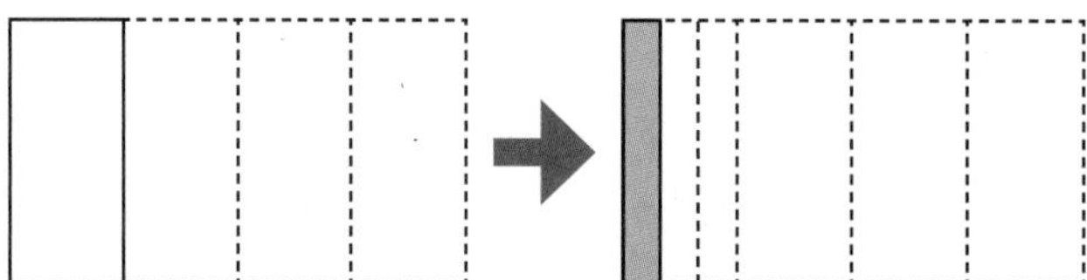

STEP 3 Unfold the paper to reveal the total number of parts.

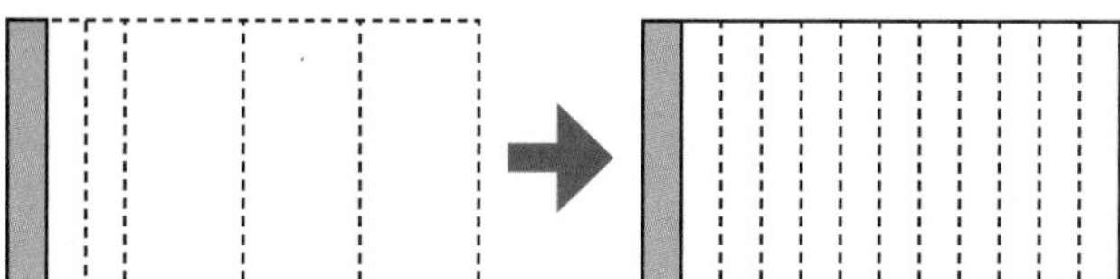

Count

a the total number of parts,

b the number of colored parts.

$\frac{1}{4} \div 3 = \frac{\square}{\square}$

Check!

$\frac{\square}{\square} \times 3 = \frac{\square}{\square}$

$= \frac{\square}{\square}$

2 Use a similar method to divide $\frac{1}{4}$ by 4.

Let's Practice

Divide. Express the quotient in simplest form. You may draw models to help you.

1. $\frac{2}{3} \div 8 = \frac{?}{?}$
2. $\frac{3}{4} \div 12 = \frac{?}{?}$
3. $\frac{6}{7} \div 9 = \frac{?}{?}$

Divide. Express the quotient in simplest form.

4. $\frac{6}{11} \div 3$
5. $\frac{8}{9} \div 4$
6. $\frac{3}{7} \div 2$

Solve. Show your work.

7. The area of a rectangular piece of fabric is $\frac{4}{9}$ square yards. Julie cuts the fabric into 3 smaller pieces of the same size. What is the area of each smaller piece of fabric?

8. Mel made a quesadilla. He cut $\frac{1}{10}$ of the quesadilla to save for later. Mel then shared the remaining portion of the quesadilla among himself and 2 friends. What fraction of the whole quesadilla did each person get?

9. Mrs. Pena spent $\frac{1}{3}$ of her paycheck on groceries and household goods and paid bills with $\frac{5}{12}$ of the paycheck. She then deposited the rest of the money equally in 3 accounts. What fraction of her paycheck did she deposit in each account?

10. Christine bought $\frac{5}{9}$ pound of granola. She repacked it equally in 20 bags to use as party favors.
    a. Find the weight of 1 bag of granola in pounds.
    b. After the party, 7 bags were left over. How many pounds of granola were left over?

ON YOUR OWN

Go to Workbook A: Practice 6, pages 149–152

Real-World Problems: Multiplying and Dividing with Fractions

Lesson Objective

- Solve real-world problems involving multiplication and division in fractions.

Learn **Find parts of a whole to solve real-world problems.**

A vendor at the farmers' market has 240 pieces of fruit. She sells $\frac{1}{2}$ of it to one customer and $\frac{1}{3}$ of it to another customer.

(a) How many pieces of fruit does the vendor sell?

(b) How many pieces of fruit does she have left?

Method 1

The least common multiple of 2 and 3 is 6. Draw a model with 6 equal units.

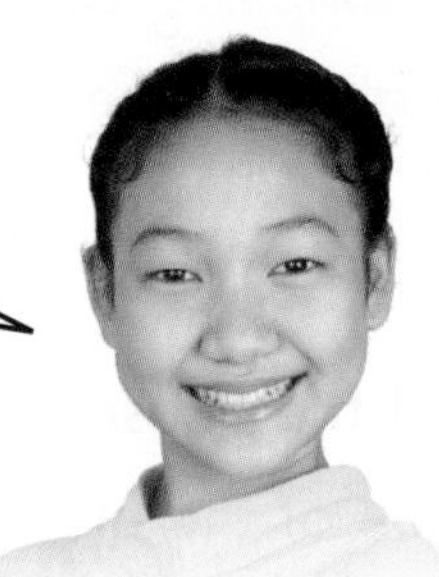

$\frac{1}{2}$ of 6 units $= \frac{1}{2} \times 6$
$= 3$ units

$\frac{1}{3}$ of 6 units $= \frac{1}{3} \times 6$
$= 2$ units

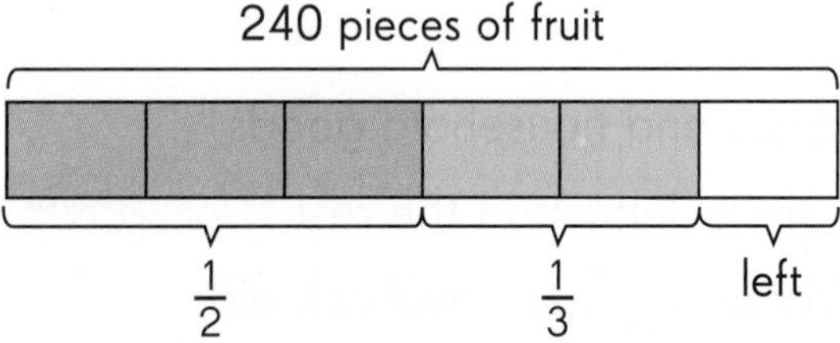

The model shows that:

6 units ⟶ 240 pieces of fruit

1 unit ⟶ $240 \div 6 = 40$ pieces of fruit

5 units ⟶ $5 \times 40 = 200$ pieces of fruit

(a) The vendor sells 200 pieces of fruit.

(b) She has 40 pieces of fruit left.

Method 2

$\frac{1}{2} = \frac{3}{6}$ $\frac{1}{3} = \frac{2}{6}$

Fraction of fruit sold:

$\frac{3}{6} + \frac{2}{6} = \frac{5}{6}$

$\frac{5}{6}$ of $240 = \frac{5}{6} \times 240 = 200$

a The vendor sells 200 pieces of fruit.

b She has $240 - 200 = 40$ pieces of fruit left.

Method 3

$\frac{1}{2} \times 240 = 120$

$\frac{1}{3} \times 240 = 80$

a The vendor sells $120 + 80 = 200$ pieces of fruit.

b She has $240 - 200 = 40$ pieces of fruit left.

Guided Practice

Solve.

1 Kim has 48 plants in her garden. Of the 48 plants, $\frac{2}{3}$ are carrots and $\frac{1}{4}$ are tomatoes. The rest of the plants are pumpkins. How many pumpkin plants are in the garden?

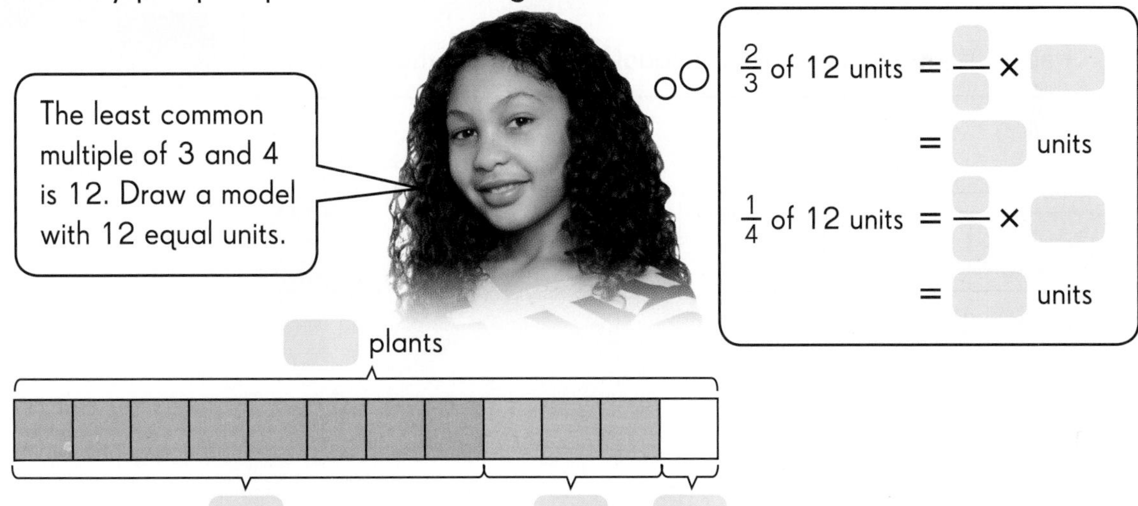

The least common multiple of 3 and 4 is 12. Draw a model with 12 equal units.
$\frac{2}{3}$ of 12 units = — ×
= units
$\frac{1}{4}$ of 12 units = — ×
= units
plants

The model shows that:

units → plants

1 unit → ÷ = plants

Kim has pumpkin plants.

Learn Find fractional parts of a whole and the remainder.

Sofia has \$480. She uses $\frac{1}{3}$ of the money to buy a winter coat. She then spends $\frac{1}{4}$ of the remainder on a pair of winter boots. How much money does she have left?

Method 1

$1 - \frac{1}{3} = \frac{2}{3}$

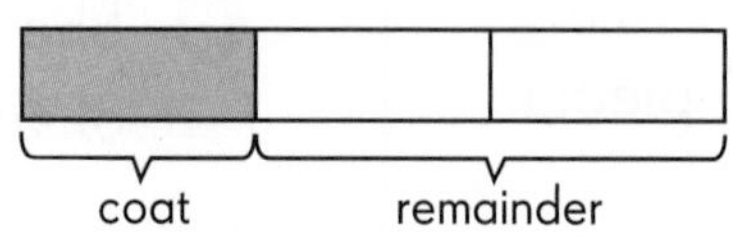

Remainder ⟶ 2 parts

To show $\frac{1}{4}$ of the remainder is spent on the boots, I have to further divide the remainder into 4 parts.

Least common multiple of 2 and 4 = 4

By equivalent fractions:

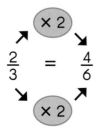

$\frac{2}{3} = \frac{4}{6}$ (× 2, × 2)

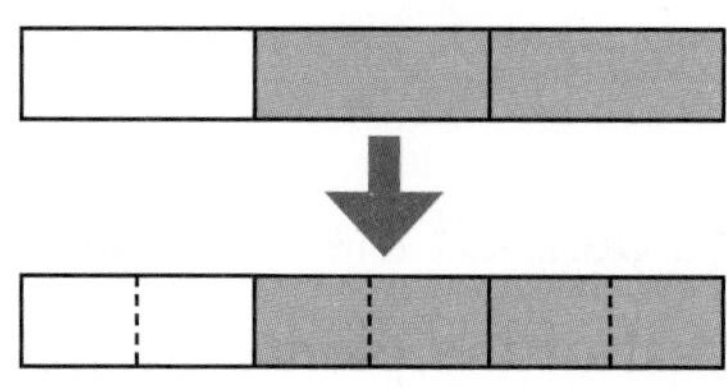

I need to draw a model with 6 equal units to show the problem.

\$480

coat boots left

$\frac{1}{3}$ of 6 units = 2 units

$\frac{1}{4}$ of 4 units = 1 unit

The model shows that:

6 units ⟶ \$480

1 unit ⟶ \$480 ÷ 6 = \$80

3 units ⟶ 3 × \$80

= \$240

She has \$240 left.

Method 2

$\frac{1}{3}$ of 480 $= \frac{1}{3} \times 480$

$= 160$

Sofia spends \$160 on the coat.

$480 - 160 = 320$

After buying the coat, she has \$320 left.

$1 - \frac{1}{4} = \frac{3}{4}$

$\frac{3}{4}$ of 320 $= \frac{3}{4} \times 320$

$= 240$

She has \$240 left.

Learn Find fractional parts and wholes given one fractional part.

Ben took a test with three sections, A, B, and C. Ben spent $\frac{1}{5}$ of his time on Section A and $\frac{1}{3}$ of the remaining time on Section B. He spent 48 minutes on Section C. How much time did Ben take to complete the whole test?

Method 1

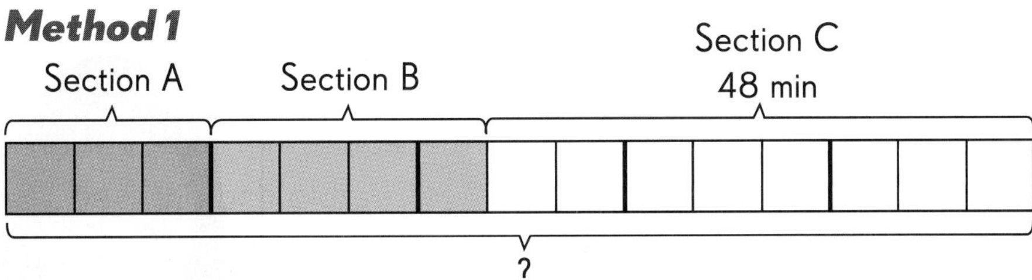

The model shows that:

8 units ⟶ 48 min

1 unit ⟶ 6 min

15 units ⟶ 90 min

Ben took 90 minutes to complete the test.

Method 2

Fraction of the total time Ben spent on Section B

$= \frac{1}{3} \times \frac{4}{5} = \frac{4}{15}$

Fraction of the total time he spent on Sections A and B

$= \frac{1}{5} + \frac{4}{15} = \frac{3}{15} + \frac{4}{15}$

$= \frac{7}{15}$

Fraction of the total time he spent on Section C

$= 1 - \frac{7}{15} = \frac{8}{15}$

$\frac{8}{15}$ ⟶ 48 min

$\frac{1}{15}$ ⟶ 6 min

$\frac{15}{15}$ ⟶ 90 min

Ben took 90 minutes to complete the test.

Method 2

Fraction of lemonade remaining $= 1 - \frac{1}{4} = \frac{3}{4}$

Amount of lemonade in 6 glasses $= \frac{3}{4} \times \frac{4}{5} = \frac{3}{5}$ gal

Amount of lemonade in 1 glass $= \frac{3}{5} \div 6$

$= \frac{3}{5} \times \frac{1}{6}$

$= \frac{1}{10}$ gal

There is $\frac{1}{10}$ gallon of lemonade in each glass.

Guided Practice

Solve.

4 Jeff buys $\frac{3}{4}$ pound of beads. $\frac{1}{6}$ of the beads are pink and the rest are green. Jeff packs the green beads equally into 10 jars. What is the weight of beads in each jar?

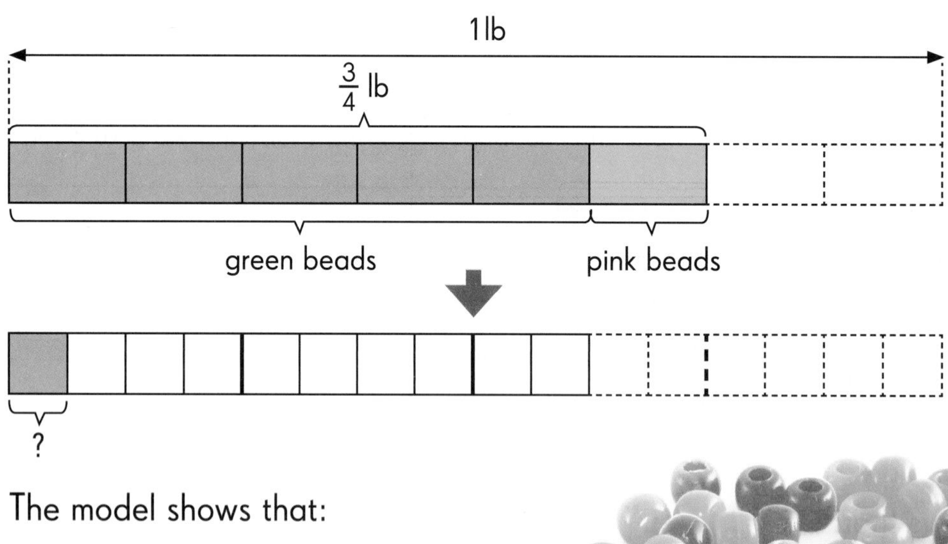

The model shows that:

16 units → ___ lb

1 unit → $\frac{\square}{\square}$ lb

There is $\frac{\square}{\square}$ pound of beads in each jar.

Let's Practice

Solve. Show your work.

1. Jan has 288 tickets to sell for charity. She sells $\frac{2}{9}$ of the tickets to her family and $\frac{1}{3}$ of them to her friends.
   a. How many tickets are sold to both her family and friends?
   b. How many tickets are not sold?

2. Maggie has \$960. She spends $\frac{1}{4}$ of it on a mountain bike and $\frac{1}{6}$ of the remainder on bicycle clothing and accessories. She keeps the rest of the money. How much money does she keep?

3. Jeb took 1 hour 40 mintues to complete a road race that was three laps around a section of the city. He took $\frac{1}{4}$ of the total time to run the first lap and $\frac{1}{3}$ of the remaining time to run the second lap. The rest of the time was used to run the third lap. How many minutes did he take to run the third lap of the race?

4. Mr. Young has a piece of rope. He uses $\frac{1}{4}$ of it to tie some boxes together. He then uses $\frac{5}{9}$ of the remainder to make a jumprope for his daughter. After this, 120 centimeters are left. What is the length of rope Mr. Young used to tie the boxes together?

5. Sean has a piece of string $\frac{7}{8}$ meter long. He uses $\frac{1}{5}$ of the piece of string to tie a package and cuts the rest into 5 equal pieces. What is the length of each piece?

6. Callie bought a bag of assorted dried fruit pieces comprising cherries, pears, and apples. In the bag, $\frac{1}{4}$ of the dried fruit is cherries and $\frac{2}{3}$ of the remainder is pears. There are 48 pear pieces. How many pieces of fruits are apples?

ON YOUR OWN

Go to Workbook A: Practice 7 and 8, pages 153–158

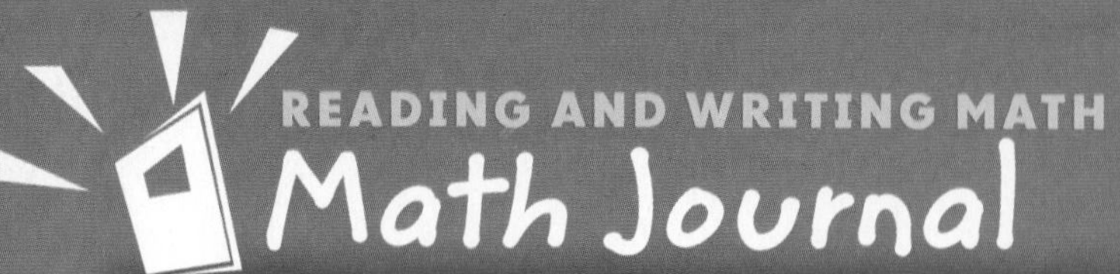

READING AND WRITING MATH
Math Journal

Amol and Bart were each given a problem to solve.

1. Amol: $\frac{2}{9} \div 3$

2. Bart: $\frac{2}{9} \times \frac{4}{11}$

They obtained answers to the problems as follows:

1. Amol: $\frac{2}{9} \div 3 = \frac{2}{3}$

2. Bart: $\frac{2}{9} \times \frac{4}{11} = \frac{6}{20}$

Their answers however are incorrect. Give explanations as to how they could have possibly arrived at these incorrect answers. Write down the correct way to solve each problem.

$\frac{2}{9} \div 3 = \frac{2}{3}$

$9 \bigcirc 3 = 3$

Amol got the answer $\frac{2}{3}$ by ______.

The correct way to solve the problem should have been:

$\frac{2}{9} \div 3 = \frac{2}{9} \bigcirc \frac{1}{\square}$

$= \frac{\square}{\square}$

$\frac{2}{9} \times \frac{4}{11} = \frac{6}{20}$

$2 \bigcirc 4 = 6$

$9 \bigcirc 11 = 20$

Bart got the answer $\frac{6}{20}$ by ______.

The correct way to solve the problem should have been:

$\frac{2}{9} \times \frac{4}{11} = \frac{\square \times \square}{\square \times \square}$

$= \frac{\square}{\square}$

CRITICAL THINKING SKILLS

Put On Your Thinking Cap!

Problem Solving

1. Find the missing mass in each pattern.

   a. 2,000 g $\quad \frac{1}{3}$ of 18 kg $\quad$ 18,000 g $\quad$ ▭ kg $\quad \frac{1}{3}$ of 486 kg

   b. 7,000 g $\quad$ ▭ kg $\quad \frac{1}{2}$ of 38 kg $\quad$ 31 kg $\quad 1\frac{1}{4}$ of 37,600 g

2. Danny was the 31st person in line at the cafeteria. His position in line was just behind $\frac{5}{9}$ of the total number of students in line. How many students were in line?

3. Keith bought 10 similar model cars. Brad bought $1\frac{1}{2}$ times as many of the same model cars as Keith. All cars were of the same price. The total cost of the model cars the two boys bought was $75. What was the cost of each model car?

ON YOUR OWN

Go to Workbook A: Put on Your Thinking Cap! pages 159–160

Chapter Wrap Up

Study Guide

You have learned...

Multiplying and Dividing Fractions and Mixed Numbers

Multiplying Proper Fractions

$\frac{3}{5} \times \frac{1}{3}$

$= \frac{3 \times 1}{5 \times 3}$

$= \frac{3}{15}$

$= \frac{1}{5}$

Multiplying Improper Fractions by Fractions

$\frac{16}{7} \times \frac{9}{8}$

$= \frac{16 \div 8}{7} \times \frac{9}{8 \div 8}$

$= \frac{2 \times 9}{7 \times 1}$

$= \frac{18}{7}$

$= 2\frac{4}{7}$

▶ Whole numbers, fractions, and mixed numbers can be multiplied or divided in any combination.

Multiplying Mixed Numbers and Whole Numbers

$12 \times 3\frac{5}{9}$

$= 12 \times \frac{32}{9}$

$= \frac{12 \times 32}{9}$

$= \frac{384}{9}$

$= 42\frac{6}{9}$

$= 42\frac{2}{3}$

Dividing a Fraction by a Whole Number

$\frac{4}{7} \div 8$

$= \frac{4}{7} \div \frac{8}{1}$

$= \frac{4}{7} \times \frac{1}{8}$

$= \frac{1}{14}$

Solve Real-World Problems

Chapter Review/Test

Vocabulary

Choose the correct word.

product
common factor
proper fraction
improper fraction
mixed number
reciprocal

1. A fraction whose numerator is greater than the denominator is called an ____.

2. A number that has a whole number part and a fractional part is called a ____.

3. When the same number is a factor of two numbers, it is called a ____.

4. The ____ of $\frac{9}{1}$ or 9 is $\frac{1}{9}$.

Concepts and Skills

Multiply. Express each product in simplest form.

5. $\frac{1}{2} \times \frac{4}{7}$

6. $\frac{2}{3} \times \frac{9}{10}$

7. $\frac{3}{8}$ of $\frac{2}{5}$

8. $\frac{11}{3} \times \frac{1}{4}$

Multiply. Express each product as a whole number or a a mixed number in simplest form.

9. $\frac{20}{6} \times \frac{12}{5}$

10. $\frac{16}{9} \times \frac{12}{8}$

Multiply. Express the product as a whole number or a mixed number in simplest form.

11. $5\frac{1}{4} \times 8$

12. $14 \times 3\frac{5}{6}$

13. $17 \times 2\frac{5}{8}$

Divide. Express the quotient in simplest form.

14. $\frac{2}{9} \div 4$

15. $\frac{7}{12} \div 2$

16. $\frac{3}{10} \div 9$

17. $\frac{15}{19} \div 5$

Problem Solving

Solve. Show your work.

18. Pat has some T-shirts. $\frac{1}{4}$ of the T-shirts are pink, $\frac{1}{2}$ of the remainder are white and the rest are purple.
What fraction of the T-shirts are purple?

19. Donald works $1\frac{3}{4}$ hours a day at a book store. If he is paid \$7 an hour, how much money does he earn in 5 days?

20. Jody has a rectangular piece of fabric $\frac{7}{8}$ yard long and $\frac{4}{5}$ yard wide.
   a. What is the area of the piece of fabric?
   b. Jody decides to share the piece of fabric equally with her friend. What is the area of the piece of fabric each person gets?

21. Of the total number of spectators at a circus show, $\frac{1}{4}$ are men. $\frac{2}{5}$ of the remaining number of spectators are women. There are 132 women at the circus show. How many children are at the circus show?

Chapter 5

Algebra

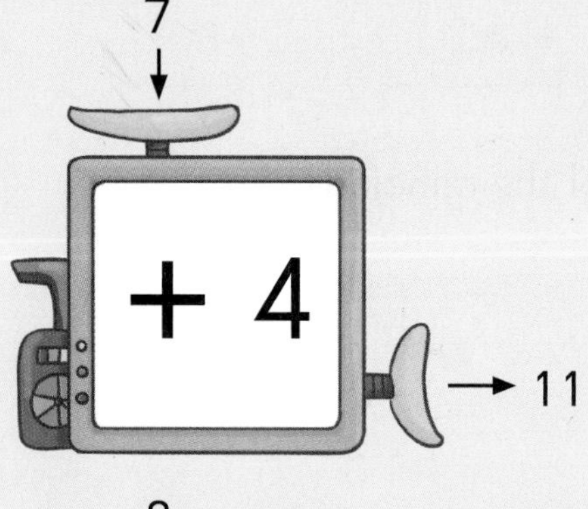

This machine adds 4 to the number put in.

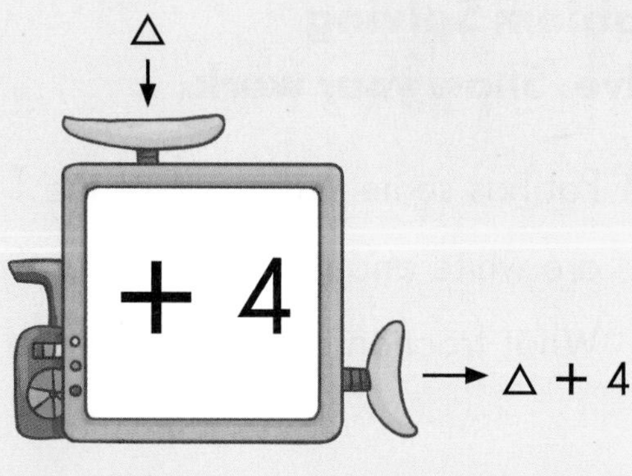

This machine multiplies the number put in by 3.

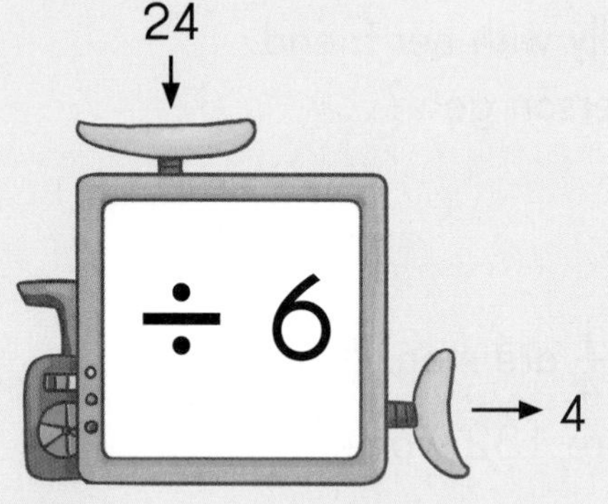

What does this machine do?

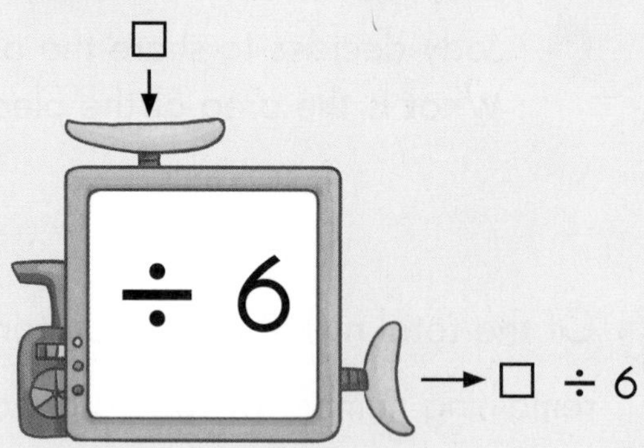

Lessons

BIG IDEA

▶ Algebraic expressions can be used to describe situations and solve real-world problems.

Recall Prior Knowledge

Comparing numbers with symbols

Symbol	Meaning	Example
$=$	is equal to	$4 + 6 = 10 \rightarrow 4 + 6$ is equal to 10.
$>$	is greater than	$15 > 6 \rightarrow 15$ is greater than 6.
$<$	is less than	$4 < 10 \rightarrow 4$ is less than 10.

Multiplication is the same as repeated addition.

8	8	8	8

$8 + 8 + 8 + 8 = 4 \times 8$

Number properties

1. Commutative properties
   $2 + 3 = 3 + 2$
   $4 \times 5 = 5 \times 4$

2. Associative properties
   $(6 + 7) + 8 = 6 + (7 + 8)$
   $(9 \times 10) \times 11 = 9 \times (10 \times 11)$

3. Identity properties
   $13 + 0 = 13$
   $14 \times 1 = 14$

4. Distributive properties
   $12 \times 2 = (10 \times 2) + (2 \times 2)$
   $9 \times 4 = (10 \times 4) - (1 \times 4)$

5. Zero property of multiplication
   $16 \times 0 = 0$

Inverse operations

Inverse operations are operations that have opposite effects.

Addition and subtraction are one pair of inverse operations.

Multiplication and division are another pair of inverse operations.

You can use inverse operations to find missing numbers.

In ☐ + 7 = 15,
☐ = 15 − 7
= 8

In ☐ × 4 = 24,
☐ = 24 ÷ 4
= 6

Order of operations

STEP 1 Work inside the parentheses.

STEP 2 Multiply and divide from left to right.

STEP 3 Add and subtract from left to right.

First expression: (30 + 42) − 3 × 8 ← Perform all operations in the parentheses first.

Second expression: 72 − 3 × 8 ← Then multiply.

Third expression: 72 − 24 ← Finally, subtract.

48

Complete with =, >, or <.

1 101 ◯ 99

2 49 ◯ 51

3 8 + 5 ◯ 4 + 9

Complete.

4 7 + 7 = ☐ × 7

5 5 + 5 + 5 = ☐ × 5

6 23 + 23 = 2 ◯ 23

7 16 + 16 + 16 + 16 = 4 ◯ 16

Write True or False.

8 25 + 39 gives the same sum as 39 + 25.

9 (3 × 4) × 9 gives a different product from 3 × (4 × 9).

10 The sum of any number and 0 is the same number.

11 64 × 9 is the same as (60 × 9) − (4 × 9).

12 The product of any number and 0 is 0.

Find the missing number.

13 7 + ☐ = 11

14 ☐ − 3 = 18

15 6 × ☐ = 54

16 ☐ ÷ 6 = 10

Simplify each expression.

17 2 + (8 − 3) × 4

18 (12 − 8) ÷ 4 + 5

Lesson 5.1 Using Letters as Numbers

Lesson Objective

- Recognize, write, and evaluate simple algebraic expressions in one variable.

Vocabulary

variable	numerical expression
evaluate	algebraic expression

Learn Write a numerical expression to show how numbers in a situation are related.

Randy is now 12 years old.

a Write an expression to show Randy's age one year from now.

	Randy's age (in years)
Now	12
1 year from now	12 + 1 = 13

An expression is a number or group of numbers with operation symbols.

Randy's age one year from now is (12 + 1) or 13 years.

b Write an expression to show Randy's age two years ago.

	Randy's age (in years)
Now	12
1 year ago	12 − 1
2 years ago	12 − 2 = 10

Randy's age two years ago was (12 − 2) or 10 years.

Learn Use **variables** to represent unknown numbers and form expressions involving addition and subtraction.

Mr. Haskin is a fifth-grade teacher. His students do not know his age.

a Write an expression to show Mr. Haskin's age one year from now.

I do not know Mr. Haskin's age. How can I write an expression to show his age one year from now?

You can use a letter, called a variable, to represent the unknown number. You can then write an expression for Mr. Haskin's age in the same way as if you know it.

Let x stand for Mr. Haskin's age now (in years).

	Mr. Haskin's age (in years)
Now	x
1 year from now	$x + 1$

Mr. Haskin's age one year from now is $(x + 1)$ years.

> A variable can take on different values. x is a variable, so it can take on different values. If Mr. Haskin is 47 years old, then x is 47. If Mr. Haskin is 38 years old, then x is 38.

b Write an expression to show Mr. Haskin's age two years ago. Use the same variable, x :

	Mr. Haskin's age (in years)
Now	x
1 year ago	$x - 1$
2 years ago	$x - 2$

Mr. Haskin's age two years ago was $(x - 2)$ years.

$x + 1$, $x - 1$ and $x - 2$ are examples of **algebraic expressions** in terms of x.

> An algebraic expression is an expression that contains at least one variable.

Guided Practice

Complete.

1 What is Mr. Haskin's age in terms of x?

	Mr. Haskin's age (in years)
Now	x
4 years from now	
10 years from now	
5 years ago	
8 years ago	

Learn **A variable can be used in place of a number in an algebraic expression.**

a Add 2 to 6.
$6 + 2$

b Add x to 6.
$6 + x$

c Subtract 3 from 4.
$4 - 3$

d Subtract 3 from y.
$y - 3$

e Find 4 more than 8.
$8 + 4$

f Find x more than 8.
$8 + x$

g Find 5 less than 9.
$9 - 5$

h Find 5 less than y.
$y - 5$

Guided Practice

Write the algebraic expression for each of the following.

2 Add 5 to z.

3 Add z to 8.

4 Subtract 7 from z.

5 Subtract z from 10.

6 Find 9 more than z.

7 Find z more than 9.

8 Find 11 less than z.

9 Find z less than 11.

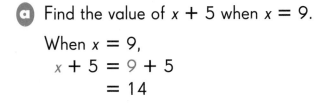

Learn Algebraic expressions can be evaluated for given values of the variable.

a Find the value of $x + 5$ when $x = 9$.

When $x = 9$,
$x + 5 = 9 + 5$
$= 14$

b Find the value of $5 + x$ when $x = 23$.

When $x = 23$,
$5 + x = 5 + 23$
$= 28$

c Find the value of $y - 7$ when $y = 15$.

When $y = 15$,
$y - 7 = 15 - 7$
$= 8$

d Find the value of $30 - y$ when $y = 7$.

When $y = 7$,
$30 - y = 30 - 7$
$= 23$

To evaluate an expression for a given value of the variable, substitute the given value for the variable and then find the value of the expression.

Guided Practice

Complete. Evaluate each algebraic expression for the given values of *x*.

10

Expression	Value of expression when	
	$x = 8$	$x = 30$
$x + 4$	$8 + 4 = 12$	$30 + 4 = 34$
$12 + x$		
$x - 6$		
$40 - x$		

Learn Use variables to form expressions involving multiplication.

A box has 12 plums. How many plums are in 2 such boxes?

$$2 \times 12 = 24$$

2 ↑ Number of boxes; 12 ↑ Number of plums in each box

There are (2×12) or 24 plums in 2 such boxes.

A box has n plums.

a How many plums are in 2 such boxes?

$$2 \times n = 2 \times n$$

2 ↑ Number of boxes; n ↑ Number of plums in each box

There are $(2 \times n)$ plums in 2 such boxes.

b How many plums are in 3 such boxes?

$$3 \times n = 3 \times n$$

3 ↑ Number of boxes; n ↑ Number of plums in each box

There are $(3 \times n)$ plums in 3 such boxes.

Write $2 \times n$ as $2n$ and $3 \times n$ as $3n$.

The expressions $2n$ and $3n$ are examples of algebraic expressions involving multiplication in terms of n.

$2n$ and $3n$ are how $2 \times n$ and $3 \times n$ are written in algebra.

$3n$ is $3 \times n$ or 3 groups of n or $n \times 3$ or n groups of 3.

$1 \times n = n \times 1$
$= 1n$
$= n$

$12p$ is $12 \times p$ or 12 groups of p or $p \times 12$ or p groups of 12.

Guided Practice

Write each of the following in at least three other ways.

11 $4k$

12 $7 \times j$

13 5 groups of p

14 q groups of 8

Complete.

15 There are n stickers in 1 package. Find the number of stickers in terms of n. Then, find the number of stickers for the given values of n.

Number of packages	Number of stickers	Number of stickers when	
		$n = 15$	$n = 20$
1	n	15	20
4			
7			
10			
15			

To find the number of stickers for any value of n, substitute the value of n into the expression for the number of stickers. Then, find the value of the expression.

Learn Use variables to form expressions involving division.

A carton has 6 juice boxes. The boxes are put into 2 equal groups. How many boxes are in each group?

$6 \div 2 = 3$

6 ↑ Number of juice boxes

2 ↑ Number of groups

There are $(6 \div 2)$ or 3 juice boxes in each group.

A carton has m juice boxes.

a If the juice boxes are put into 2 equal groups, how many boxes are in each group?

$m \div 2$

m ↑ Number of juice boxes

2 ↑ Number of groups

There are $(m \div 2)$ juice boxes in each group.

b If the juice boxes are put into 3 equal groups, how many boxes are in each group?

$m \div 3$

m ↑ Number of juice boxes

3 ↑ Number of groups

There are $(m \div 3)$ juice boxes in each group.

Write $m \div 2$ as $\frac{m}{2}$ and $m \div 3$ as $\frac{m}{3}$.

The expressions $\frac{m}{2}$ and $\frac{m}{3}$ are examples of algebraic expressions involving division in terms of m.

$\frac{m}{2}$ and $\frac{m}{3}$ are how $m \div 2$ and $m \div 3$ are written in algebra.

$\frac{m}{1}$ is equal to m.

$\frac{s}{6}$ means $s \div 6$.

Guided Practice

Complete.

16 A packet of m pretzel sticks is to be shared equally among some children. Find the number of pretzel sticks each child gets in terms of m. Then, find the number of pretzel sticks for the given values of m.

Number of children	Number of pretzel sticks each child gets	Number of pretzel sticks each child gets when	
		$m = 24$	$m = 48$
1	m	24	48
3	$\frac{m}{3}$	$\frac{24}{3} = 8$	
6			
8			
12			

17 Find the expression that belongs to each box in terms of p. For each circle on the right, find the value of the expression in the box next to it when $p = 6$.

Start	Operation	Box	Operation	Box		Circle
p	$\times 1$ →	p	$+ 7$ →	$p + 7$	when $p = 6$ →	
3	$\times p$ →		$- 8$ →		when $p = 6$ →	
p	$+ 4$ →		$\div 2$ →		when $p = 6$ →	
p	$\div 2$ →		$+ 2$ →		when $p = 6$ →	
11	$- p$ →		$\div 5$ →		when $p = 6$ →	

Find the value of each expression when $r = 1,728$.

18 $23r - 89$

19 $\frac{11,640 - r}{28}$

20 $\frac{11r}{24} + 2,399$

21 $\frac{14r + 7,392}{32}$

Hands-On Activity

WORK IN PAIRS

Materials:

- 5 letter cards
- 5 number cards

STEP 1 Choose one letter card and one number card.

STEP 2 Write as many algebraic expressions as you can with the two cards. For example, if you draw the cards x and 8, you can write: '$x + 8$', '$8 + x$', '$x - 8$', '$8 - x$', '$8x$', '$\frac{x}{8}$' and '$\frac{8}{x}$'.

STEP 3 Repeat **STEP 1** and **STEP 2** until all the cards have been chosen.

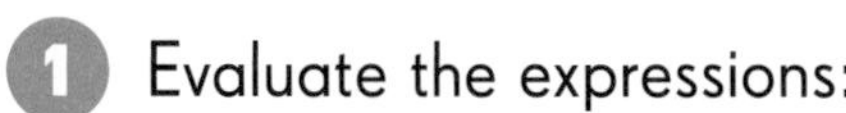

Let's Explore!

1. Evaluate the expressions:

   a. $\frac{y}{2}$

   b. $\frac{1}{2} \times y$

   for $y = 6$ and $y = 14$.

   Choose any other three values for y and use your calculator to evaluate the expressions. What can you conclude about the expressions?

2. Evaluate the expressions:

   a. $\frac{y - 2}{3}$

   b. $(y - 2) \div 3$

   c. $\frac{1}{3} \times (y - 2)$

   for $y = 8$ and $y = 17$.

   Choose any other three values for y and use your calculator to evaluate the expressions. What can you conclude about the expressions?

3. Write the expression $(x + 4) \div 6$ in two other ways.

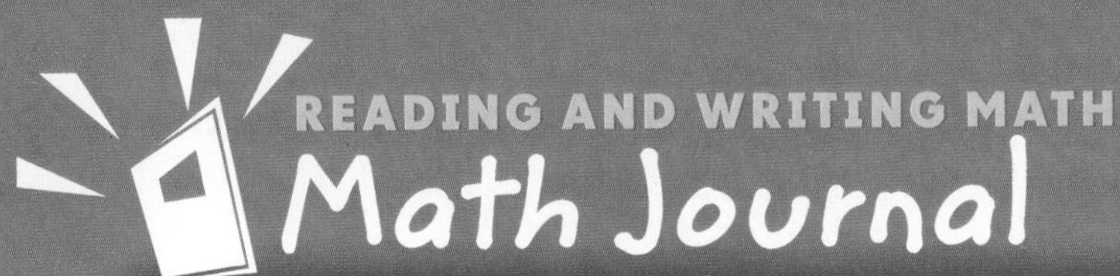

READING AND WRITING MATH

Math Journal

Write two real-world problems that can be described by these expressions.

1. $m - 20$
2. $5m$

Let's Practice

Write each expression in one or two other ways.

1. $5 \times w$
2. $v \times 15$
3. $x \div 3$
4. $\frac{1}{4} \times y$
5. $\frac{z + 4}{5}$
6. $\frac{1}{2} \times (a - 7)$

Write an expression for each of the following.

7. Add b to 9.
8. Subtract 4 from b.
9. Subtract b from 10.
10. Multiply b by 3.
11. Multiply 7 by b.
12. Divide b by 5.
13. Half of b.
14. Add 10 to b, then divide by 7.
15. Multiply b by 6, then subtract 11.
16. Divide b by 3, then add 8.

Write an expression in terms of x for each of the following. Then evaluate the expression when $x = 18$.

John is now x years old.

17 The age of his brother, who is 5 years older.

18 The age of his sister, who is 3 years younger.

19 The age of his aunt, who is twice as old as him.

20 The age of his cousin, who is half his age.

Write an expression in terms of n for each of the following. Then evaluate the expression when $n = 24$.

There are n strawberries in a carton.

21 The number of strawberries left after 6 pieces have been eaten.

22 The number of strawberries each child gets when the carton of strawberries is shared equally among 4 children.

23 The total number of strawberries in 10 similar cartons.

24 The number of strawberries each child gets when one carton and 11 strawberries are shared equally among 5 children.

Evaluate each expression when $y = 18{,}324$.

25 $y + 967$

26 $y - 1{,}259$

27 $25{,}283 - y$

28 $5y$

29 $y \div 4$

ON YOUR OWN

Go to Workbook A: Practice 1, pages 175–182

Simplifying Algebraic Expressions

Lesson Objective

- Simplify algebraic expressions in one variable.

Vocabulary
simplify
like terms

Learn Algebraic expressions can be simplified.

A rod of length a centimeters is joined to another rod of the same length. What is the total length of the 2 rods?

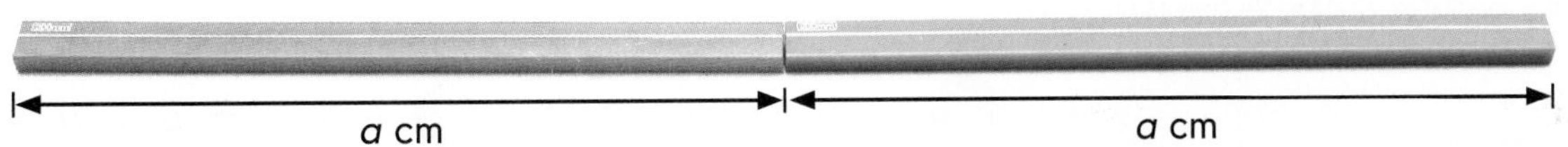

$a + a = 2 \times a$

Simplify $(a + a)$ by writing:

$a + a = 2a$

The total length of the 2 rods is $2a$ centimeters.

3	3

$3 + 3 = 2 \times 3$

4	4

$4 + 4 = 2 \times 4$

a	a

$a + a = 2 \times a$

$2 \times a$ is the same as $2a$.

The picture shows 3 rods, each b centimeters long. What is the total length of the 3 rods?

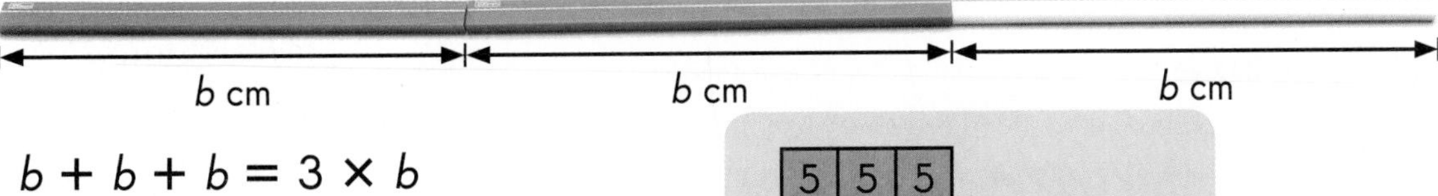

$b + b + b = 3 \times b$

Simplify $(b + b + b)$ by writing:

$b + b + b = 3b$

5	5	5

$5 + 5 + 5 = 3 \times 5$

b	b	b

$b + b + b = 3 \times b$

$3 \times b$ is the same as $3b$.

The total length of the 3 rods is $3b$ centimeters.

Continued on next page

The figure shows 5 sticks, each r centimeters long.
What is the total length of the 5 sticks?

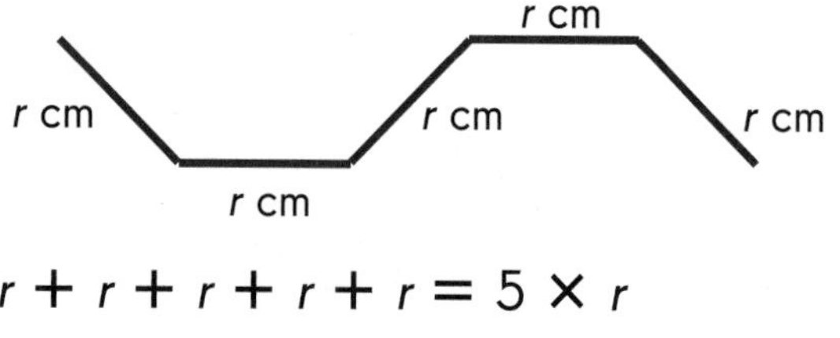

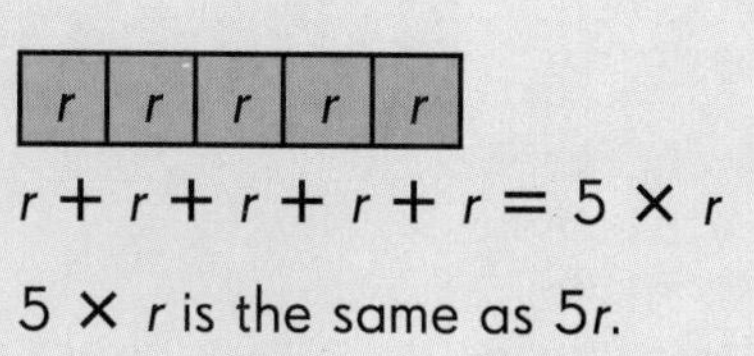

$r + r + r + r + r = 5 \times r$
$= 5r$

The total length of the 5 sticks is $5r$ centimeters.

Guided Practice

Simplify each expression.

1. $x + x$
2. $y + y + y$
3. $a + a + a + a + a$
4. $b + b + b + b + b + b$
5. $c + c + c + c + c + c + c$

Learn Like terms can be added.

Simplify $a + 2a$.

$a + 2a = a + a + a$
$= 3a$

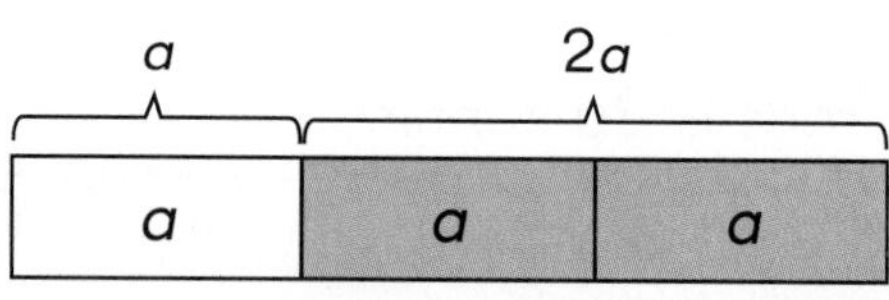

a and $2a$ are the terms of the expression, $a + 2a$. You call a and $2a$ like terms because they are both multiples of a.

Guided Practice

Complete.

6. Simplify $2a + 3a$.

$2a + 3a =$ ______

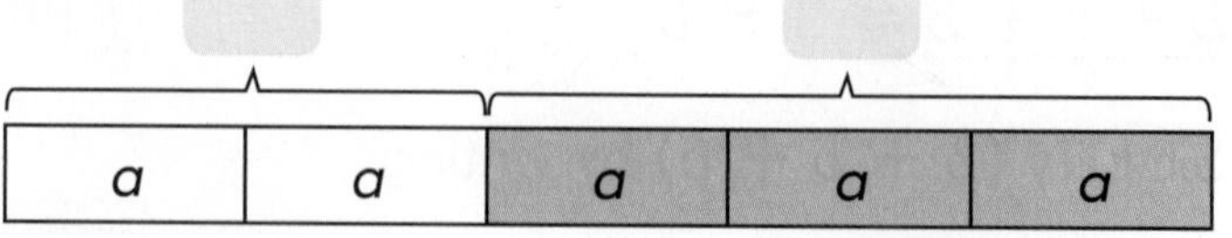

Simplify each expression.

7. $a + 3a$
8. $4x + x$
9. $2z + 5z$
10. $3y + 6y$
11. $b + 2b + 3b$
12. $4c + 2c + 10c$

Learn A variable subtracted from itself results in zero.

A ribbon is a centimeters long. Jenny uses the whole ribbon to decorate a present.
How much ribbon is left?

$a - a = 0$

There are 0 centimeters of ribbon left.

Compare this with:
$2 - 2 = 0$
$7 - 7 = 0$
$14 - 14 = 0$

Guided Practice

Simplify each expression.

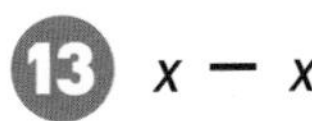

13. $x - x$

14. $2y - 2y$

15. $10z - 10z$

Learn Like terms can be subtracted.

Simplify $3a - a$.

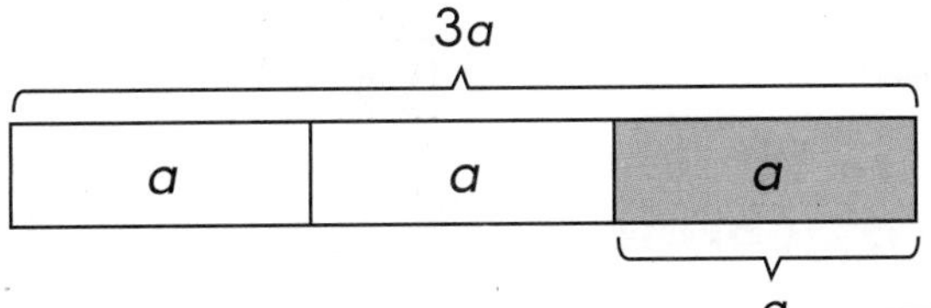

$3a - a = 2a$

From the model,
$3a - a = a + a$
$a + a = 2 \times a = 2a$
So, $3a - a = 2a$

Simplify $4a - 2a$.

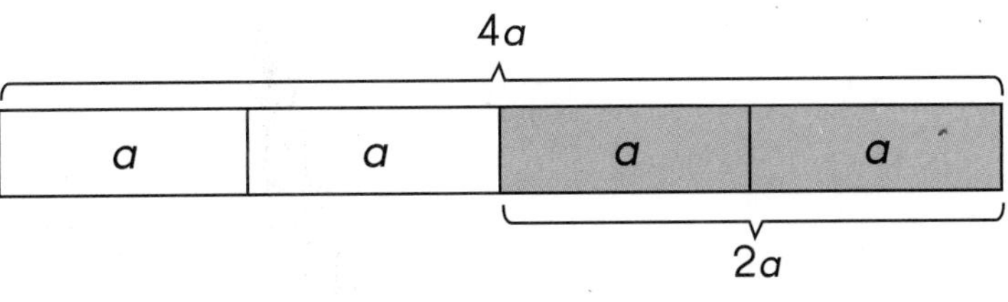

$4a - 2a = 2a$

From the model,
$4a - 2a = a + a$
$a + a = 2 \times a = 2a$
So, $4a - 2a = 2a$

Guided Practice

Complete.

16 Simplify $5a - 2a$.

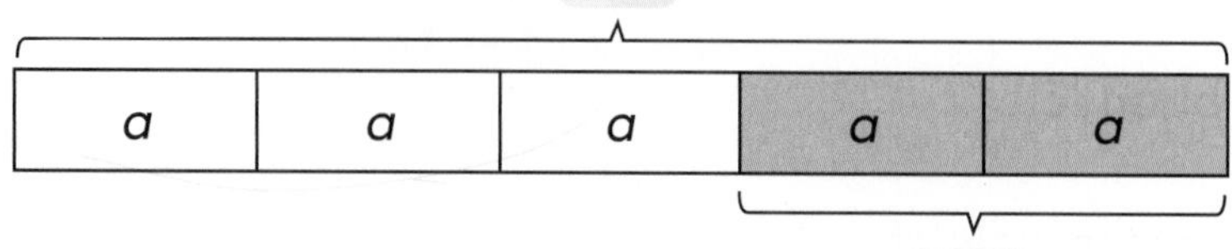

$5a - 2a = \square$

Simplify each expression.

17 $4a - a$

18 $7a - 3a$

19 $5x - 4x$

20 $10x - 6x$

21 $8y - 3y - 5y$

22 $12y - 7y - y$

Learn Use order of operations to simplify algebraic expressions.

a Simplify $6a + 3a - 2a$.

Working from left to right,

$$6a + 3a - 2a = 9a - 2a$$
$$= 7a$$

b Simplify $6a - 2a + 3a$.

Working from left to right,

$$6a - 2a + 3a = 4a + 3a$$
$$= 7a$$

Guided Practice

Simplify each expression.

23 $2x + 3x - 4x$

24 $x + 5x - 6x$

25 $9a - 3a + 4a$

26 $12a - 7a + 2a$

Learn

Collect like terms to simplify algebraic expressions.

Find the distance between point A and point B.

A |— a km —|— 4 km —|— a km —|— 2 km —| B

$a + 4 + a + 2$ ← Identify like terms.

$= a + a + 4 + 2$ ← Change the order of terms to collect like terms. Then simplify.

$= 2a + 6$

The distance between point A and point B is $(2a + 6)$ kilometers.

Commutative Property of Addition:

Two numbers can be added in any order.

So, $4 + a = a + 4$.

Simplify $4x + 6 - 2x$.

$4x + 6 - 2x$ ← Identify like terms.

$= 6 + 4x - 2x$ ← Change the order of terms to collect like terms. Then simplify.

$= 6 + 2x$

$4x + 6 = 6 + 4x$

Guided Practice

Simplify each expression.

27 $b + 5 + b + 5$

28 $3b + 4b + 2 + 6$

29 $5s + 9 - 3s$

30 $8s + 6 - 2s - 1$

Hands-On Activity

WORK IN PAIRS

Materials:
- 20 craft sticks

Let the length of each craft stick equal p units.

STEP 1 Form a closed figure using 3 or more craft sticks.

Example

STEP 2 Write the total length of the craft sticks used.

Example

Total length of craft sticks $= p + p + p$

$= 3p$ units

STEP 3 Remove, then add craft sticks to form another figure.

Example

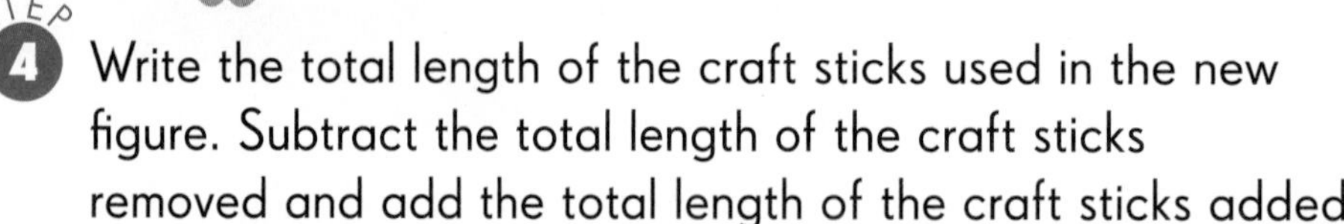

STEP 4 Write the total length of the craft sticks used in the new figure. Subtract the total length of the craft sticks removed and add the total length of the craft sticks added.

Example

To form a second figure, 1 craft stick was removed and 3 craft sticks were added.

Total length of craft sticks $= 3p - p + 3p$

$= 5p$ units

STEP 5 Check your answer in STEP 4 by counting the number of craft sticks used in the new figure to find the total length.

Example

Total number of craft sticks used = 5

Total length of craft sticks = $5 \times p$

= $5p$ units

STEP 6 Repeat the activity with other figures.

Let's Practice

Simplify each expression.

1. $2a + 5a$
2. $a + 7a$
3. $3a + 3a + 6a$
4. $4x - 2x$
5. $6x - 5x$
6. $10x - 2x - 8x$
7. $7y - 5y + 4y$
8. $9y + 3y - 5y$
9. $a + a + 5$
10. $b + 4 + 4 + b$
11. $2s + 7 - 6 + s$
12. $9r + 10 + 2 - 3r$

ON YOUR OWN

Go to Workbook A: Practice 2, pages 183–186

Lesson 5.3 Inequalities and Equations

Lesson Objectives

- Write and evaluate inequalities.
- Solve simple equations.

Vocabulary

inequality	equation
solve	true
Equality Properties	

Learn Algebraic expressions can be used in inequalities and equations.

Serena buys 2 bags of apples and 1 bag of 8 oranges. There is the same number of apples in each bag. Are there more oranges or apples?

Let each bag of apples contain x apples.

$x + x = 2x$

There are $2x$ apples.

To compare $2x$ and 8, you need to know the value of x.

When $x = 3$, $\quad 2x = 2 \times 3 = 6$

$6 < 8$, so $2x < 8$.

When $x = 3$, there are more oranges than apples.

When $x = 4$, $\quad 2x = 2 \times 4 = 8$

$8 = 8$, so $2x = 8$.

When $x = 4$, there is the same number of oranges and apples.

When $x = 5$, $\quad 2x = 2 \times 5 = 10$

$10 > 8$, so $2x > 8$.

When $x = 5$, there are more apples than oranges.

The statement $2x = 8$ is an equation.
The statements $2x < 8$ and $2x > 8$ are inequalities.

Guided Practice

Complete with >, <, or =.

1. When $y = 6$, $3y$ ◯ 18.
2. When $y = 10$, $3y$ ◯ 18.
3. When $y = 5$, $3y$ ◯ 18.
4. When $y = 9$, $3y$ ◯ 18.

Learn

Algebraic expressions can be compared by evaluating them for a given value of the variable.

When $b = 8$, is $4b - 6$ greater than, less than, or equal to 26?

Evaluate the expression to compare:

When $b = 8$,

$$\begin{aligned} 4b - 6 &= (4 \times 8) - 6 \\ &= 32 - 6 \\ &= 26 \end{aligned}$$

$26 = 26$

So, when $b = 8$, $4b - 6 = 26$.

Two expressions that have the same value are said to be equal.
When two equal expressions are related by an '=' sign, they form an equation.

When $c = 15$, is $3c \div 5$ greater than, less than, or equal to $c - 8$?

Evaluate both expressions to compare:

When $c = 15$,

$$\begin{aligned} 3c \div 5 &= (3 \times 15) \div 5 \\ &= 45 \div 5 \\ &= 9 \end{aligned}$$

$$\begin{aligned} c - 8 &= 15 - 8 \\ &= 7 \end{aligned}$$

$9 > 7$

So, when $c = 15$, $3c \div 5 > c - 8$.

When two expressions with different values are related by an '>' or '<' sign, they form an inequality.

Guided Practice

Complete.

5 When $d = 6$, is $2d + 10$ greater than, less than or equal to $4d$?

When $d = 6$, $2d + 10 = (2 \times$ ____ $) + 10$ $\qquad$ $4d = 4 \times$ ____

$=$ ____ $+ 10$ $\qquad$ $=$ ____

$=$ ____

So, $2d + 10$ is ____ $4d$, when $d = 6$.

Complete with >, <, or =.

6 When $e = 4$, $3e \div 6$ ____ $e - 2$. $\qquad$ **7** When $f = 9$, $8f - 4$ ____ $6f + 10$.

Learn: Equality Properties

You can add the same number to or subtract the same number from both sides of an equation. The new equation will still be **true** for the same value of variable.

Look at the balance.

(counter) represents 1.

(box a) represents a counters.

a counters together with 4 counters on the left side balance 5 counters on the right side.

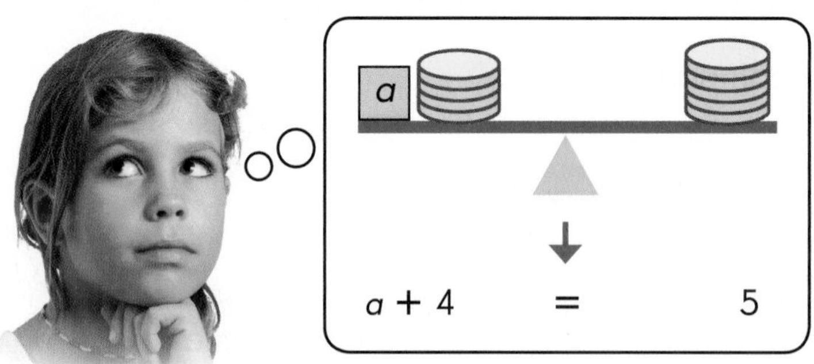

You have the equation $a + 4 = 5$.

Compare $a + 4 = 5$ with $1 + 4 = 5$, it can be seen that $a = 1$.

This equation is true for $a = 1$.

a Add 2 counters to both sides of the equation.
The two sides still balance.

You have a new equation:
$a + 4 + 2 = 5 + 2$, that is, $a + 6 = 7$.

Substitute 1 for a:
$a + 6 = 1 + 6 = 7$

The new equation $a + 6 = 7$ is still true for $a = 1$.

b Take away 2 counters from both sides of the equation.
The two sides still balance.

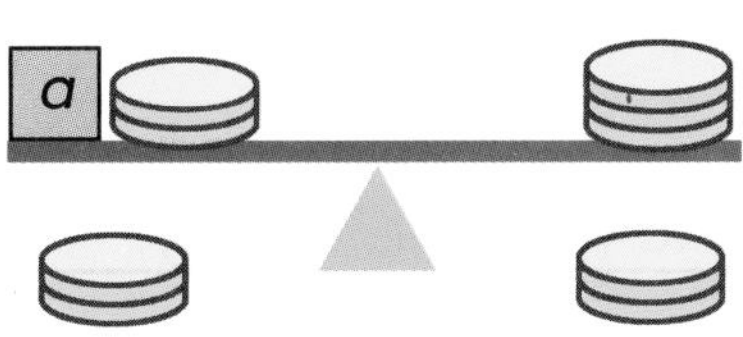

You have a new equation:
$a + 4 - 2 = 5 - 2$, that is, $a + 2 = 3$.

Substitute 1 for a:
$a + 2 = 1 + 2 = 3$

The new equation $a + 2 = 3$ is still true for $a = 1$.

You can multiply or divide both sides of an equation by the same number. The new equation will still be true for the same value of the variable.

Look at the balance.

$4a$ counters on the left side balance 8 counters on the right side.

You have the equation, $4a = 8$.

Compare $4a = 8$ with $4 \times 2 = 8$, it can be seen that $a = 2$.

This equation is true for $a = 2$.

a Multiply the number of counters on both sides by 2.
The two sides still balance.

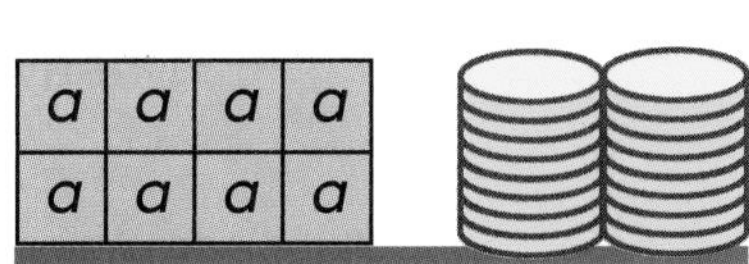

You have a new equation:
$4a \times 2 = 8 \times 2$, that is, $8a = 16$.

Substitute 2 for a:
$8a = 8 \times 2 = 16$

The new equation $8a = 16$ is still true for $a = 2$.

Learn: Solve equations with variables on both sides of the equal sign.

For what value of y will $6y - 7 = 2y + 9$ be true?

Guess and check.

Method 1

y	$6y - 7$	$2y + 9$	Both sides equal?
2	$6 \times 2 - 7 = 12 - 7$ $= 5$	$2 \times 2 + 9 = 4 + 9$ $= 13$	No
3	$6 \times 3 - 7 = 18 - 7$ $= 11$	$2 \times 3 + 9 = 6 + 9$ $= 15$	No
4	$6 \times 4 - 7 = 24 - 7$ $= 17$	$2 \times 4 + 9 = 8 + 9$ $= 17$	Yes

$6y - 7 = 2y + 9$ is true when $y = 4$.

Method 2

$$6y - 7 = 2y + 9$$

$$6y - 7 + 7 = 2y + 9 + 7$$ ← Add 7 to both sides of the equation.

$$6y = 2y + 16$$

$$6y - 2y = 2y - 2y + 16$$ ← Subtract $2y$ from both sides of the equation.

$$4y = 16$$

$$4y \div 4 = 16 \div 4$$ ← Divide both sides of the equation by 4.

$$y = 4$$

$6y - 7 = 2y + 9$ is true when $y = 4$.

Check!

Substitute the value of y into both sides of the equation.

Left side:

$6y - 7 = 6 \times 4 - 7$
$= 24 - 7$
$= 17$

Right side:

$2y + 9 = 2 \times 4 + 9$
$= 8 + 9$
$= 17$

$y = 4$ is the correct answer.

Solve $3p + 4 = 5p - 6$.

Method 1

y	$3p + 4$	$5p - 6$	Both sides equal?
2	$3 \times 2 + 4 = 6 + 4$ $= 10$	$5 \times 2 - 6 = 10 - 6$ $= 4$	No
4	$3 \times 4 + 4 = 12 + 4$ $= 16$	$5 \times 4 - 6 = 20 - 6$ $= 14$	No
5	$3 \times 5 + 4 = 15 + 4$ $= 19$	$5 \times 5 - 6 = 25 - 6$ $= 19$	Yes

$p = 5$

Method 2

$$3p + 4 = 5p - 6$$
$$3p + 4 + 6 = 5p - 6 + 6$$ ← Add 6 to both sides of the equation.
$$3p + 10 = 5p$$
$$3p - 3p + 10 = 5p - 3p$$ ← Subtract $3p$ from both sides of the equation.
$$10 = 2p$$
$$2p = 10$$
$$2p \div 2 = 10 \div 2$$ ← Divide both sides of the equation by 2.
$$p = 5$$

I can either subtract 4 from both sides of the equation or add 6 to both sides. Which do I know how to do?

Subtract 4:
$3p + 4 - 4 = 5p - 6 - 4$ (?)

Add 6:
$3p + 4 + 6 = 5p - 6 + 6$

I do not know how to simplify '$- 6 - 4$'. I will add 6 to both sides instead.

Check!

Substitute the value of p into both sides of the equation.

Left side:
$3p + 4 = 3 \times 5 + 4$
$= 15 + 4$
$= 19$

Right side:
$5p - 6 = 5 \times 5 - 6$
$= 25 - 6$
$= 19$

$p = 5$ is the correct answer.

Guided Practice

Fill in ◯ with +, −, ×, or ÷ and ▭ with the correct number.

11 For what value of q will $8q - 7 = 5q + 11$ be true?

$8q - 7 = 5q + 11$

$8q - 7$ ◯ ▭ $= 5q + 11$ ◯ ▭

$8q = 5q$ ◯ ▭

$8q$ ◯ $5q = 5q$ ◯ $5q$ ◯ ▭

$3q =$ ▭

$3q$ ◯ ▭ $=$ ▭ ◯ ▭

$q =$ ▭

$8q - 7 = 5q + 11$ is true when $q =$ ▭.

12 For what value of m will $3m + 9 = 5m - 11$ be true?

$3m + 9 = 5m - 11$

$3m + 9$ ◯ ▭ $= 5m - 11$ ◯ ▭

$3m$ ◯ ▭ $= 5m$

$3m$ ◯ $3m +$ ▭ $= 5m$ ◯ $3m$

▭ $= 2m$

$2m =$ ▭

$2m$ ◯ ▭ $=$ ▭ ◯ ▭

$m =$ ▭

$3m + 9 = 5m - 11$ is true when $m =$ ▭.

I can either subtract ▭ from both sides of the equation or add ▭ to both sides. Which do I know how to do?

Subtract ▭:

$3m + 9 -$ ▭ $= 5m - 11 -$ ▭

?

Add ▭:

$3m + 9 +$ ▭ $= 5m - 11 +$ ▭

I do not know how to simplify '− ▭ ◯ ▭'. I will add ▭ to both sides instead.

Let's Practice

Complete with $>$, $<$, or $=$.

1. When $z = 5$, $4z$ ◯ 24.
2. When $z = 8$, $4z$ ◯ 24.
3. When $z = 6$, $4z$ ◯ 24.
4. When $z = 2$, $4z$ ◯ 24.

Complete with $=$, $>$, or $<$ for $a = 9$.

5. $a + 7$ ◯ 16
6. $2a - 5$ ◯ 11
7. $(12 + a) - 21$ ◯ 1
8. $15 - a$ ◯ $a - 2$
9. $4a \div 6$ ◯ $17 - a$
10. $13 + (72 \div a)$ ◯ $2a + 2$

Solve each equation.

11. $6j - 24 = 12$
12. $8k + 19 = 35$
13. $5m - 9 = 3m + 7$
14. $10n + 6 = 15n - 9$

Check your solution by substituting it for the variable in the given equation.

ON YOUR OWN

Go to Workbook A: Practice 3, pages 187–188

Lesson 5.4 Real-World Problems: Algebra

Lesson Objective

- Solve real-world problems involving algebraic expressions.

Learn **Write an addition or subtraction expression for a real-world problem and evaluate it.**

Tyrone has y compact discs (CDs). John has 3 times as many CDs as Tyrone. John buys another 7 CDs.

a. How many more CDs does John have than Tyrone?

John has $(3y + 7)$ CDs.

$$3y + 7 - y = 7 + 3y - y$$
$$= 7 + 2y$$

John has $(7 + 2y)$ more CDs than Tyrone.

b. If Tyrone has 25 CDs, how many more CDs does John have than Tyrone?

$$7 + 2y = 7 + 2 \times 25$$
$$= 7 + 50$$
$$= 57$$

John has 57 more CDs than Tyrone.

Guided Practice

Complete.

1. Ray has m dollars. Ben has \$15 more than Ray.

   a. Find the amount of money they have altogether in terms of m.

   Ben has ____ dollars.

   They have ____ dollars altogether.

   b. If Ray has \$75, how much money do they have altogether?

   If $m = 75$, they have \$____ altogether.

Learn Write a multiplication or division expression for a real-world problem and evaluate it.

Salma has x dollars in her wallet. She buys a shirt for \$15 and spends the rest of her money on 3 movie tickets.

a Find the price of 1 movie ticket in terms of x.

Price of 3 movie tickets $= \$(x - 15)$

$(x - 15) \div 3 = \frac{x - 15}{3}$

The price of 1 movie ticket is $\frac{x - 15}{3}$ dollars.

b If Salma has \$39, what is the price of 1 movie ticket?

$$\begin{aligned}\frac{x - 15}{3} &= \frac{39 - 15}{3} \\ &= \frac{24}{3} \\ &= 8\end{aligned}$$

The price of 1 movie ticket is \$8.

Guided Practice

Complete.

2 A man has y dollars in his wallet. He withdraws \$200 from an ATM and spends half the total amount on groceries.

a Find the amount of money he has left in terms of y.

Total amount the man had upon withdrawing \$200 from the ATM $= \$(\ \ ?\ \ )$

? $\div 2 = \frac{?}{?}$

He has $\frac{?}{?}$ dollars left.

b If $y = 80$, how much money does he have left?

If $y = 80$, he has \$? left.

Learn Use algebraic expressions to compare quantities and solve equations.

Andy and Cathy each have some pencils. Andy has his pencils in 4 boxes. 3 of the boxes have an equal number of pencils. There are p pencils in each of the 3 boxes. The remaining box has 3 pencils fewer. Cathy has 2 boxes of pencils each with p pencils and 13 extra pencils.

a Write the number of pencils Andy and Cathy each have, in terms of p.

Andy has $3p + (p - 3)$ pencils. So, Andy has $(4p - 3)$ pencils.
Cathy has $(2p + 13)$ pencils.

b Write an inequality to show who has more pencils if $p = 9$.

If $p = 9$,

$$\begin{aligned} 4p - 3 &= (4 \times 9) - 3 \\ &= 36 - 3 \\ &= 33 \end{aligned} \qquad \begin{aligned} 2p + 13 &= (2 \times 9) + 13 \\ &= 18 + 13 \\ &= 31 \end{aligned}$$

$4p - 3 > 2p + 13.$

Andy has more pencils if $p = 9$.

c For what value of p will Andy and Cathy have the same number of pencils?

$$\begin{aligned} 4p - 3 &= 2p + 13 \\ 4p - 3 + 3 &= 2p + 13 + 3 \\ 4p &= 2p + 16 \\ 4p - 2p &= 2p + 16 - 2p \\ 2p &= 16 \\ 2p \div 2 &= 16 \div 2 \\ p &= 8 \end{aligned}$$

Andy and Cathy will have the same number of pencils, if $p = 8$.

Guided Practice

Fill in ◯ with +, −, ×, or ÷ and ▭ with the correct number.

3 Lenny has $2y - 7$ marbles. Max has $y + 9$ marbles.

a Write an inequality to show who has more marbles if $y = 18$.

If $y = 18$,

$2y - 7 = (2 \times \square) - 7$ $\quad$ $y + 9 = \square + 9$

$= \square - 7$ $\quad$ $= \square$

$= \square$

$2y - 7 \bigcirc y + 9$

▭ has more marbles if $y = 18$.

b For what value of y will Lenny and Max have the same number of marbles?

$2y - 7 = y + 9$

$2y - 7 + \square = y + 9 + \square$

$2y = y + \square$

$2y \bigcirc \square = y + \square \bigcirc \square$

$y = \square$

They will have the same number of marbles if $y = \square$.

Let's Practice

Solve. Show your work.

1 José is r years old. Keith is 3 times as old as he is. Lara is 4 years younger than Keith.

a Find Keith's age in terms of r.

b Find Lara's age in terms of r.

c If $r = 5$, how old is Lara?

2 Aida bought a belt for x dollars and a handbag that cost twice as much as the belt. She gave the cashier \$100.

a Find the amount that Aida spent in terms of x.

b Find the amount of change Aida received in terms of x.

c If $x = 15$, how much change did Aida receive?

3 Paul scored z points playing a math game. Meghan scored 4 times as many points as Paul. Kieran scored 5 more points than Meghan.

a Find the number of points Meghan scored in terms of z.

b Find the number of points Kieran scored in terms of z.

c Find the total number of points the three players scored in terms of z.

4 A plumber has a copper pipe and a steel pipe. The copper pipe is $(3p + 2)$ feet long and the steel pipe is $(4p - 3)$ feet long.

a If $p = 8$, which pipe is longer?

b For what value of p will the two pipes be of the same length?

5 A group of 3 friends made m bracelets. They sold the bracelets for \$14 each and shared the money equally.

a How much did each person get? Give your answer in terms of m.

b If there were 18 bracelets, how much did each person get?

6 A pail and a pitcher contain q quarts of water altogether. The pail contains 9 times as much water as the pitcher.

a Find the amount of water in the pitcher in terms of q.

b If the pail and the pitcher contain 25 quarts of water altogether, find the amount of water in the pail in quarts. Express your answer as a decimal.

ON YOUR OWN

Go to Workbook A:
Practice 4, pages 189–194

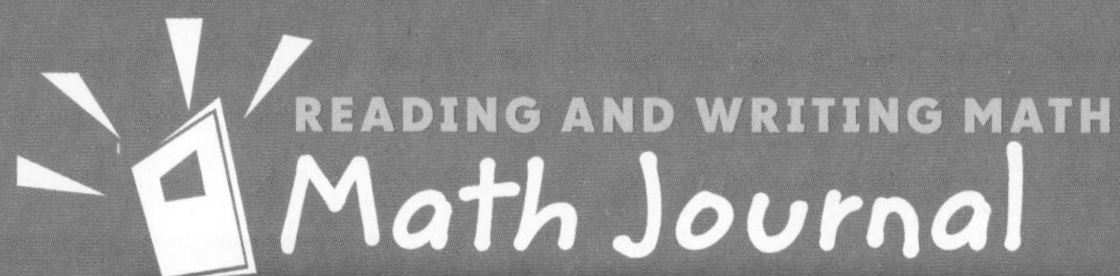

READING AND WRITING MATH
Math Journal

1. Explain in words what the expression $3x$ means.

2. Rita says that $a + a = 2a$ can be thought of as:
   1 apple + 1 apple = 2 apples.
   Is her thinking correct? If not, what is the correct way to think of $a + a = 2a$?

CRITICAL THINKING SKILLS
Put On Your Thinking Cap!

PROBLEM SOLVING

Grace thinks of a number. First, she multiplies it by 2. Then, she adds 12. Finally, she subtracts twice the number that she originally thought of. What is the answer that she will get?

ON YOUR OWN

Go to Workbook A: Put on Your Thinking Cap! pages 195–196

Chapter Wrap Up

Study Guide

You have learned...

Algebraic Expressions

Using Letters as Numbers

- Letters in algebra, called variables, stand for numbers.
- $x + 4$, $2y - 5$, $4z$ and $\frac{b}{3}$ are examples of algebraic expressions.
- Operations can be performed on variables.
- Algebraic expressions can be evaluated for given values of the variable.

  For $x = 4$,

  $$\begin{aligned} 2x + 3 &= (2 \times 4) + 3 \\ &= 8 + 3 \\ &= 11 \end{aligned}$$

Simplifying Algebraic Expressions

Algebraic expressions can be simplified.

$y + y + y = 3y$

$3y + 2y = 5y$

$8y + 10 - 4y - 5 = 4y + 5$

Solve Real-World Problems

▶ Algebraic expressions can be used to describe a situation and solve real-world problems.

Inequalities and Equations

- Algebraic expressions can be compared by evaluating them for a given value of the variable.

  When $a = 3$, $4a + 2 > 2a + 4$
- When two equal expressions are related by an '=' sign, they form an equation.
- When two expressions with different values are related by an '>' or '<' sign, they form an inequality.
- Equations can be solved.

$$\begin{aligned} 6a - 5 &= 4a + 3 \\ 6a &= 4a + 8 \\ 2a &= 8 \\ a &= 4 \end{aligned}$$

Learn A triangle is measured by its base and its height.

You measure a triangle by its base and its height:
— the base being the side chosen as such;
— the height being the **perpendicular** distance from the base to the opposite vertex.

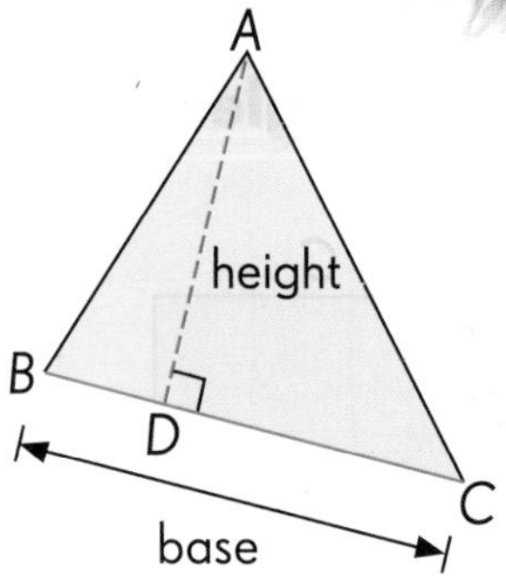

You can take the length of $\overline{BC}$ and the height, *AD* to be the measurements of triangle *ABC*.

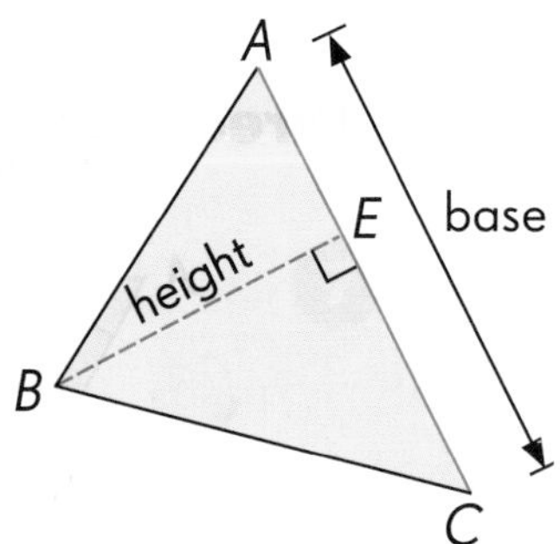

You can take the length of $\overline{AC}$ and the height, *BE* to be the measurements of triangle *ABC*.

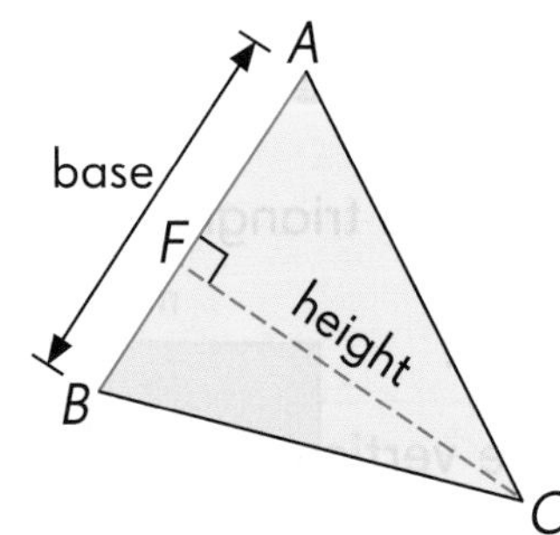

You can take the length of $\overline{AB}$ and the height, *CF* to be the measurements of triangle *ABC*.

Learn Sometimes the height is not part of the triangle.

In triangle *PQR*:

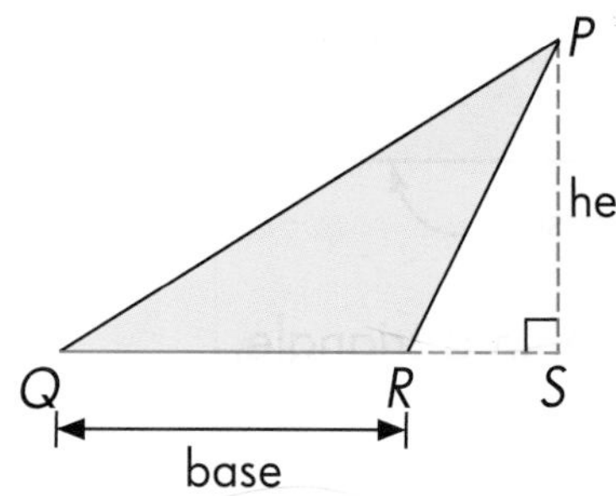

If the base is $\overline{QR}$, then the height is *PS*.

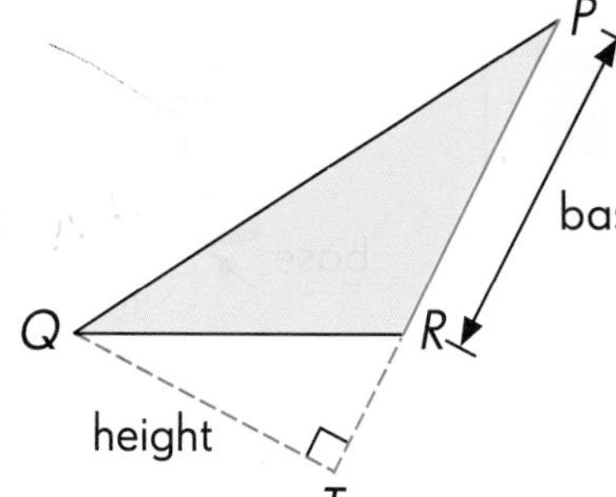

If the base is $\overline{PR}$, then the height is *QT*.

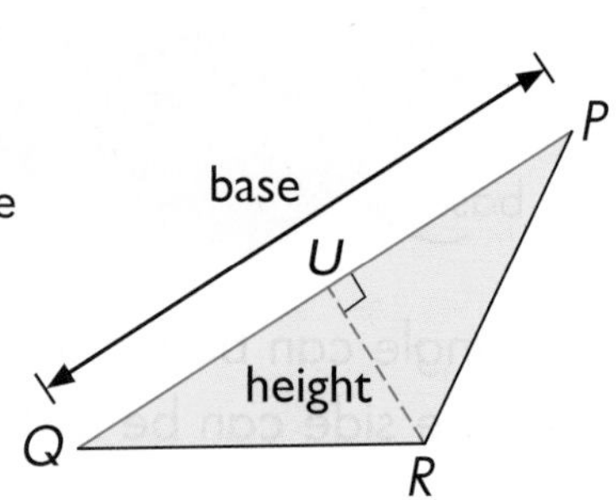

If the base is $\overline{QP}$, then the height is *RU*.

The height of a triangle is always perpendicular to its base.

Guided Practice

Complete to give both the base and the height in each triangle.

1
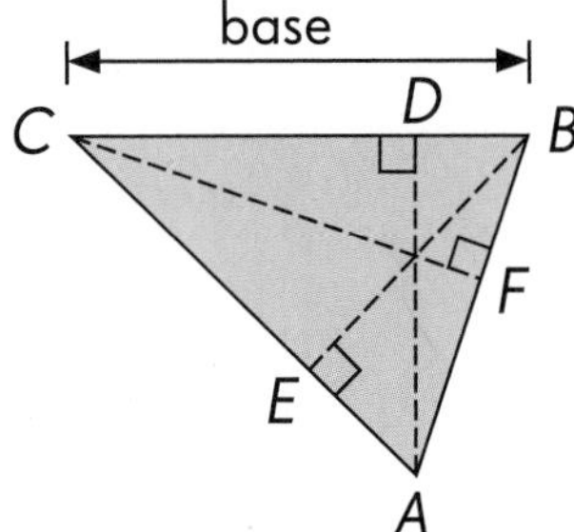

Base:

Height:

2
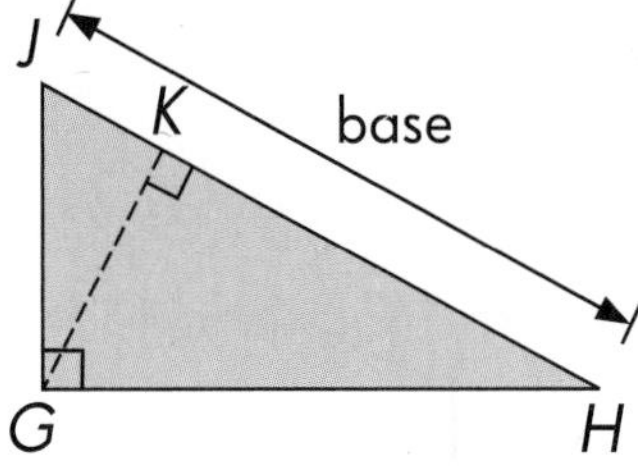

Base:

Height:

3
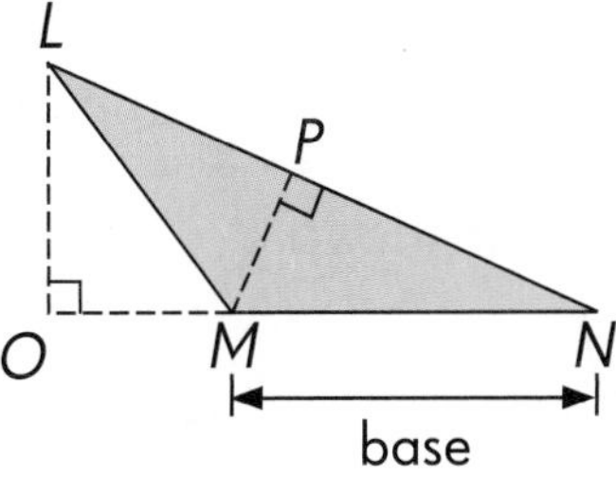

Base:

Height:

4
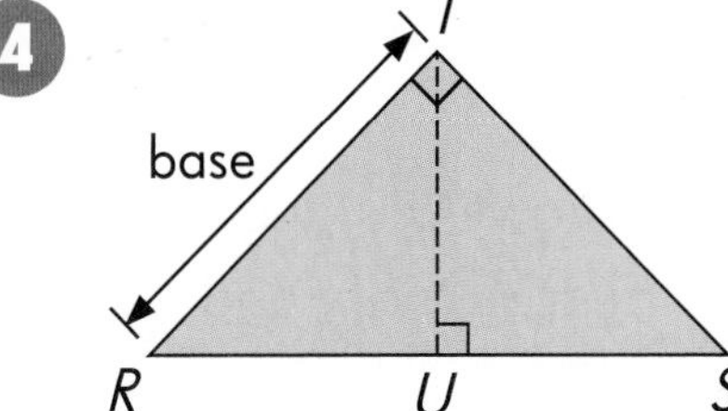

Base:

Height:

5
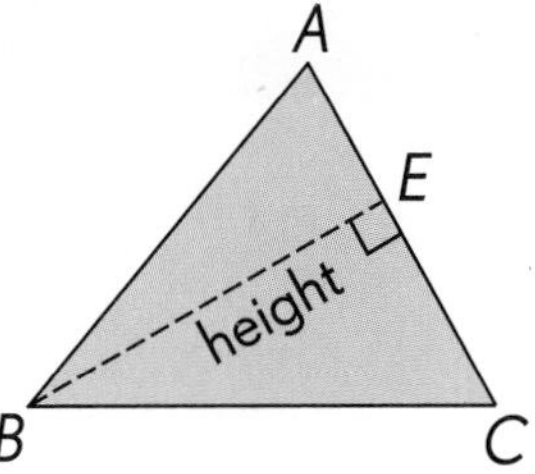

Height:

Base:

6
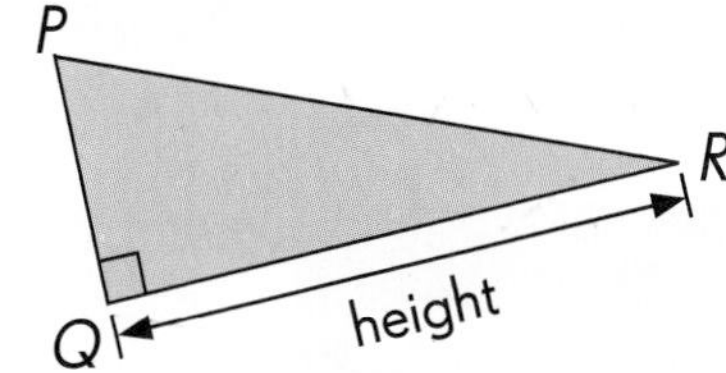

Height:

Base:

7
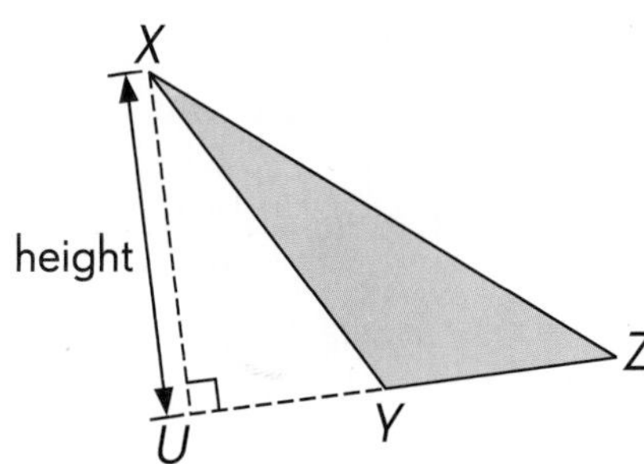

Height:

Base:

Hands-On Activity

WORKING TOGETHER

STEP 1 Draw a triangle and label it ABC.

Examples

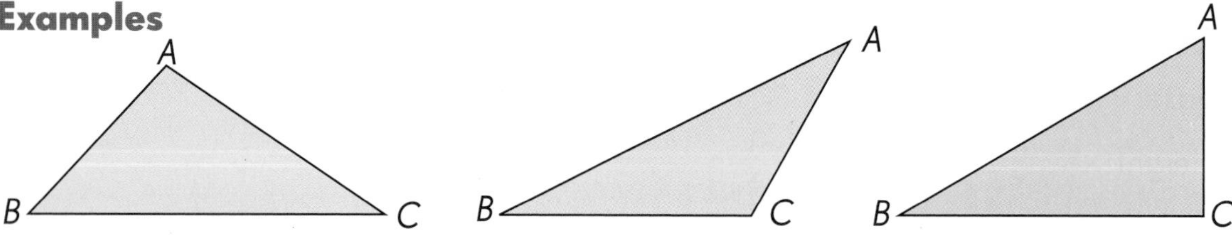

STEP 2 For each base, AB, BC and CA, identify the height.

STEP 3 Using a drawing triangle, draw the three heights of your triangle. Label them AD, BE, and CF.

STEP 4 Look at all the triangles drawn. What do you notice about the heights AD, BE, and CF?

Let's Practice

Complete to give both the base and the height in each triangle.

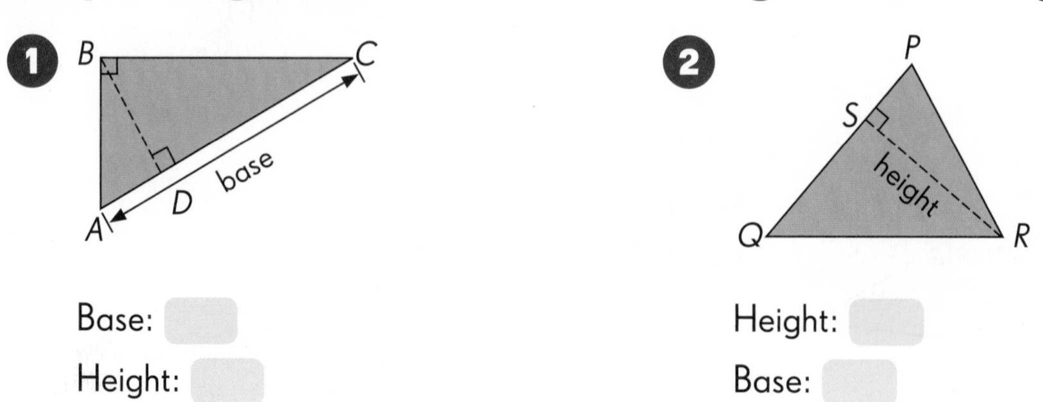

1. Base: ____
   Height: ____

2. Height: ____
   Base: ____

The height of triangle *ABC* is as given. Name its base.

3

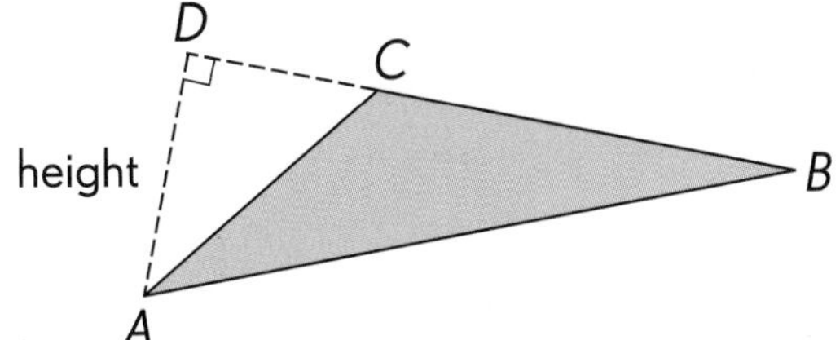

Height: *AD*

Base: ______

The base of triangle *DEF* is as labeled. Make a copy of triangle *DEF* and mark its height on the copy.

4

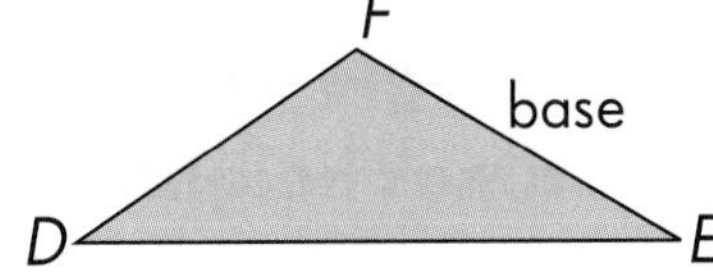

List all the possible pairs of bases and heights for triangle *ABC*.

5

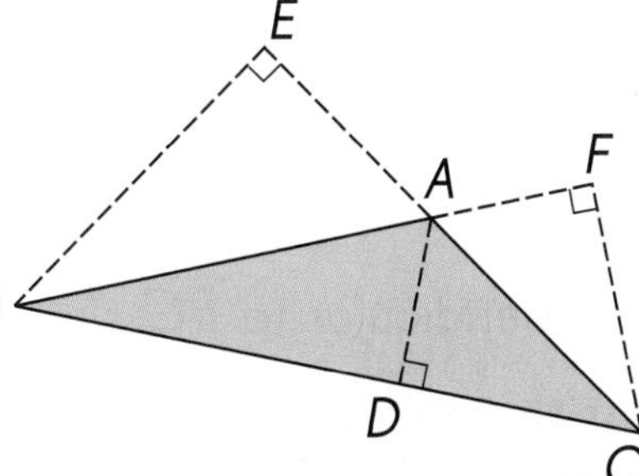

Base: ______ ; Height: ______

Base: ______ ; Height: ______

Base: ______ ; Height: ______

Complete.

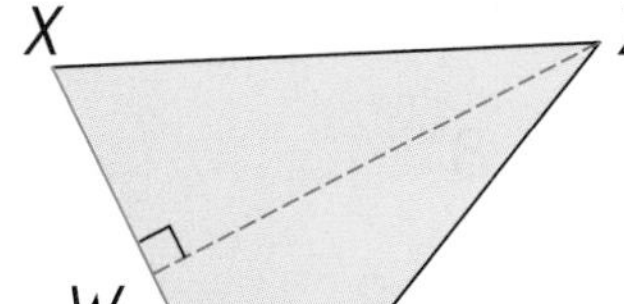
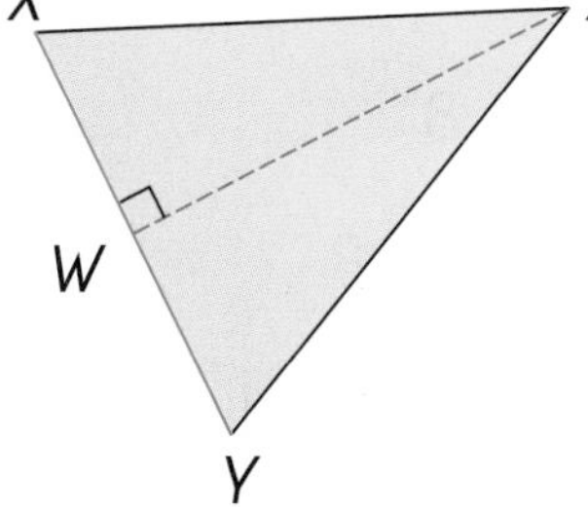

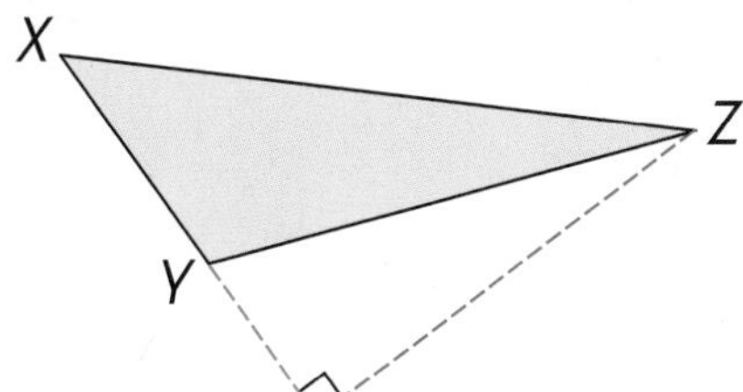

6 In both triangles, ______ is perpendicular to $\overline{XY}$.

7 In both triangles, ______ is the height and ______ is the base.

ON YOUR OWN

Go to Workbook A:
Practice 1, pages 197–198

Lesson

6.2 Finding the Area of a Triangle

Lesson Objective

- Find the area of a triangle given its base and its height.

Vocabulary

area | acute triangle
right triangle | obtuse triangle

Learn

The area of a triangle is half the area of a rectangle with the same 'base' and 'height' or half its base times height.

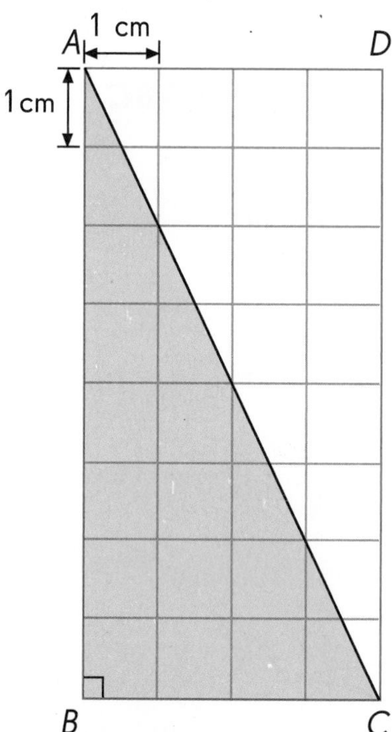

The area of triangle *ABC* is half the area of rectangle *ABCD*.

ABCD is a rectangle.

In triangle *ABC*, $\overline{AB}$ is perpendicular to $\overline{BC}$.

$\overline{BC}$ is the base and *AB* is the height.

The length of the base $\overline{BC}$ = 4 cm and the height *AB* = 8 cm.

$$\begin{aligned}\text{Area of triangle } ABC &= \frac{1}{2} \times \text{area of rectangle } ABCD\\ &= \frac{1}{2} \times 4 \times 8\\ &= \frac{1}{2} \times BC \times AB\\ &= \frac{1}{2} \times \text{base} \times \text{height}\end{aligned}$$

The length 4 cm and the width 8 cm of rectangle *ABCD* are exactly the base and the height of triangle *ABC*.

So, $\frac{1}{2} \times 4 \times 8 = \frac{1}{2} \times BC \times AB$

$= \frac{1}{2} \times \text{base} \times \text{height}$

Hands-On Activity

WORKING TOGETHER

Triangles can be identified by type:

Right triangle — A triangle with exactly one right angle.

Acute triangle — A triangle with all angles measuring less than 90°.

Obtuse triangle — A triangle with one angle measuring greater than 90°.

On page 256, you saw that a right triangle *ABC* has an area that is half the area of the corresponding rectangle or $\frac{1}{2}$ × base × height. You shall now check if the same is true of the area of the two other types of triangles.

1 In triangle *DEF*, $\overline{EF}$ is the base and *DG* is the height.

STEP **1** Use a copy of Figure 1. Cut out triangles *DLM* and *DMN*. Rearrange the two triangles as shown in Figure 2.

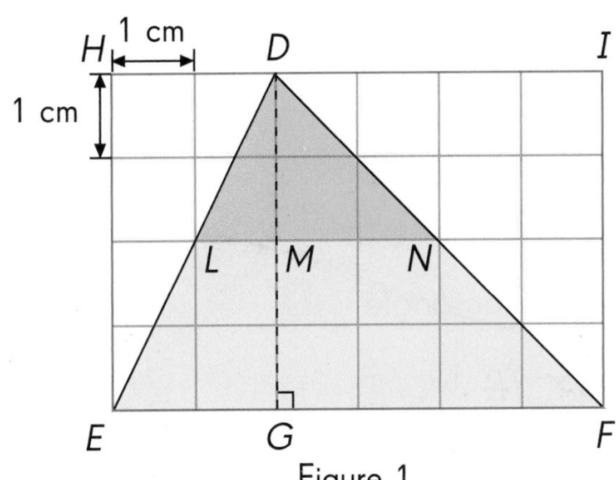

Figure 1

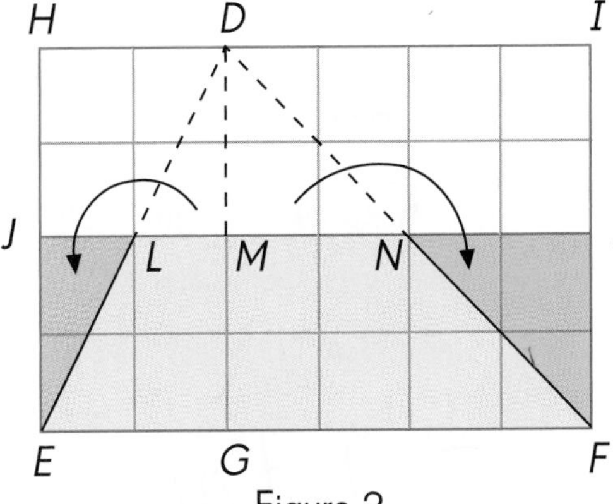

Figure 2

STEP **2** Complete.

Area of triangle *DEF* = area of rectangle ____

$= \frac{1}{2} \times$ area of rectangle ____

$= \frac{1}{2} \times EF \times IF$

$= \frac{1}{2} \times EF \times$ ____

$= \frac{1}{2} \times$ base $\times$ ____

2 In triangle *PQR*, $\overline{QR}$ is the base and *PS* is the height.

STEP 1 Use a copy of Figure 3. Cut out triangles *PVX* and *VRX*. Then rearrange the two triangles as shown in Figure 4.

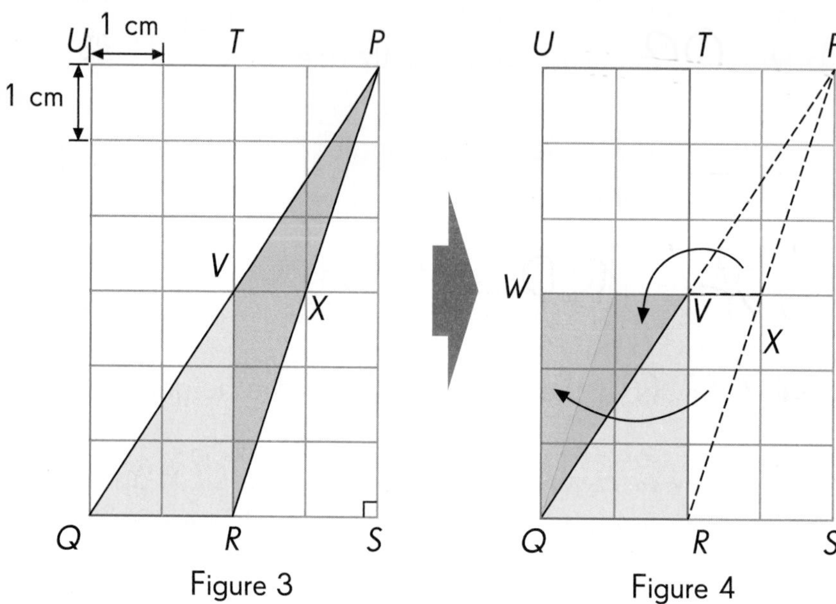

Figure 3

Figure 4

STEP 2 Complete.

Area of triangle *PQR* = area of rectangle ___

$= \frac{1}{2} \times$ area of rectangle ___

$= \frac{1}{2} \times QR \times TR$

$= \frac{1}{2} \times QR \times$ ___

$= \frac{1}{2} \times \text{base} \times$ ___

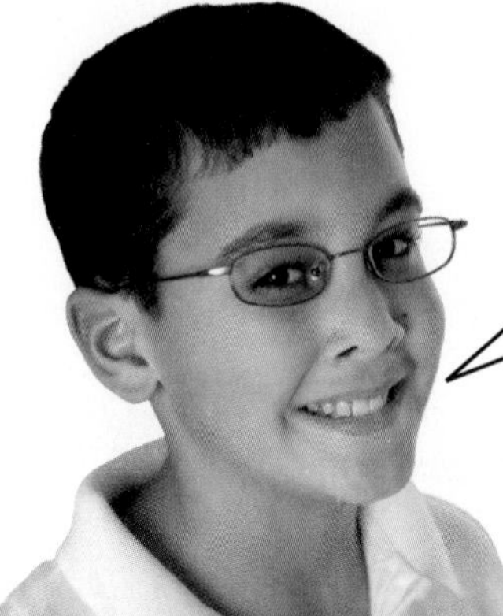

What can you say of the area of triangle *DEF*? How about triangle *PQR*?

Learn Find the area of a triangle using the 'area of a triangle' formula.

Find the area of triangle PQR.

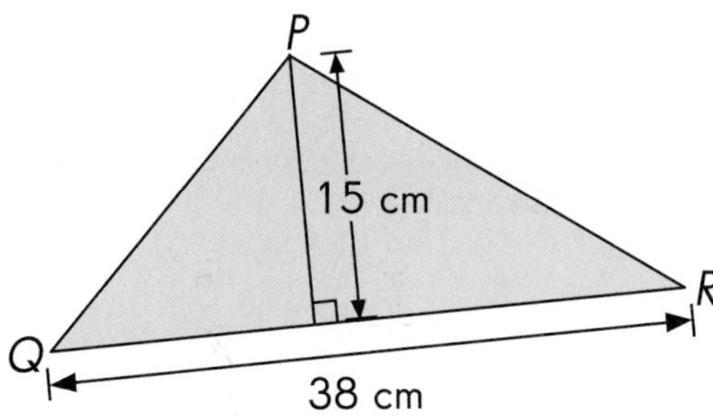

$$\text{Area of triangle PQR} = \frac{1}{2} \times \text{base} \times \text{height}$$
$$= \frac{1}{2} \times 38 \times 15$$
$$= 285 \text{ cm}^2$$

Hands-On Activity

WORK IN PAIRS

Try this.

In triangle *ABC*, ∠BAC is a right angle and *AD* is perpendicular to *BC*.

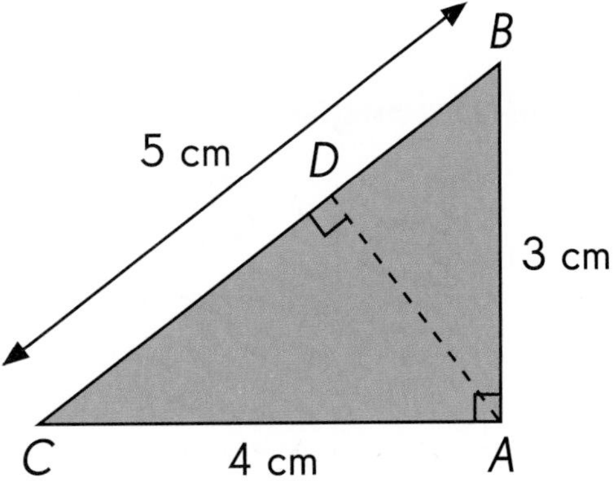

STEP 1 Measure the height *AD* in centimeters to the nearest tenth.

STEP 2 Using each side *AB*, *AC* and *BC* as the base, find the area of the triangle. Are all three answers the same?

Guided Practice

Find the area of each shaded triangle.

1. 17 cm; 16 cm

2. 7 in.; 52 in.

3. 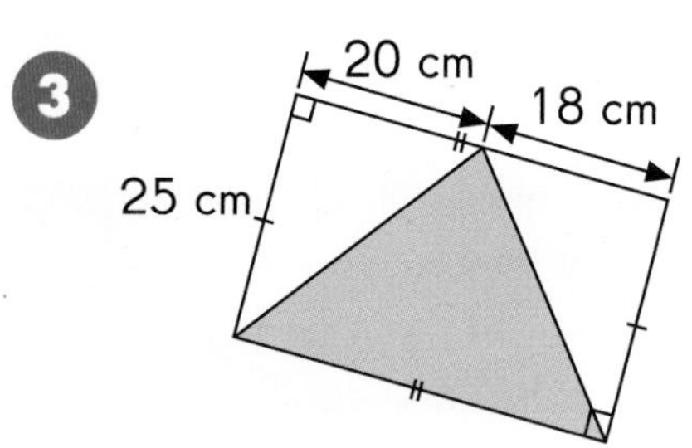

4. 28 yd; 14 yd; 23 yd

5. 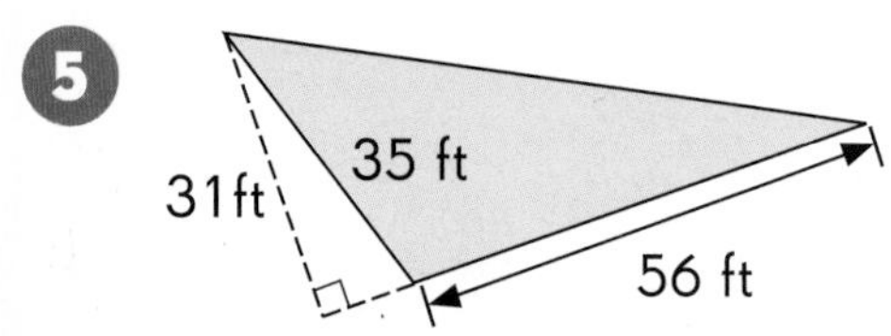

6. 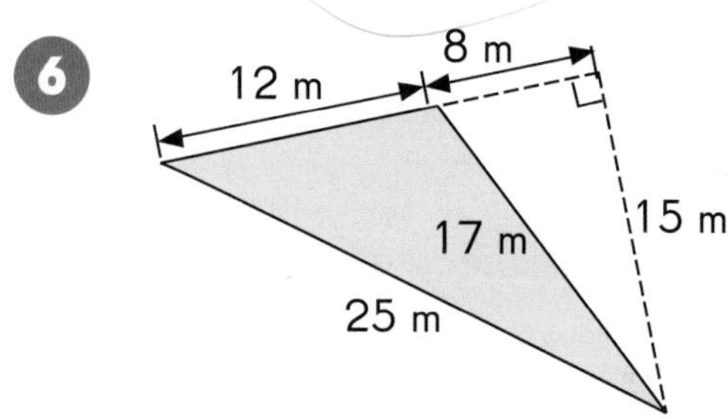

Let's Practice

Find the area of each shaded triangle.

1. 14 cm; 4 cm

2. 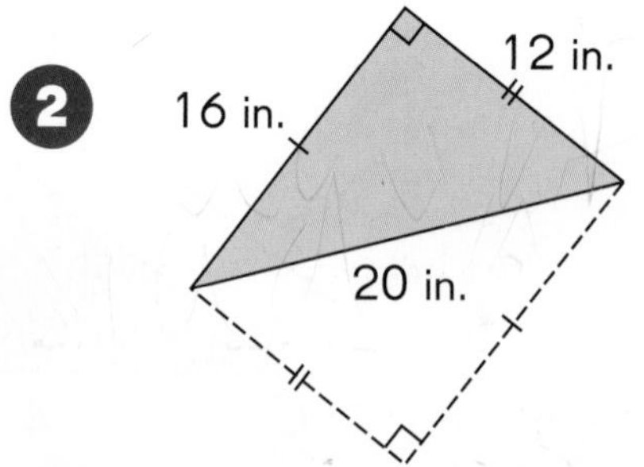

3. 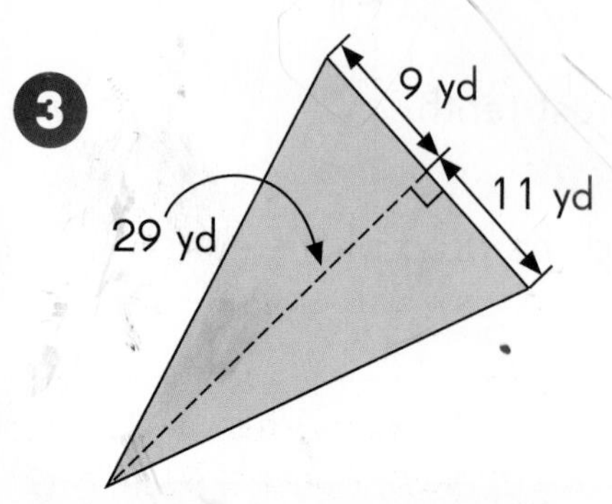

4. 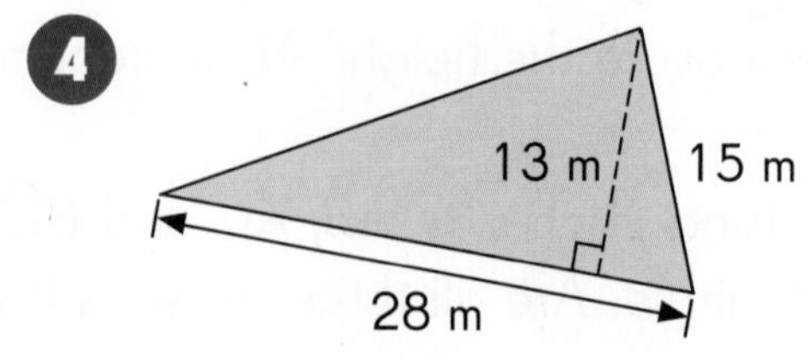

5 In triangle ABC, $BC = 44$ cm and $AD = 27$ cm. Find the area of triangle ABC.

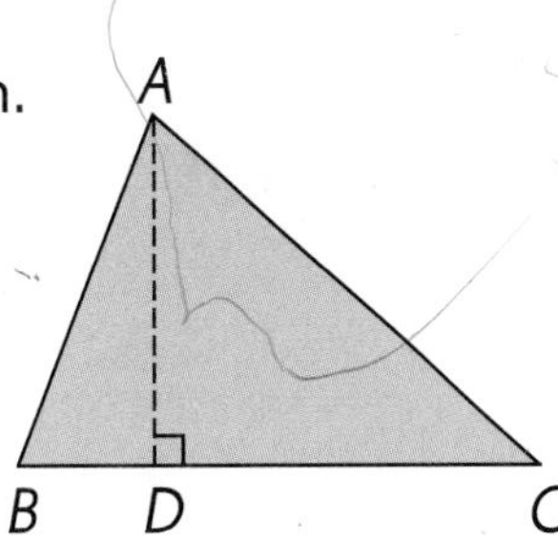

6 In the figure, $QR = 26$ in., $QS = 20$ in. and $PS = 26$ in. Find the area of triangle PQR.

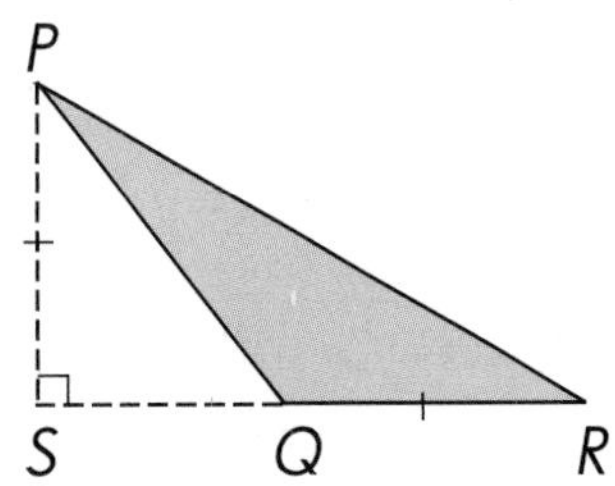

7 In the figure, $LM = 18$ ft, $KM = 16$ ft and $KN = 14$ ft. Find the area of triangle KLM.

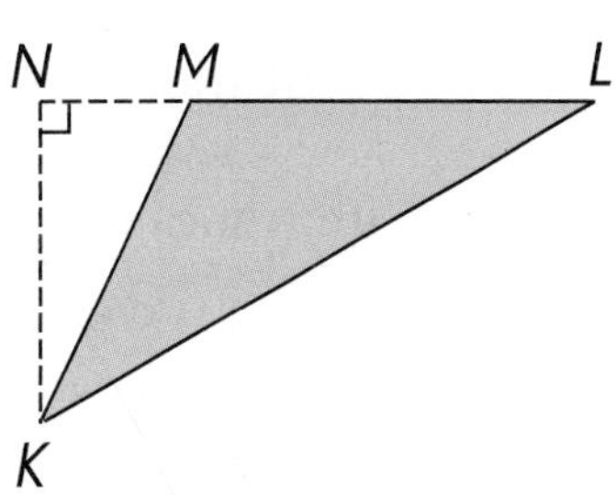

8 Triangle STU represents a triangular table top. It is given that $SU = 32$ in. and $UT = 25$ in. Find the area of the triangular table top.

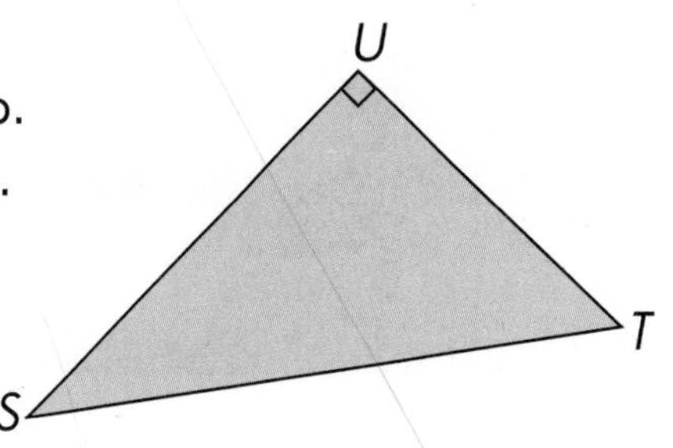

9 In the figure, triangle PQR represents a plot of land. $PQ = 10$ yds, $RS = 21$ yds and $PQ = QS$. Find the area of the land.

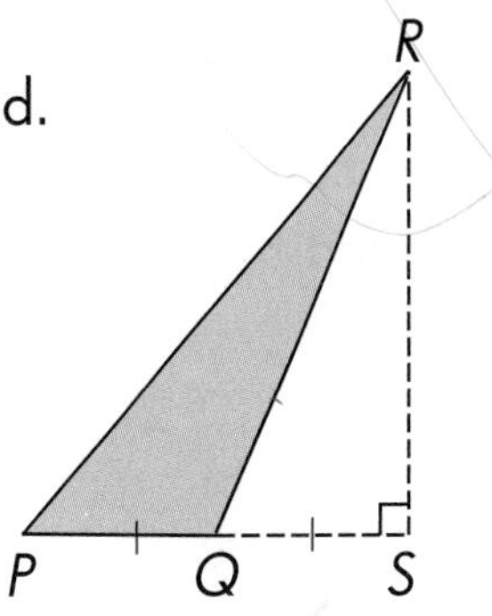

ON YOUR OWN

Go to Workbook A: Practice 2, pages 199–203

Let's Explore!

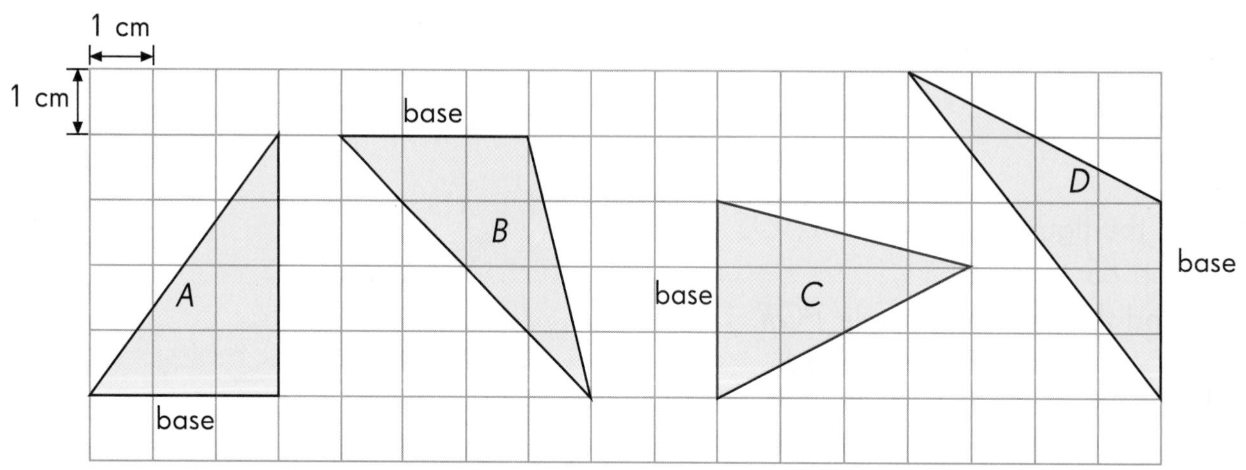

For each triangle, find the height. Then find its area.
What can you say about the bases and heights of these triangles?

Different triangles with equal bases and equal ___ have the same ___.

CRITICAL THINKING SKILLS

Put On Your Thinking Cap!

PROBLEM SOLVING

ABCD is a rectangle. *BE* = *ED*.
Explain how you can find the area of the shaded triangle *ABE*.

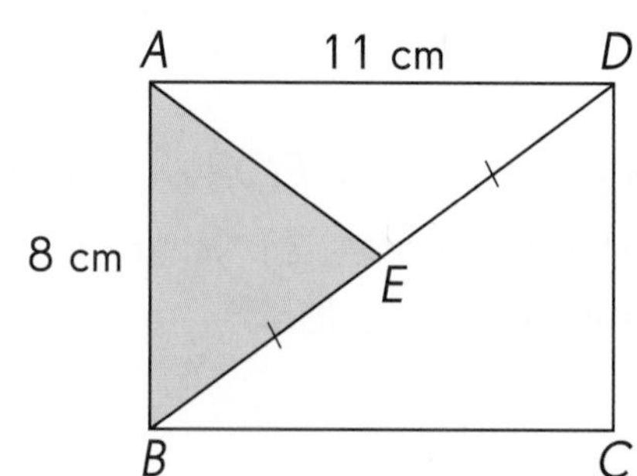

ON YOUR OWN

Go to Workbook A: Put on Your Thinking Cap! pages 203–208

Find the area

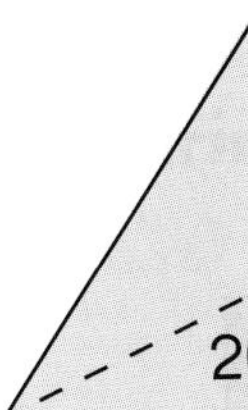

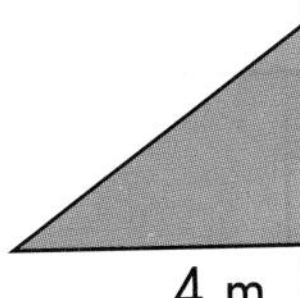

4 m

Problem So

Use the figu

ABCD is a re

13 Find the

14 Find the

15 Find the

Chapter Wrap Up

Study Guide

You have learned...

▶ Base and height are measurements that are used to find the area of a triangle.

Area of a Triangle

Base and Height

- The base of any object is the face or the side on which it lies. In a triangle, any one side can be its base.

- You measure a triangle by its base and its height:
  - the base is the side chosen as such;
  - the height is the perpendicular distance from the base to the opposite vertex.

Example

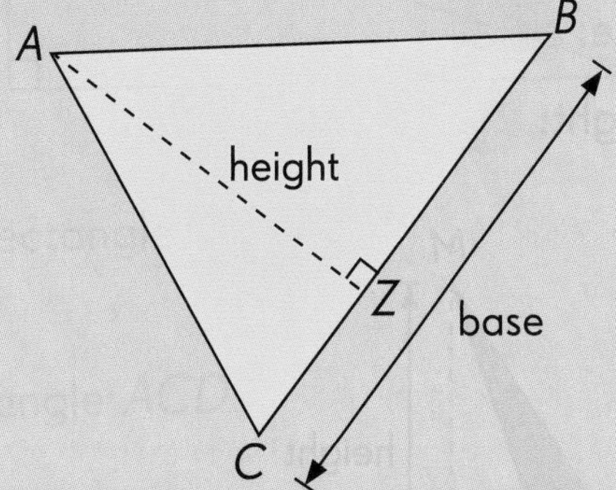

- You can take the length of $\overline{BC}$ and the height, *AZ* to be the measurements of triangle *ABC*.

Finding the Area

- The area of a triangle is half the area of a rectangle with the same 'base' and 'height' or $\frac{1}{2}$ × base × height.

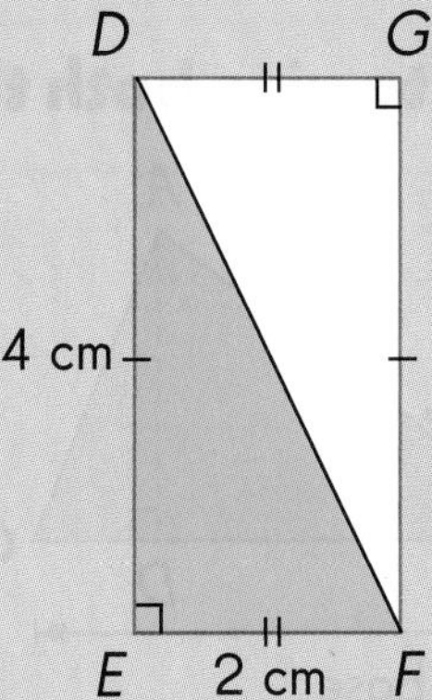

Area of triangle *DEF*

$= \frac{1}{2} \times$ area of rectangle *DEFG*

$= \frac{1}{2} \times EF \times DE$

$= \frac{1}{2} \times$ base × height

$= \frac{1}{2} \times 2 \times 4$

$= 4 \text{ cm}^2$

Using models to solve problems

Find the value of each set using the model.

a) 4 units
b) 1 unit
c) 3 units
d) 7 units

From the model,

a) 4 units ⟶ 24
b) 1 unit ⟶ 6
c) 3 units ⟶ 18
d) 7 units ⟶ 42

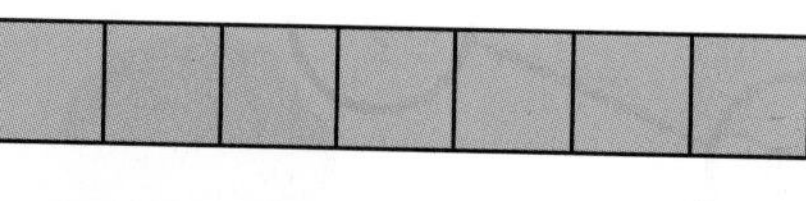

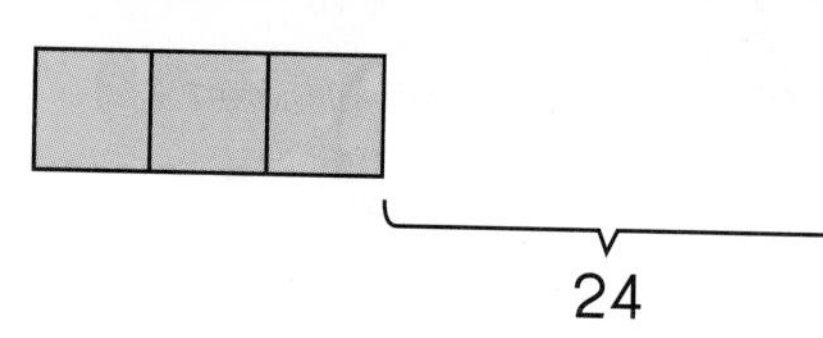

✔ Quick Check

Complete using the number bond on the right.

1) ___ is 9 less than 17.

2) 17 is 8 more than ___.

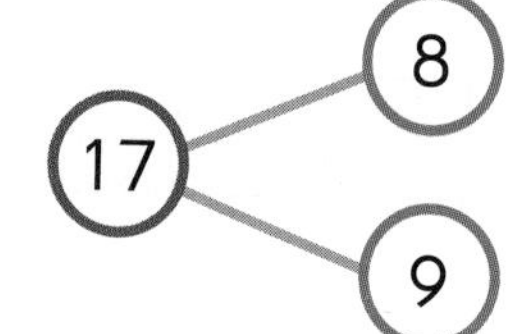

State how many parts of the whole are represented by each fraction.

3) $\frac{1}{3}$

4) $\frac{4}{8}$

Write each fraction in simplest form.

5) $\frac{15}{20}$

6) $\frac{4}{24}$

Find the value of each set using the model.

7) 7 units

8) 1 unit

9) 2 units

10) 9 units

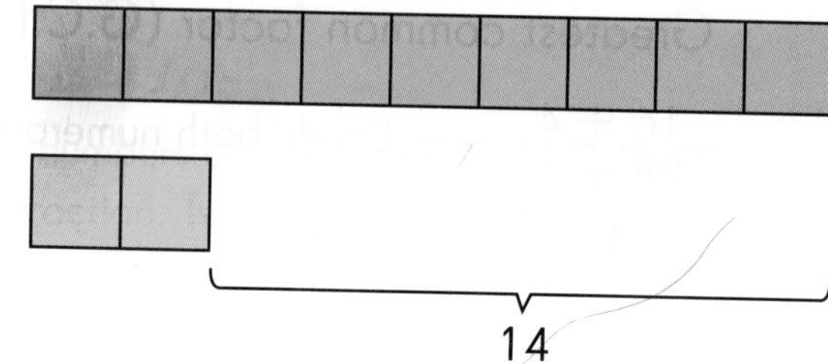

Lesson 7.1 Finding Ratio

Lesson Objective

- Read and write ratios.

Vocabulary
ratio term

Learn Use ratios to compare two numbers or quantities by division.

You can compare two quantities or numbers by division.
To compare two quantities or numbers by division, you write them as a ratio.

There are 2 bran muffins and 1 blueberry muffin. You can compare the number of one type of muffin to the number of the other by division.

a To compare the number of bran muffins to the number of blueberry muffins, you write them as a ratio as shown.

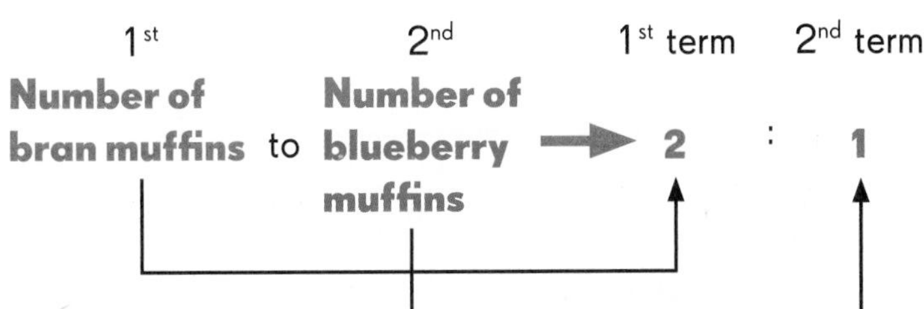

Say: The ratio of the number of bran muffins to the number of blueberry muffins is '2 to 1'.

The two quantities you are comparing form the **terms** of the ratio.

The first term of the ratio is the first quantity in the comparison. The second term of the ratio is the second quantity.

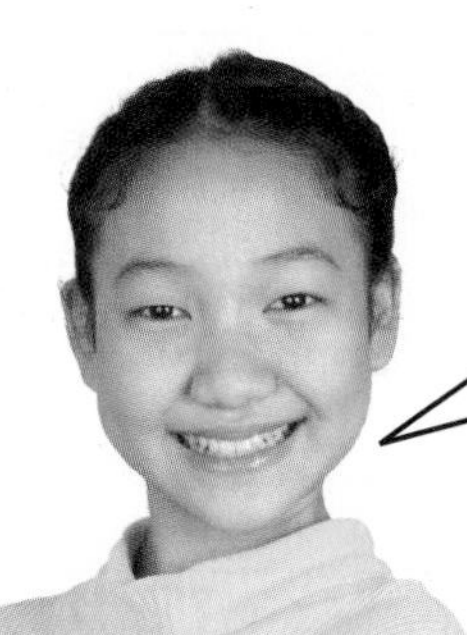

The ratio '2 : 1' tells us that 'there are 2 bran muffins to 1 blueberry muffin' or 'there is 1 blueberry muffin to 2 bran muffins'.

Continued on next page

b To compare the number of blueberry muffins to the number of bran muffins, you write them as a ratio as shown.

1st		2nd		1st term		2nd term
Number of blueberry muffins	to	**Number of bran muffins**	→	**1**	:	**2**

Say: The ratio of the number of blueberry muffins to the number of bran muffins is '1 to 2'.

The ratio '1 to 2' tells us similarly that 'there is 1 blueberry muffin to 2 bran muffins' or 'there are 2 bran muffins to 1 blueberry muffin.'

Guided Practice

Complete.

1. The ratio of the number of blue pennants to the number of yellow pennants is ___ : ___.

2. The ratio of the number of yellow pennants to the number of blue pennants is ___ : ___.

The ratio ___ : ___ tells us that 'there are ___ blue pennants to ___ yellow pennants' or 'there are ___ yellow pennants to ___ blue pennants'.

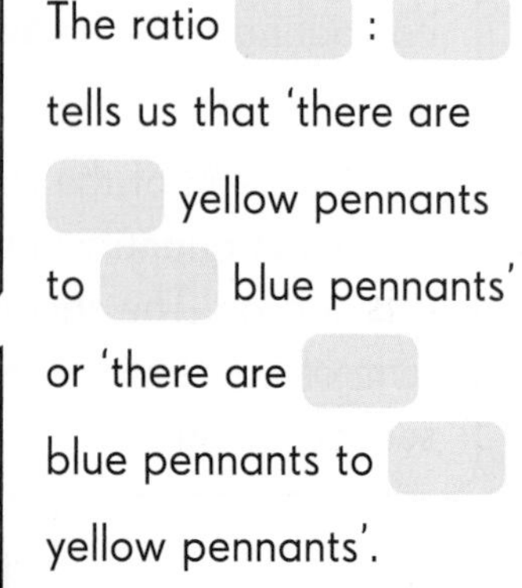

The ratio ___ : ___ tells us that 'there are ___ yellow pennants to ___ blue pennants' or 'there are ___ blue pennants to ___ yellow pennants'.

Learn A ratio need not give the actual quantities compared.

The manager of a sporting goods store set up bins of baseballs and lacrosse balls for a sale. There are 2 bins of lacrosse balls and 3 bins of baseballs. Each bin has an equal number of balls.

2 bins to 3 bins is 2 : 3.

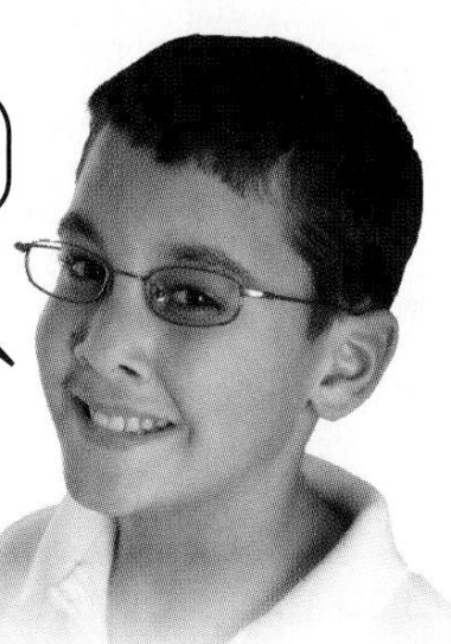

You know that there is an equal number of balls in each bin. The ratio does not give us the actual number of balls.

The ratio of the number of lacrosse balls to the number of baseballs is 2 : 3.

The ratio of the number of baseballs to the number of lacrosse balls is 3 : 2.

1 unit

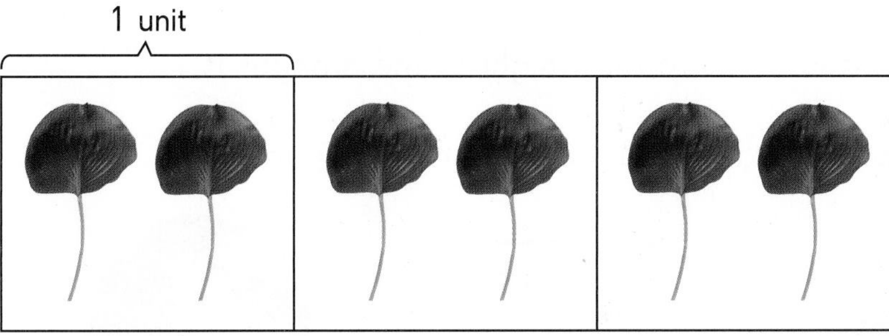

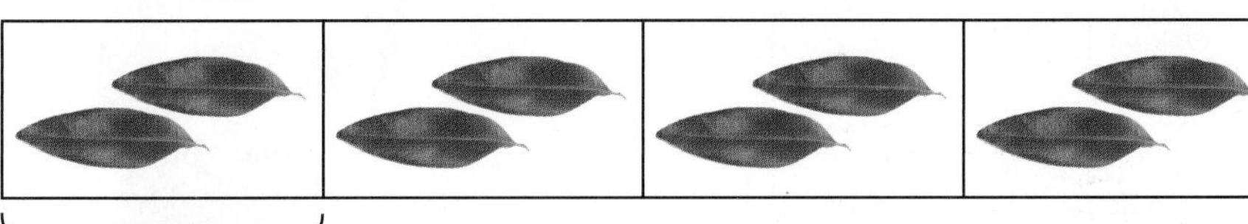

1 unit

1 unit = 2 leaves
So, a ratio need not give the actual quantities compared.

The ratio of the number of fan-shaped leaves to the number of lance-shaped leaves is 3 : 4.

The ratio of the number of lance-shaped leaves to the number of fan-shaped leaves is 4 : 3.

Guided Practice

Complete.

3. The ratio of the number of grape juice boxes to the number of apple juice boxes is ___ : ___.

4. The ratio of the number of apple juice boxes to the number of grape juice boxes is ___ : ___.

Ronald bought 2 pounds of pears and 5 pounds of oranges.

To compare as a ratio, the items must be in the same unit. The ratio however has no units.

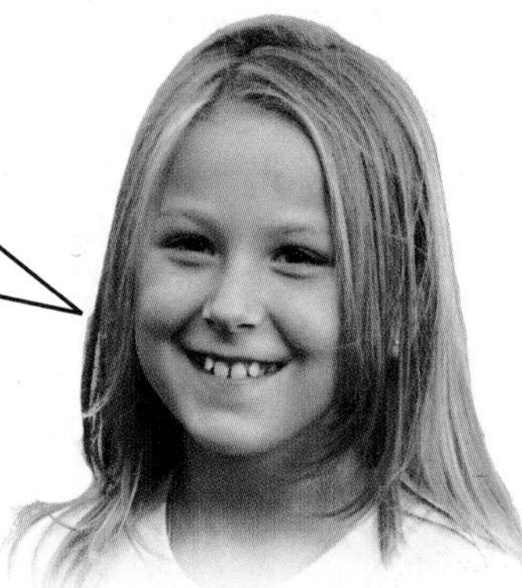

5. The ratio of the weight of the pears to the weight of the oranges is ___ : ___.

6. The ratio of the weight of the oranges to the weight of the pears is ___ : ___.

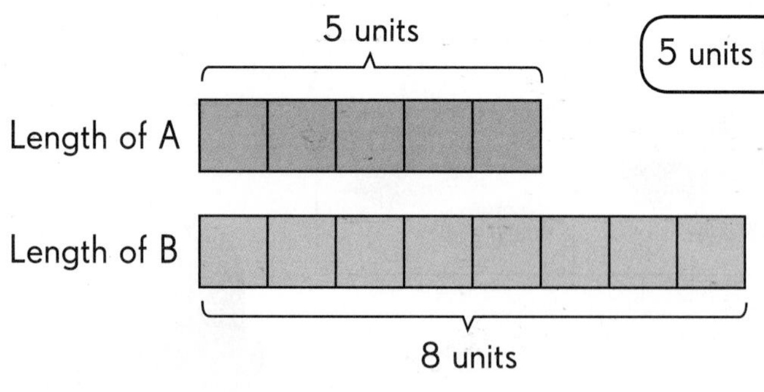

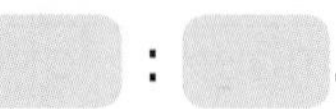

7. The ratio of the length of A to the length of B is ___ : ___.

8. The ratio of the length of B to the length of A is ___ : ___.

Learn Use a part-whole model to show a ratio.

Jim cuts a piece of wood, 24 centimeters long, into two pieces. The shorter piece is 7 centimeters long. Find the ratio of the length of the shorter piece to the length of the longer piece.

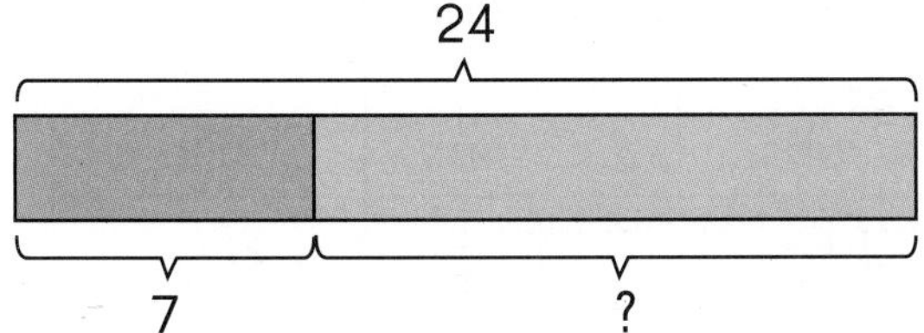

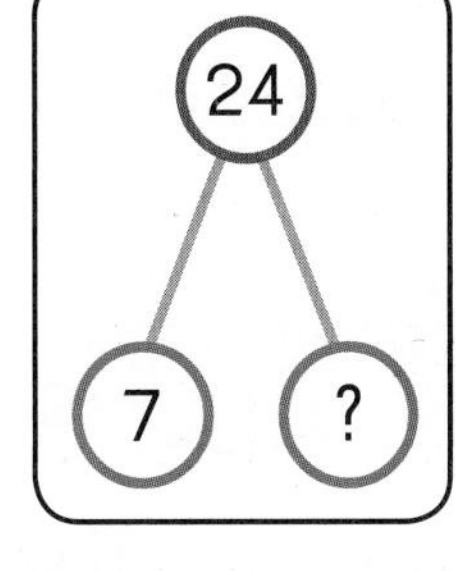

The length of the shorter piece of wood is 7 centimeters.

$24 - 7 = 17$

The length of the longer piece of wood is 17 centimeters.

The ratio of the length of the shorter piece to the length of the longer piece is 7 : 17.

Guided Practice

Solve.

9. Mr. Larson had 15 pounds of green beans to sell at his vegetable stand. He sold 7 pounds of green beans. Find the ratio of the weight of beans sold to the weight of beans left.

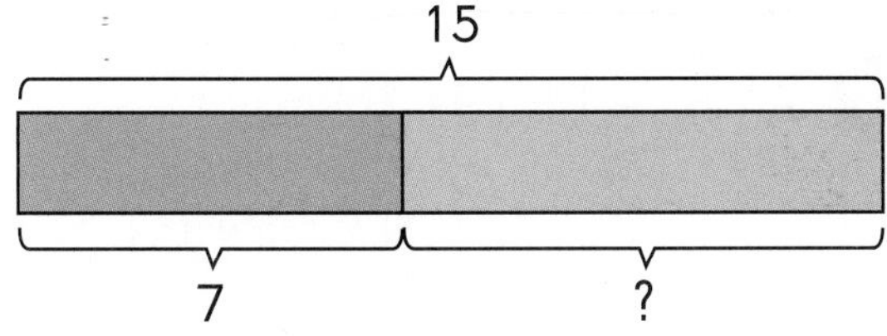

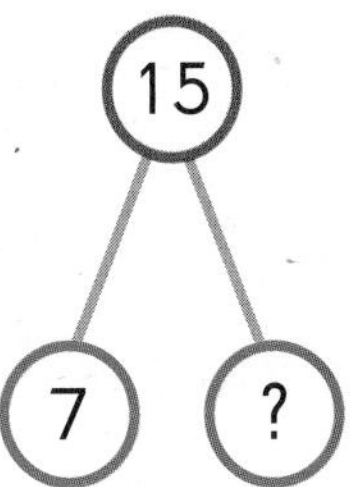

The weight of beans sold is 7 pounds.

___ − 7 = ___

The weight of beans left is ___ pounds.

The ratio of the weight of beans sold to the weight of beans left is ___ : ___.

Let's Practice

Complete.

1 The table shows the masses of shellfish sold at a seafood market one afternoon.

Shellfish	Mussels	Shrimp	Crabs	Lobsters	Scallops
Mass	2 kg	5 kg	3 kg	11 kg	8 kg

Copy and complete the table. Then write as many ratios as you can from the data.

Example

	Ratio
Mass of mussels to mass of shrimp	2 : 5
Mass of lobsters to mass of scallops	:
⋮	⋮
Mass of crabs to mass of shellfish in total	:

Draw a model to show each ratio.

Example

A : B = 2 : 5

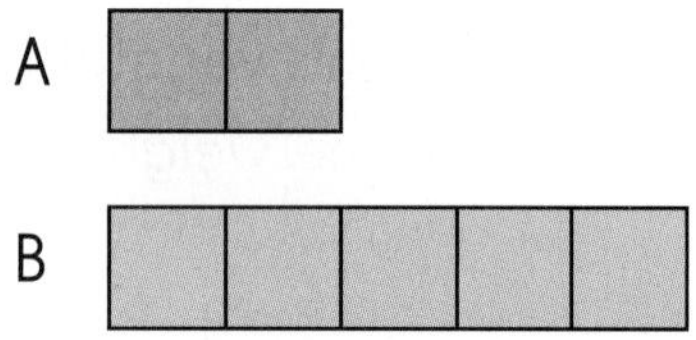

2 A : B = 4 : 9

3 A : B = 11 : 7

Write two ratios to compare the sets.

4

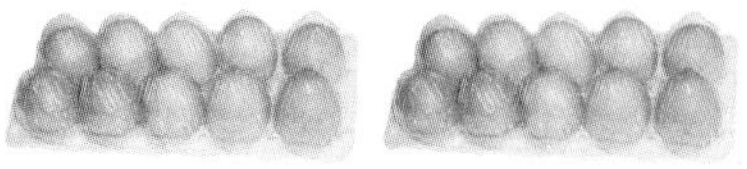

Set A

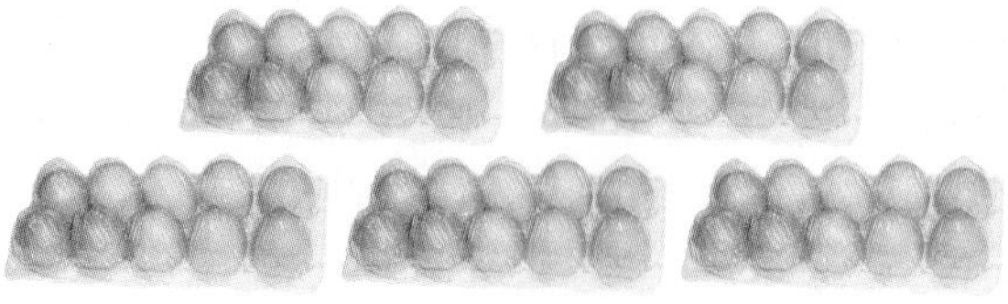

Set B

Write two ratios to compare the sets.

5

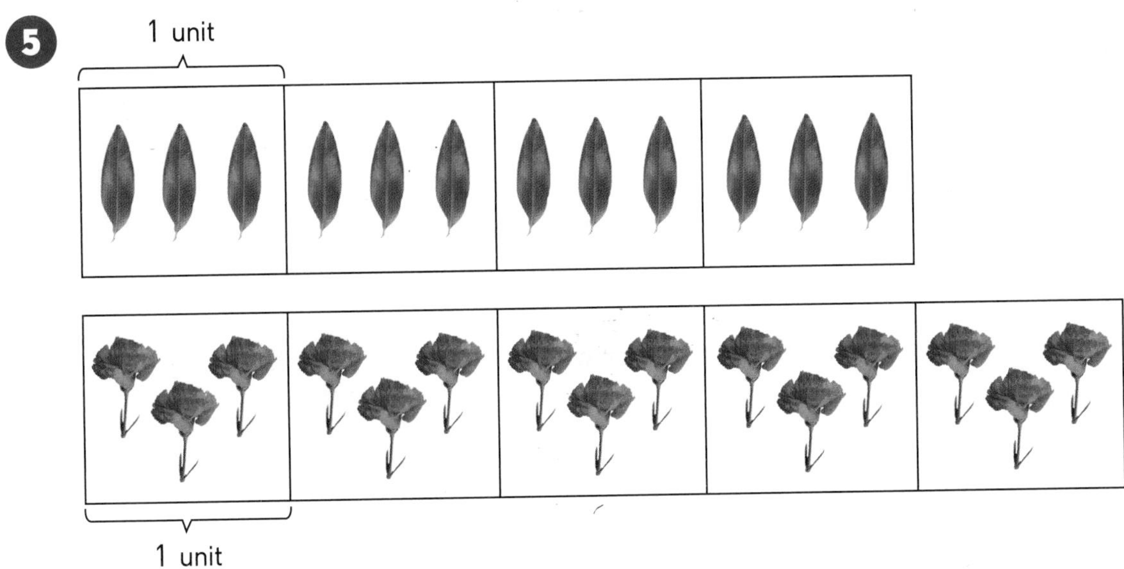

Solve.

6 A large checkered tablecloth is 5 feet wide and 7 feet long. Find the ratio of the length of the tablecloth to its width.

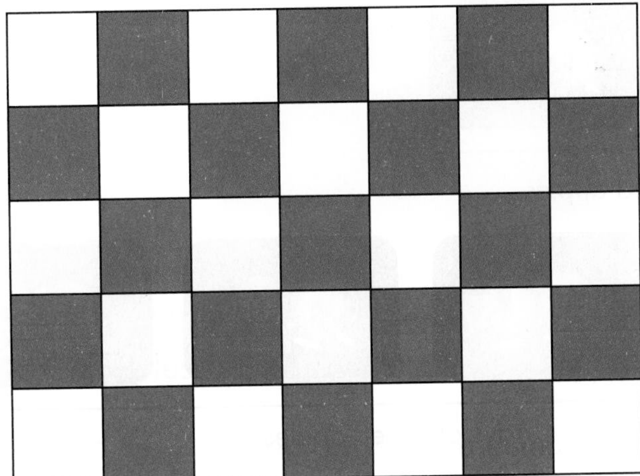

7 James has $88. He gives $35 to charity A and the rest to charity B. Find the ratio of the amount of money he gives to charity A to the amount of money he gives to charity B.

ON YOUR OWN

Go to Workbook A: Practice 1, pages 209–214

Learn Use multiplication to find missing terms in equivalent ratios.

Find the missing term in these equivalent ratios.

2 : 5 = 6 : ?

Look at the first terms of the equivalent ratios — **2** : 5 = **6** : ?.

First, find the multiplying factor. Then multiply the second term by the multiplying factor.

Method 1

$2 \times 3 = 6$

2 : 5

× 3 × 3

= **6** : 15

The missing term is 15.

Method 2

$6 \div 2 = 3$

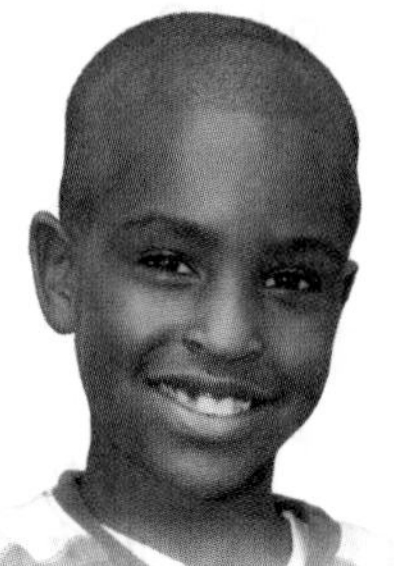

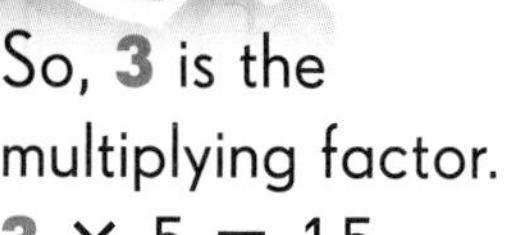

So, **3** is the multiplying factor.

$3 \times 5 = 15$

Learn Use division to find missing terms in equivalent ratios.

Find the missing term in these equivalent ratios.

15 : 12 = ? : 4

Look at the second terms of the equivalent ratios — 15 : **12** = ? : **4**.

First, find a common factor of the terms in the first ratio. Then divide the first term by the common factor.

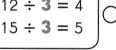

Method 1

$12 \div 3 = 4$
$15 \div 3 = 5$

15 : **12**

÷ 3 ÷ 3

= 5 : **4**

The missing term is 5.

Method 2

$12 \div 4 = 3$

So, **3** is the factor.

$15 \div 3 = 5$

Guided Practice

Find the missing terms in each set of equivalent ratios.

9 $4 : 3 \xrightarrow{\times \square,\ \times \square} = 20 : \square$

$20 \div 4 = \square$

$3 \times \square = \square$

10 $7 : \square \xrightarrow{\times \square,\ \times \square} = 21 : 12$

$21 \div 7 = \square$

$12 \div \square = \square$

11 $\square : 16 \xrightarrow{\div \square,\ \div \square} = 3 : 2$

$16 \div 2 = \square$

$3 \times \square = \square$

Hands-On Activity

Materials:
- 14 yellow cubes
- 28 red cubes

Work in groups of two or four.

STEP 1 Put the cubes in groups so that each group has the same number of cubes. (Do not mix yellow cubes and red cubes in a group.)

STEP 2 Write the ratio of the number of groups of yellow cubes to the number of groups of red cubes.

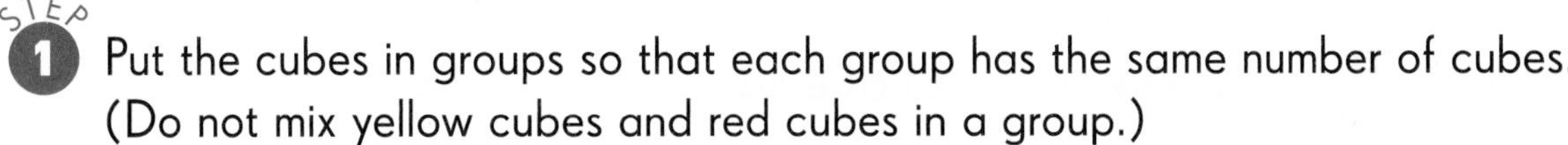

STEP 3 Repeat **STEP 1** and **STEP 2** with different numbers of cubes in each group to get another two ratios.
What can you say about these ratios?

STEP 4 Repeat the activity using 8 yellow cubes and 24 red cubes. What can you say about these ratios?

Why is this so? Explain your reasoning.

Let's Practice

Solve.

Mrs. Jefferson has 3 boxes of yellow chalk and 8 boxes of white chalk. Each box contains 5 pieces of chalk.

1. Find the total number of pieces of yellow chalk.
2. Find the total number of pieces of white chalk.
3. Find the ratio of the number of pieces of yellow chalk to the number of pieces of white chalk.
4. Find the ratio of the number of boxes of yellow chalk to the number of boxes of white chalk.
5. What can you say about the ratios in 3 and 4?

Express each ratio in simplest form.

6. 4 : 14 = ___ : ___
7. 18 : 8 = ___ : ___
8. 8 : 32 = ___ : ___
9. 42 : 12 = ___ : ___

Find the missing term in each set of equivalent ratios.

10. 4 : 7 = 12 : ___
11. 3 : 8 = ___ : 32
12. 27 : 15 = ___ : 5
13. 6 : 42 = 2 : ___

Find the missing term in each set of equivalent ratios.

14. 3 : ___ = 48 : 80
15. ___ : 51 = 4 : 3
16. 70 : ___ = 2 : 4
17. ___ : 7 = 128 : 224

ON YOUR OWN

Go to Workbook A: Practice 2, pages 215–216

Real-World Problems: Ratios

Lesson Objective

- Solve real-world problems involving ratios.

Learn Find simplest-form ratios to compare quantities in real-world problems.

There are 6 angelfish and 18 tetras in an aquarium. Find the ratio of the number of angelfish to the number of tetras in the aquarium.

The ratio of the number of angelfish to the number of tetras is 6 : 18.

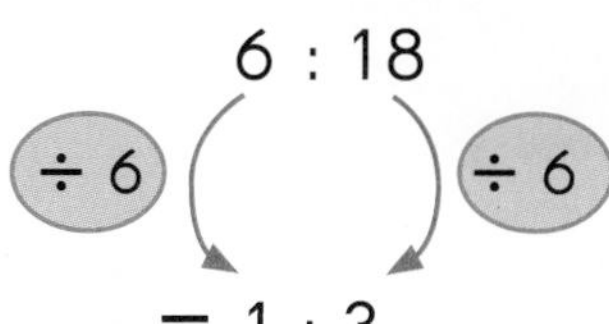

Write the ratio 6 : 18 in simplest form. Divide 6 and 18 by their greatest common factor, 6.

The ratio of the number of angelfish to the number of tetras in the aquarium is 1 : 3.

Guided Practice

Complete.

There are 12 pink roses and 15 yellow roses in Beth's garden.

1. What is the ratio of the number of pink roses to the number of yellow roses?

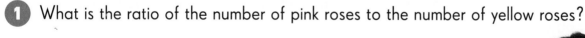

12 : 15

÷ ___ ÷ ___

= ___ : ___

Write the ratio 12 : 15 in simplest form. Divide 12 and 15 by the greatest common factor, 3.

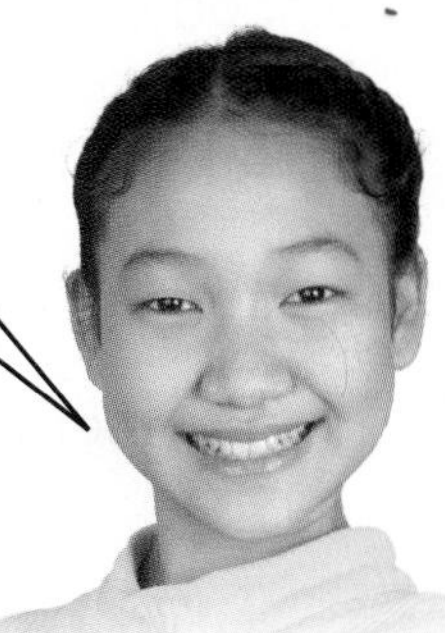

The ratio of the number of pink roses to the number of yellow roses is ___ : ___.

2. The ratio of the number of yellow roses to the number of pink roses is ___ : ___.

Learn Use the whole to find the missing part in a ratio.

There are 48 children in a soccer program, and 16 of them are girls.
Find the ratio of the number of girls to the number of boys in the program.

$48 - 16 = 32$

There are 32 boys in the program.

$16 : 32 = 1 : 2$

16 : 32
÷ 16 ÷ 16
= 1 : 2

The ratio of the number of girls to the number of boys in the program is 1 : 2.

Give the answer in simplest form.

Guided Practice

Complete.

On a rainy day, the All-Weather Goods store sold 56 umbrellas and raincoats altogether. The number of raincoats sold was 24.

3 Find the ratio of the total number of umbrellas and raincoats sold to the number of raincoats sold.

___ : ___ = ___ : ___

The ratio of the total number of umbrellas and raincoats sold to the number of raincoats sold is ___ : ___.

4 Find the ratio of the number of umbrellas sold to the number of raincoats sold.

56 − ___ = ___

The number of umbrellas sold was ___.

___ : 24 = ___ : ___

The ratio of the number of umbrellas sold to the number of raincoats sold is ___ : ___.

Learn Find the new ratio after one of the terms changes.

Ernesto has 25 football cards and 40 baseball cards. He gives away 5 baseball cards. What is the ratio of the number of football cards to the number of baseball cards Ernesto has now?

$40 - 5 = 35$

Ernesto has 35 baseball cards now.

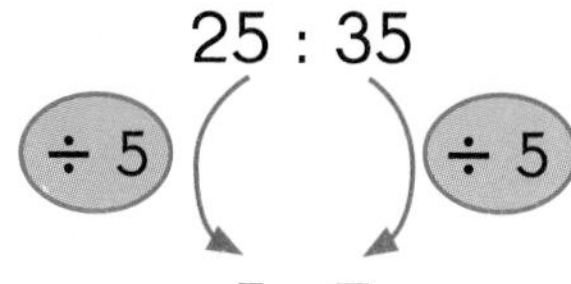

The ratio of the number of football cards to the number of baseball cards Ernesto has now is 5 : 7.

Guided Practice

Complete.

Gerald donated 30 quarters and 16 dimes to a charity collection. He then donated another 18 quarters.

5. Find the ratio of the total number of quarters to the number of dimes Gerald donated.

   30 + ___ = ___

   Gerald donated a total of ___ quarters.

   ___ : 16 = ___ : ___

   The ratio of the total number of quarters Gerald donated to the number of dimes he donated is ___ : ___.

6. Find the ratio of the total number of quarters Gerald donated to the total number of coins he donated.

   From 5, the total number of quarters Gerald donated is ___.

   ___ + 16 = ___

   Gerald donated a total of ___ coins.

   ___ : ___ = ___ : ___

   The ratio of the total number of quarters Gerald donated to the total number of coins he donated is ___ : ___.

Learn: Use models to find a ratio.

Amy has 96 comic and story books altogether. She has 60 comic books. Find the ratio of the number of comic books to the number of story books.

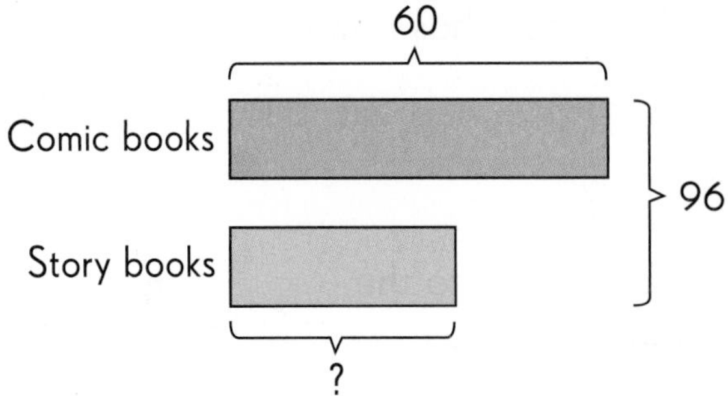

96 − 60 = 36

There are 36 story books.

60 : 36 = 5 : 3

The ratio of the number of comic books to the number of story books is 5 : 3.

Guided Practice

Complete.

Stanley collects stamps as a hobby. In his collection, he has 56 foreign and 196 U.S. stamps.

7 What is the ratio of the number of U.S. stamps to the total number of stamps he has?

196

U.S. stamps

Foreign stamps

?

56

196 + 56 = ____

The total number of stamps in Stanley's collection is ____.

____ : ____ = ____ : ____

The ratio of the number of U.S. stamps to the total number of stamps Stanley has is ____ : ____.

Learn Find the other term given the ratio and one term.

Harold divides a carton of tomatoes into two portions. The ratio of the mass of the bigger portion to the mass of the smaller portion is 5 : 2. The mass of the bigger portion is 15 pounds. Find the mass of the smaller portion.

Method 1

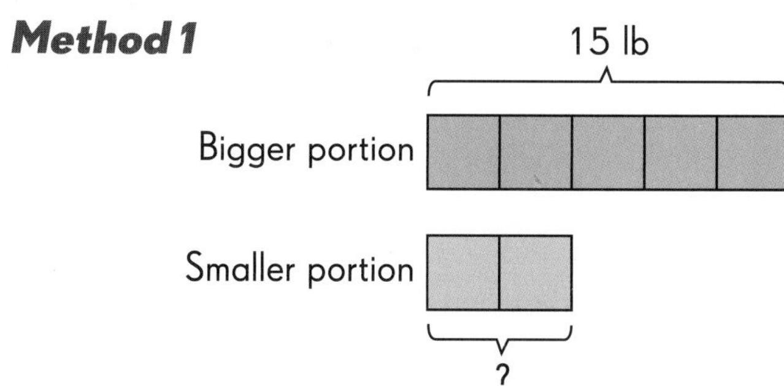

5 units ⟶ 15 lb

1 unit ⟶ $15 \div 5 = 3$ lb

2 units ⟶ $2 \times 3 = 6$ lb

The mass of the smaller portion of tomatoes is 6 pounds.

Method 2

5 : 2

× 3 × 3

= 15 : 6

The mass of the smaller portion of tomatoes is 6 pounds.

Guided Practice

Complete.

8 Mrs. Gardner has the milk she is going to use to make a smoothie and a shortcake in two portions. The ratio of the volume of portion 1 to the volume of portion 2 is 3 : 4. The volume of portion 1 is 120 milliliters. Find the total volume of both portions.

Method 1

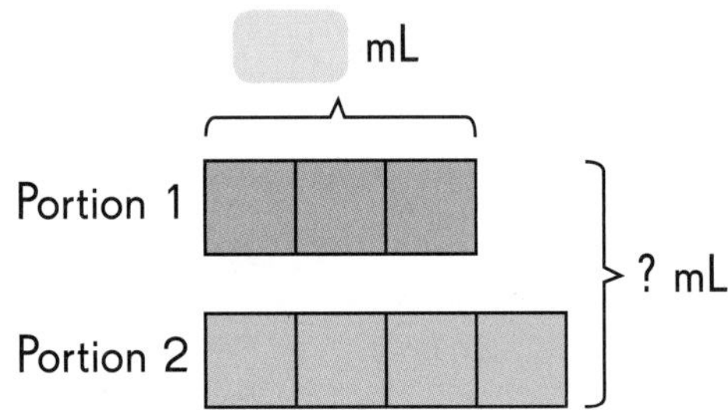

3 units → ___ mL

1 unit → ___ ÷ ___ = ___ mL

7 units → ___ × ___ = ___ mL

The total volume of both portions is ___ milliliters.

Method 2

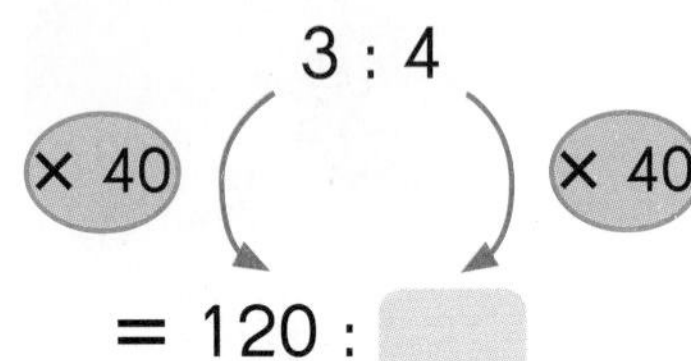

3 × 40 = 120
4 × 40 = ___

The volume of portion 1 is ___ milliliters.

120 + ___ = ___

The total volume of both portions is ___ milliliters.

READING AND WRITING MATH

Math Journal

Look at the model.
Write a real-world problem that includes a ratio. Then, solve your real-world problem.

Stephanie
Tania
$24

Let's Practice

Solve. Show your work.

1. Lindsay spent \$24 and had \$11 left. Find the ratio of the amount of money she spent to the total amount of money she had at first.
2. A box contained 42 apples and 12 of them were green. The rest of the apples were red. Find the ratio of the number of green apples to the number of red apples.
3. Stella mixed 20 milliliters of cranberry juice with 30 milliliters of blackcurrant juice. She then added another 15 milliliters of cranberry juice. Find the ratio of the amount of cranberry juice to the amount of blackcurrant juice in the end.
4. Mr. Wong cuts a coil of wire into two pieces in the ratio 3 : 4. The length of the longer piece of wire is 32 centimeters. What is the total length of the coil of wire?
5. The ratio of the number of students at the zoo in the morning to the number of students at the zoo in the afternoon was 5 : 3. There were 145 students at the zoo in the morning. What was the number of students at the zoo in the afternoon?
6. The total time that Ken and Bob worked in a week was 63 hours. Ken worked 36 hours. What is the ratio of Bob's working hours to Ken and Bob's total working hours?

ON YOUR OWN

Go to Workbook A: Practice 3, pages 217–220

Lesson 7.4 Ratio in Fraction Form

Lesson Objectives

- Interpret ratios given in fraction form.
- Write ratios in fraction form to find how many times as large as one number another number is.

Learn Ratios can also be written in fraction form.

Jason has two colored pencils: one red, the other blue.

The ratio of the length of his red pencil to the length of his blue pencil is as represented in the model.

3 units

Length of red pencil

Length of blue pencil

5 units

Total number of units $= 3 + 5 = 8$

a The ratio of the length of the red pencil to the length of the blue pencil is 3 : 5.

The same ratio can also be written in fraction form as:

$$\frac{\text{Length of the red pencil}}{\text{Length of the blue pencil}} = \frac{3}{5}$$

b The ratio of the length of the blue pencil to the length of the red pencil is 5 : 3.

The same ratio can also be written in fraction form as:

$$\frac{\text{Length of the blue pencil}}{\text{Length of the red pencil}} = \frac{5}{3}$$

c The ratio of the length of the red pencil to the total length of the two pencils is 3 : 8.

The same ratio can also be written in fraction form as:

$$\frac{\text{Length of the red pencil}}{\text{Total length of the two pencils}} = \frac{3}{8}$$

Guided Practice

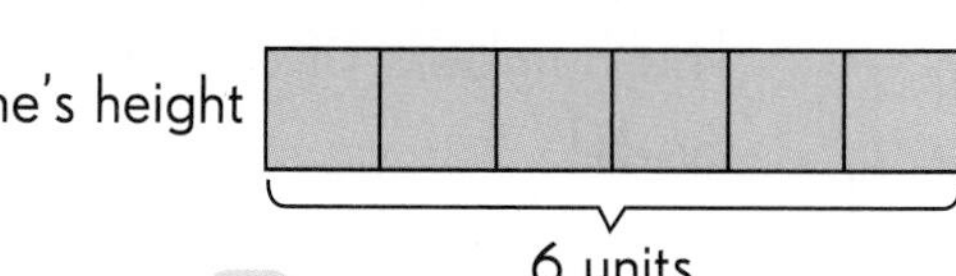

Complete. You may draw models to help you.

The ratio of Sam's height to Gene's height is as represented in the model.

1. The ratio of Sam's height to Gene's height is ___ : ___ or $\frac{\square}{\square}$.

2. The ratio of Sam's height to the total height of the two boys is ___ : ___ or $\frac{\square}{\square}$.

Let's Explore!

In this table, you are given the ratio of a quantity to another quantity.

	Ratio form	Fraction form
A to B	3 : 8	$\frac{3}{8}$
C to D	4 : 7	$\frac{4}{7}$
E to F	5 : 9	$\frac{5}{9}$

1. Look at the fraction form of each ratio. Note the quantity in the numerator. Locate the same quantity in the corresponding ratio form. Where is its position?

2. Look at the fraction form of each ratio. Note the quantity in the denominator. Locate the same quantity in the corresponding ratio form. Where is its position?

What can you say about the relationship between the ratio form and fraction form of a ratio?

Learn Write ratios in fraction form to find how many times as large as one number another number is.

The numbers of adults and children watching a show are as represented in the model.

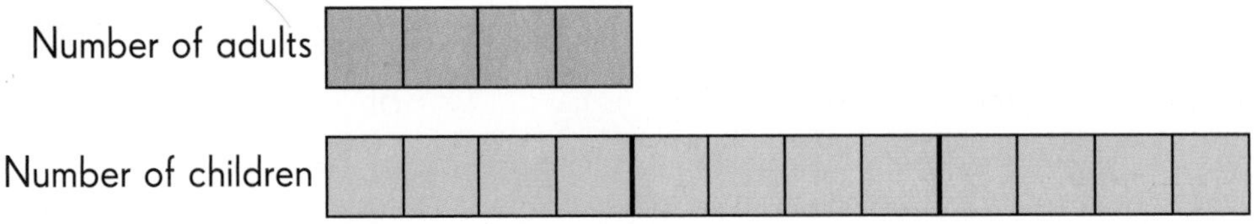

a How many times the number of children is the number of adults?

$$\frac{\text{Number of adults}}{\text{Number of children}} = \frac{4}{12} = \frac{1}{3}$$

The number of adults is $\frac{1}{3}$ times the number of children.

b How many times the number of adults is the number of children?

$$\frac{\text{Number of children}}{\text{Number of adults}} = \frac{3}{1}$$

The number of children is 3 times the number of adults.

Guided Practice

Complete. Give all answers in simplest form.

Felice spent \$21 and Brad spent \$42.

3 $\frac{\text{Amount of money Felice spent}}{\text{Amount of money Brad spent}} = \frac{__}{__}$

The amount of money Felice spent is $\frac{__}{__}$ times the amount of money Brad spent.

4 $\frac{\text{Amount of money Brad spent}}{\text{Amount of money Felice spent}} = \frac{__}{__}$

The amount of money Brad spent is ___ times the amount of money Felice spent.

Learn Draw a model to represent a ratio given in fraction form.

Steve saved $\frac{3}{4}$ as much money as Chyna.

Steve's savings

Chyna's savings

In fraction form:
Steve's savings: Chyna's savings = $\frac{3}{4}$

So, in ratio form:
Steve's savings: Chyna's savings = 3 : 4

I can draw a model with 3 units to represent Steve's savings and 4 units to represent Chyna's savings respectively.

Total number of units = 3 + 4 = 7

From the model:

a The ratio of Chyna's savings to Steve's savings is 4 : 3 or $\frac{4}{3}$.

b The ratio of Chyna's savings to their total savings is 4 : 7 or $\frac{4}{7}$.

Guided Practice

Complete. Use the model to help you.

Ryan cut a rope into two pieces. The length of the first piece was $\frac{4}{7}$ of the length of the second piece.

Length of first piece

Length of second piece

5 The ratio of the length of the second piece to the length of the first piece is ___ : ___ or $\frac{\quad}{\quad}$.

6 The ratio of the length of the second piece to the total length of the two pieces is ___ : ___ or $\frac{\quad}{\quad}$.

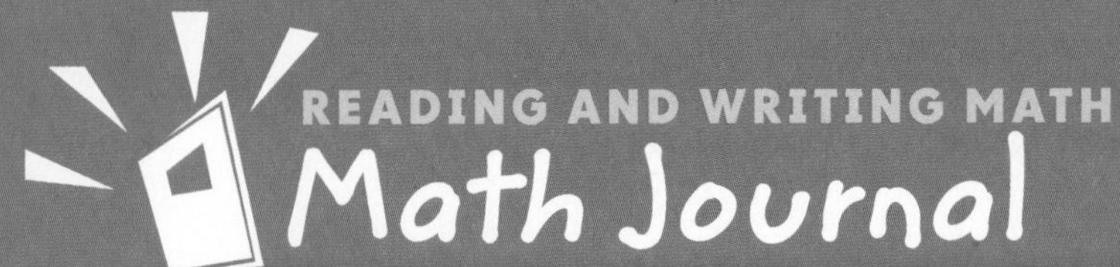

Write, in fraction form, three ratios for each scenario.

1. There is $\frac{4}{7}$ times as many large eggs as there are medium eggs at Mim's convenience store.

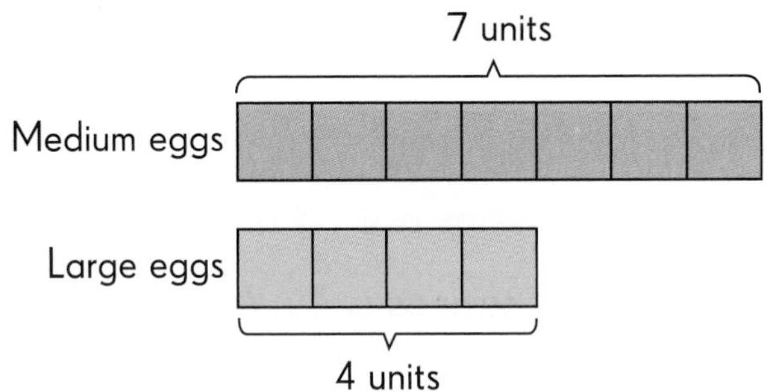

Example

Number of large eggs : number of medium eggs $= \frac{4}{7}$

2. Fang saves $450 every month while Lily saves $150 every month.

Let's Practice

Complete.

2 units
X
Y
7 units

1. The ratio of X to Y is  ___ : ___ or $\frac{\square}{\square}$.

2. X is $\frac{\square}{\square}$ times Y.

3. Y is $\frac{\square}{\square}$ times X.

Solve. Use the model to help you.

The ratio of the length of pole A to the length of pole B is as represented in the model.

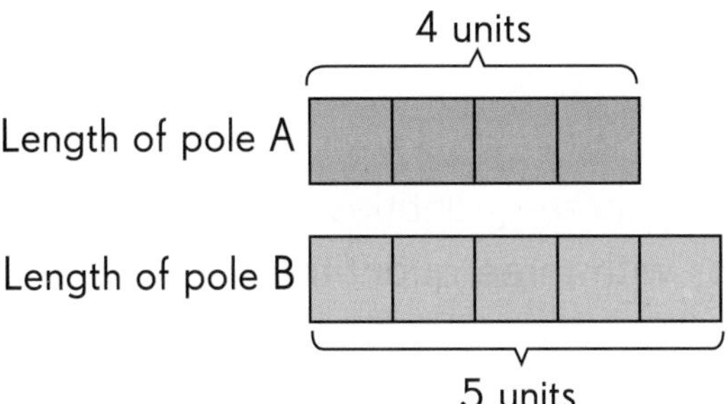

4. Find the ratio of pole A's length to the total length of the two poles. Give your answer in fraction form.
5. How many times pole A's length is pole B's length?
6. How many times pole B's length is pole A's length?
7. How many times pole A's length is the total length of both poles?
8. How many times pole B's length is the total length of both poles?

Solve. You may draw a model to help you.

Jessie has $15. Kimberley has $21.

9. Find the ratio of the amount of money Jessie has to the amount of money that Kimberley has. Give your answer in fraction form.
10. How many times the amount of money Kimberley has is the amount of money Jessie has?
11. How many times the amount of money Jessie has is the amount of money Kimberley has?
12. How many times the total amount of money they have altogether is the amount of money Jessie has?
13. How many times the amount of money Kimberley has is the total amount of money they have altogether?

ON YOUR OWN

Go to Workbook A: Practice 4, pages 221–226

Lesson 7.5 Comparing Three Quantities

Lesson Objectives

- Read and write ratios with three quantities.
- Express equivalent ratios with three quantities.

Learn Use ratios to compare three quantities.

Wendy has 4 red carnations, 8 pink carnations, and 12 yellow carnations. The ratio of the number of red carnations to the number of pink carnations to the number of yellow carnations is 4 : 8 : 12.

Method 1

The greatest common factor of 4, 8, and 12 is 4.

I can take

to be 1 unit.

Wendy puts 4 carnations into each box.

1 box of red carnations

2 boxes of pink carnations

3 boxes of yellow carnations

The ratio of the number of red carnations to the number of pink carnations to the number of yellow carnations is 1 : 2 : 3.

Method 2

$$4 : 8 : 12 \xrightarrow{\div 4} = 1 : 2 : 3$$

1 : 2 : 3 is 4 : 8 : 12 in simplest form.

The ratio of the number of red carnations to the number of pink carnations to the number of yellow carnations is 1 : 2 : 3.

Guided Practice

Complete to express each ratio in simplest form.

1 15 : 12 : 18

15 : 12 : 18 ÷ ___ ÷ ___ ÷ ___

= ___ : ___ : ___

The greatest common factor of 15, 12, and 18 is ___. Divide 15, 12, and 18 by ___.

2 12 : 8 : 20

12 : 8 : 20 ÷ ___ ÷ ___ ÷ ___

= ___ : ___ : ___

Learn Use multiplication to find missing terms in equivalent ratios.

Find the missing terms in these equivalent ratios.
2 : 3 : 5 = ? : 12 : ?

Look at the second terms of the equivalent ratios.
2 : **3** : 5 = ? : **12** : ?

First, find the multiplying factor. Then, multiply the first and third terms by this multiplying factor.

Method 1

3 × **4** = 12
Multiply by **4** throughout.

Method 2

12 ÷ 3 = **4**

2 : **3** : 5
× 4 × 4 × 4
= 8 : **12** : 20

So, **4** is the multiplying factor.
4 × 2 = 8
4 × 5 = 20

So, 2 : 3 : 5 = 8 : 12 : 20.

Guided Practice

3 **Find the missing terms in these equivalent ratios.**

3 : 5 : 7 = 9 : ? : ?

Look at the first terms of the equivalent ratios — **3** : 5 : 7 = **9** : ? : ?.

First, find the multiplying factor. Then, multiply the second and third terms by the multiplying factor.

Method 1

3 × ___ = 9
Multiply by ___ throughout.

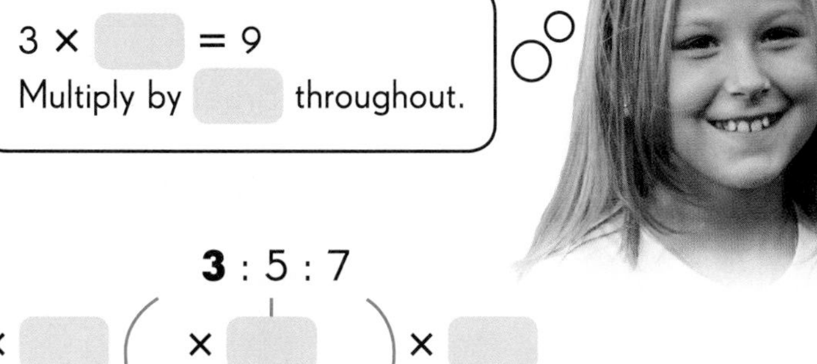

Method 2

9 ÷ 3 = ___

So, ___ is the multiplying factor.

___ × 5 = ___

___ × 7 = ___

3 : 5 : 7

× ___ × ___ × ___

= **9** : ___ : ___

Learn: Use division to find missing terms in equivalent ratios.

Find the missing numbers in these equivalent ratios.

18 : 12 : 9 = ? : ? : 3

Look at the third terms of the equivalent ratios —
18 : 12 : **9** = ? : ? : **3**

First, find the greatest common factor of the third terms. Then, divide the first and second terms by the greatest common factor.

9 ÷ 3 = 3
3 is the greatest common factor.

18 : 12 : **9**

÷ 3 ÷ 3 ÷ 3

= 6 : 4 : **3**

So, 18 : 12 : 9 = 6 : 4 : 3.

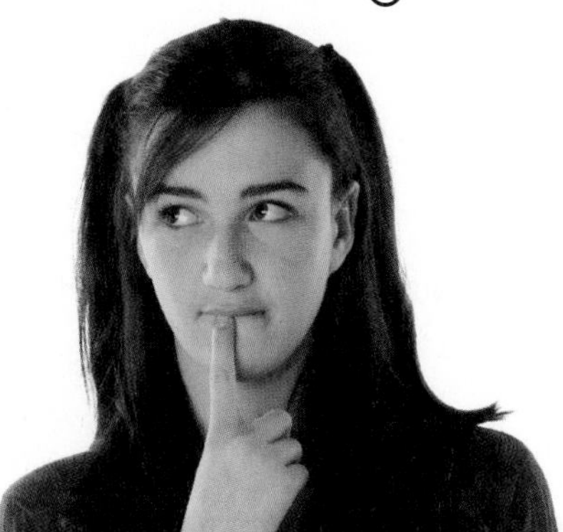

Guided Practice

Find the missing terms in each set of equivalent ratios.

4 15 : 5 : 20 = ___ : 1 : ___

5 7 : 21 : 14 = ___ : ___ : 2

Hands-On Activity

WORKING TOGETHER

Materials:

- 3 green counters
- 12 blue counters
- 18 yellow counters
- 5 ten frames

Work in groups.

STEP **1** Arrange 3 green counters, 12 blue counters, and 18 yellow counters in s.

STEP **2** Write the ratio of the number of green counters to the number of blue counters to the number of yellow counters.

STEP **3** Take away some counters of any two colors. Find the new ratio of the number of green counters to the number of blue counters to the number of yellow counters. Give your ratio in simplest form.

Example

Take away 1 green and 2 yellow counters.

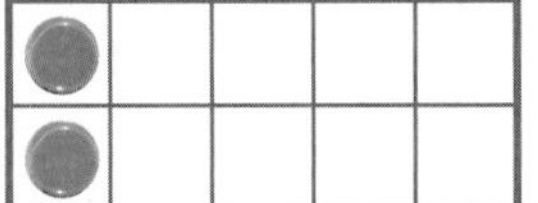
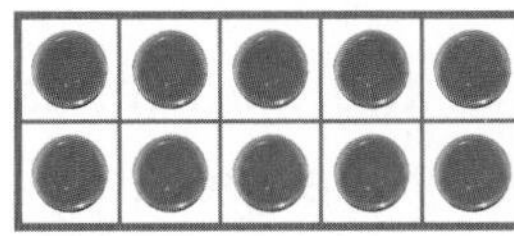
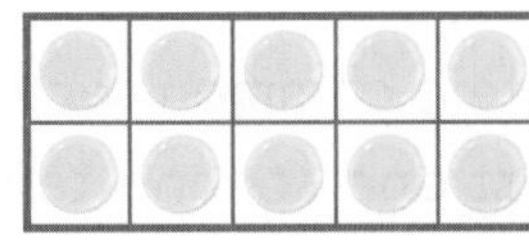

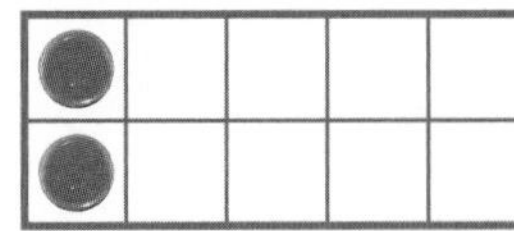
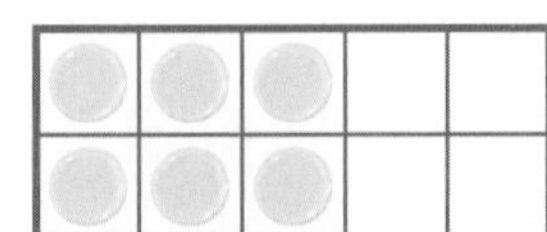

Number of  : Number of  : Number of ◯ (in simplest form) = 1 : 6 : 8

Let's Practice

Complete to express each ratio in simplest form.

1. 5 : 15 : 20

   5 : 15 : 20
   ÷ ___ ÷ ___ ÷ ___
   = ___ : ___ : ___

2. 4 : 18 : 24

   4 : 18 : 24
   ÷ ___ ÷ ___ ÷ ___
   = ___ : ___ : ___

3. 12 : 16 : 28

   12 : 16 : 28
   ÷ ___ ÷ ___ ÷ ___
   = ___ : ___ : ___

4. 36 : 45 : 72

   36 : 45 : 72
   ÷ ___ ÷ ___ ÷ ___
   = ___ : ___ : ___

Find the missing terms in each set of equivalent ratios.

5. 1 : 4 : 5

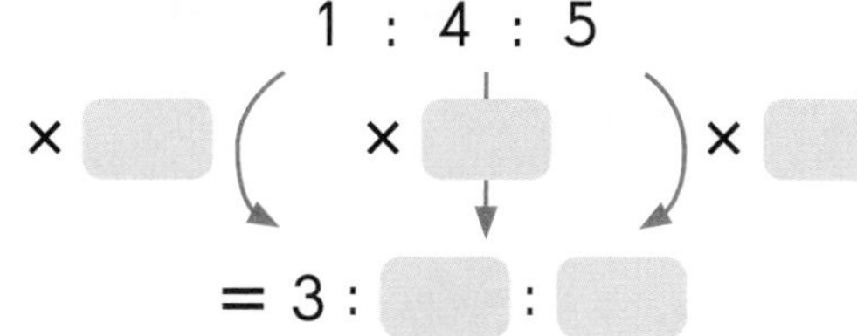

   1 : 4 : 5
   × ___ × ___ × ___
   = 3 : ___ : ___

6. 32 : 56 : 16

   32 : 56 : 16
   ÷ ___ ÷ ___ ÷ ___
   = ___ : ___ : 2

7. 2 : 3 : 8 = ___ : 18 : ___

8. 4 : 5 : 9 = ___ : ___ : 63

9. 45 : 72 : 18 = ___ : 8 : ___

10. 15 : 100 : 125 = ___ : ___ : 25

ON YOUR OWN

Go to Workbook A:
Practice 5, pages 227–228

Lesson 7.6

Real-World Problems: More Ratios

Lesson Objectives

- Solve real-world problems involving ratios and fractions.
- Solve real-world problems involving ratios with three quantities.

Learn

Find simplest-form ratios to compare quantities in real-world problems.

At a toy shop, Bernice bought 3 pink toy cars, 6 blue toy cars, and 9 yellow toy cars. What is the ratio of the number of pink toy cars to the number of blue toy cars to the number of yellow toy cars that Bernice bought?

Method 1

Put 3 toy cars into each box.

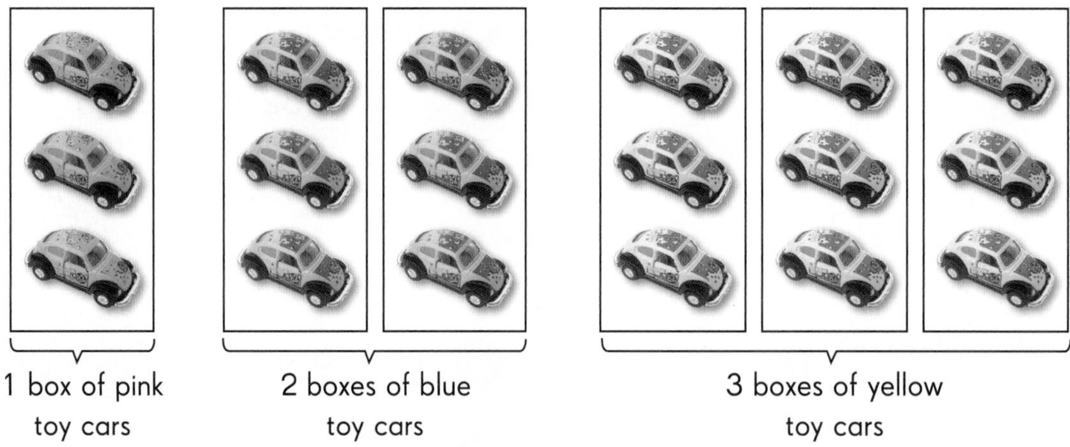

The ratio of the number of pink toy cars to the number of blue toy cars to the number of yellow toy cars that Bernice bought is 1 : 2 : 3.

Method 2

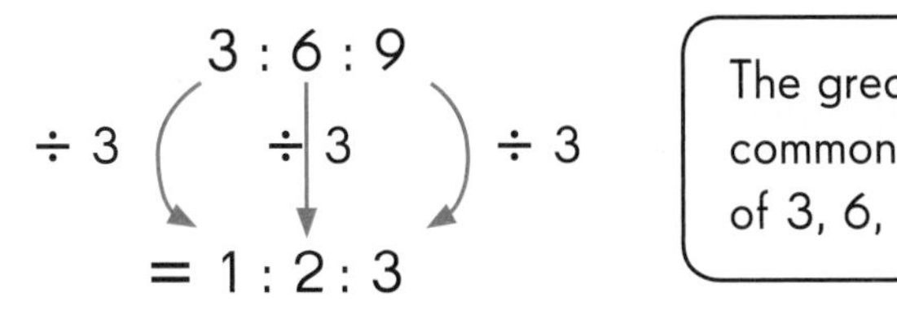

The greatest common factor of 3, 6, and 9 is 3.

1 : 2 : 3 is 3 : 6 : 9 in simplest form.

The ratio of the number of pink toy cars to the number of blue toy cars to the number of yellow toy cars that Bernice bought is 1 : 2 : 3.

Guided Practice

Complete.

1 During a track event, Darren ran 200 meters, Shelby ran 800 meters, and Antonio ran 3,000 meters. What was the ratio of the distance Darren ran to the distance Shelby ran to the distance Antonio ran?

200 : 800 : 3,000

÷ ___ ÷ ___ ÷ ___

= ___ : ___ : ___

Find the common factor of 200, 800 and 3,000.

The ratio of the distance Darren ran to the distance Shelby ran to the distance Antonio ran was ___ : ___ : ___.

Learn Find equivalent ratios or use models to solve real-world problems.

Rebecca filled three containers, A, B, and C, completely with orange juice. The containers' capacities were in the ratio 2 : 3 : 4. The capacity of the largest container was 12 cups. Find the capacity of the smallest container.

Method 1

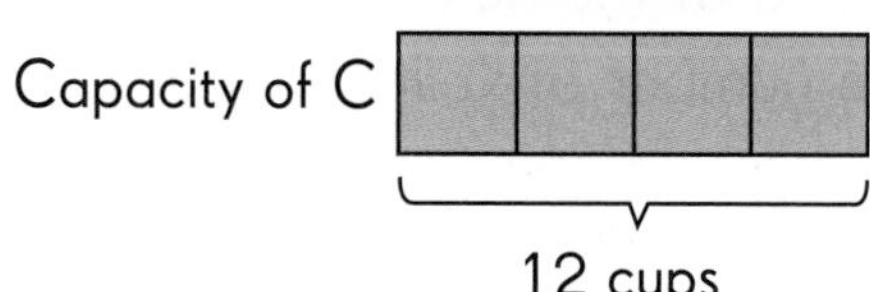

4 units → 12 cups

1 unit → $12 \div 4 = 3$ cups

2 units → $2 \times 3 = 6$ cups

The capacity of the smallest container is 6 cups.

Method 2

A B C

2 : 3 : 4

× 3 × 3 × 3

= 6 : 9 : 12

The capacity of the smallest container is 6 cups.

Guided Practice

Complete.

2 Raymond cut a roll of ribbon into three pieces, X, Y, and Z, in the ratio 4 : 2 : 1. The length of the longest piece is 28 centimeters. Find the total length of the three pieces of ribbons.

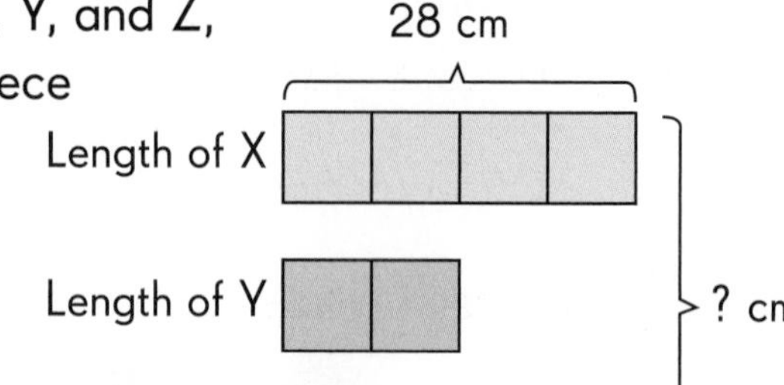

4 units → 28 cm

1 unit → ___ ÷ ___ = ___ cm

Total number of units = 4 + 2 + 1 = ___

___ × ___ = ___

The total length of the three pieces of ribbon is ___ centimeters.

Guided Practice

Complete.

3. The amounts of Mrs. Caito's monthly car payment, electric bill, and grocery bill last month were in the ratio 5 : 4 : 6. The grocery bill was $432. How much was the total amount of all three bills?

6 units → $432

1 unit → $ ___ ÷ ___ = $ ___

Total number of units = 5 + 4 + 6

= 15

___ × $ ___ = $ ___

The total amount of all three bills was $ ___.

car payment

electric bill

grocery bill

?

$432

Learn **Draw models to solve problems involving ratios in fraction form.**

Camille's salary is $\frac{2}{5}$ times Belinda's salary.

a. Find the ratio of Belinda's salary to Camille's salary. Give your answer in fraction form.

b. Belinda earned $895. How much did they earn altogether?

Belinda's salary

Camille's salary

Total number of units = 5 + 2 = 7

From the model:

a. $\frac{\text{Belinda's salary}}{\text{Camille's salary}} = \frac{5}{2}$

The ratio of Belinda's salary to Camille's salary is $\frac{5}{2}$.

b. 5 units → $895

1 unit → $895 ÷ 5 = $179

7 units → 7 × $179 = $1,253

They earned $1,253 altogether.

Guided Practice

Complete.

5 In a swim-and-run biathlon, Raul ran 5 times the distance that he swam.

a What is the ratio of the distance Raul ran to the distance he swam to the total distance of the biathlon?

b How many times the total distance of the biathlon is the distance Raul ran?

c Raul ran 3,200 meters more than he swam. What was the total distance of the biathlon?

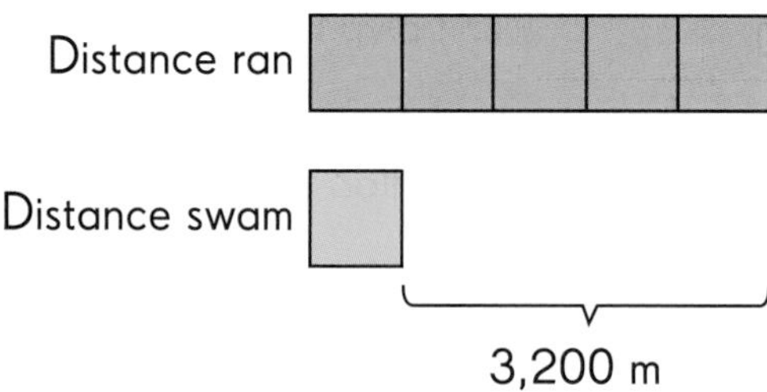

From the model:

a The ratio of the distance Raul ran to the distance he swam to the total distance of the biathlon is ___ : ___ : ___.

Total number of units is $5 + 1 = 6$

b $\frac{\text{Distance Raul ran}}{\text{Total distance of the biathlon}} = \frac{\square}{\square}$

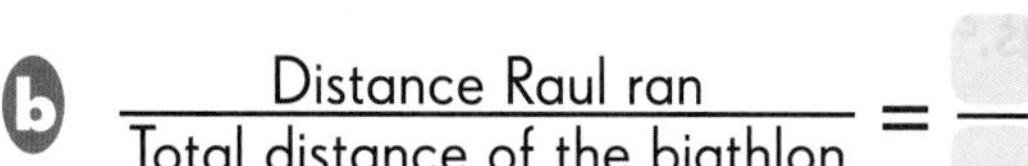

The distance Raul ran is $\frac{\square}{\square}$ times the total distance of the biathlon.

c ___ units → ___

___ unit → ___

___ units → ___

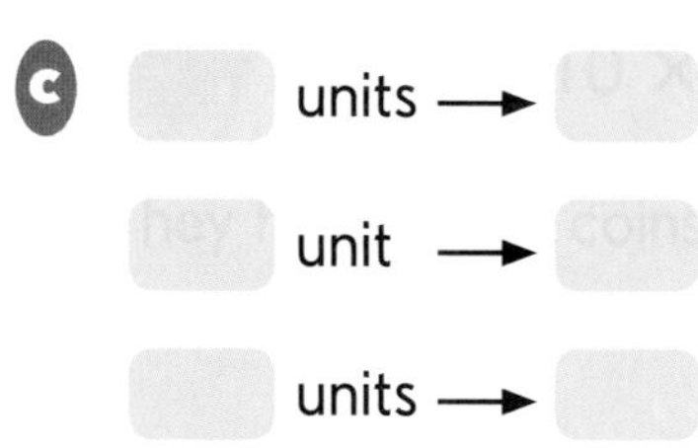

The total distance of the biathlon was ___ meters.

Let's Practice

Solve. Show your work. Give all answers in simplest form.

1. At an office supply store, Rachel bought 5 erasers, 15 pens, and 40 pencils. What is the ratio of the number of erasers to the number of pens to the number of pencils she bought?

2. Nita mixes 200 milliliters of cranberry juice, 300 milliliters of grapefruit juice, and 700 milliliters of spring water to make a fruit punch. What is the ratio of cranberry juice to grapefruit juice to spring water?

3. Ronald draws three lines in different colors — red, yellow and green. The ratio of the length of the red line to the length of the yellow line to the length of the green line is 1 : 3 : 5. The yellow line is 18 centimeters long. How long is the green line?

4. Apple, carrot and celery juices are mixed in the ratio 3 : 1 : 2. The amount of apple juice is 720 milliliters.
   - a. How much more apple juice is used in the mixture than carrot juice?
   - b. What is the total amount of the mixture?

5. The amount of savings that Anna, Beth and Cynthia each has is in the ratio 2 : 3 : 15. Cynthia has $1,575 in savings.
   - a. Who has the least amount saved?
   - b. What is the total amount that all three of them have in savings?

6. On a Saturday, La Petite Bakery sold tortillas, bagels and rolls in the ratio 12 : 5 : 7. The number of tortillas sold was 50 more than the number of rolls sold.
   - a. How many tortillas did La Petite sell on that Saturday?
   - b. How many tortillas, bagels and rolls in all did La Petite sell on that Saturday?

7 Lilian's present age is $\frac{2}{3}$ times May's age.

a Find the ratio of May's age to Lilian's age. Give your answer in fraction form.

b How many times the total age of the two girls is Lilian's age?

c How many times the total age of the two girls is May's age?

d Their combined age is 25 years. Find the age of each girl.

8 The weight of potatoes used by Mrs. Wilson in her cooking is $\frac{5}{2}$ times the weight of carrots used.

a Find the ratio of the weight of potatoes used to the weight of carrots used to the total weight of both ingredients.

b How many times the total weight of both ingredients was the weight of the potatoes?

c The weight of potatoes used was 9 pounds more than the weight of carrots used. Find the total weight of both ingredients.

9 A wall is painted yellow and brown. The area painted yellow is 3 times the area painted brown.

a What is the ratio of the area painted yellow to the area painted brown? Give your answer in fraction form.

b What is the ratio of the area painted yellow to the area of the entire wall? Give your answer in fraction form.

c How many times the area of the entire wall is the area painted brown?

d The wall has an area of 8 square meters. Find the area of the wall painted yellow.

10 Peter collects U.S. and foreign stamps. He has 5 times as many U.S. stamps as foreign stamps.

a What is the ratio of the number of U.S. stamps to the number of foreign stamps to the total number of stamps in his collection?

b How many times the total number of stamps is the number of U.S. stamps?

c How many times the total number of stamps is the number of foreign stamps?

d Peter has 140 more U.S. stamps than foreign stamps. How many stamps does he have in his collection?

ON YOUR OWN

Go to Workbook A: Practice 6, pages 229–236

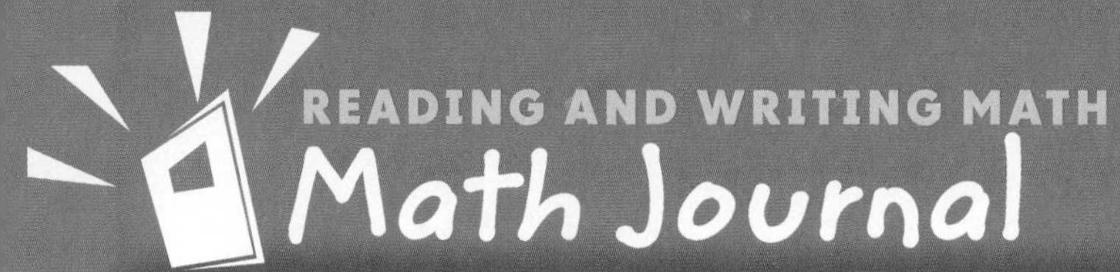

Yolanda has 6 white balloons and 15 pink balloons. Explain how to find the ratio of the number of white balloons to the number of pink balloons. Can the ratio be simplified? If so, explain how to simplify the ratio. Draw a model to help you.

1 Using these numbers, write sets of equivalent ratios in the form $a : b$. Use each number only once.

2	3	5	6	7	8	9	10
12	14	15	20	21	25	35	

Example $2 : 3 = 6 : 9 = 8 : 12$

2 Using the same numbers in 1, write as many sets of equivalent ratios in the form $a : b : c$ as you can. Use each number only once.

How did you find the numbers for each set of equivalent ratios? Explain your answer.

CRITICAL THINKING SKILLS

Put On Your Thinking Cap!

PROBLEM SOLVING

1. The ratio of the money Chris has to the money Tina has is 5 : 2. Chris has $30.

   a. How much money does Tina have?

   b. If Tina's money consists of only quarters, how many quarters does Tina have?

2. The ratio of the number of quarters to the number of dimes in Lin's pocket is 3 : 2. Lin has 4 dimes. How much money does Lin have in all?

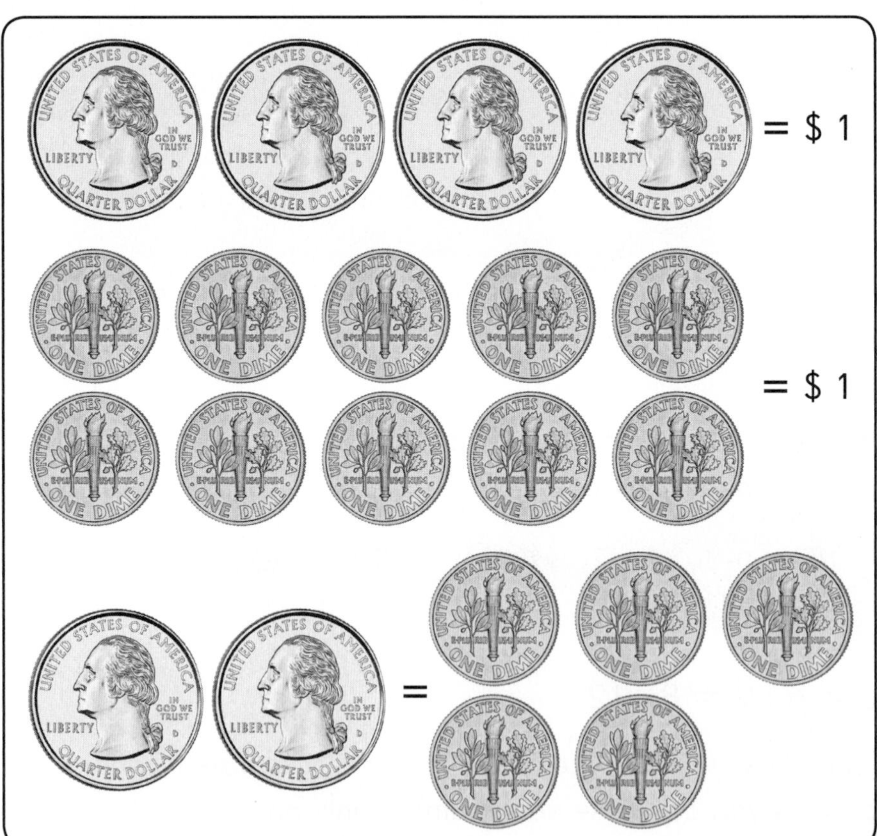

ON YOUR OWN

Go to Workbook A:
Put on Your Thinking Cap!
pages 237–238

Chapter Wrap Up

Study Guide

You have learned...

▶ Two numbers can be compared by subtraction. Two or more numbers or quantities can also be compared by division and the comparison expressed as a ratio.

Ratio

Comparing Numbers or Quantities

- A ratio is a comparison by division.
- Ratios can be used to compare 2 or 3 numbers or quantities.
- A ratio need not give the actual quantities compared.

Forms of a Ratio

- Ratios can be written in three forms.
  Ratio form : 1 : 5
  Fraction form : $\frac{1}{5}$
  Word form : 1 to 5
- Ratios in fraction form tell us how many times one number or quantity is as large as another.
- In '$\frac{\text{Number of adults}}{\text{Number of children}} = \frac{3}{12} = \frac{1}{4}$', the number of adults is $\frac{1}{4}$ times the number of children.

Equivalent Ratios

- Divide by the greatest common factor to find the simplest form of a ratio.

$$10 : 8 \xrightarrow{\div 2} = 5 : 4$$

- Multiply by the same factor to find equivalent ratios.

$$1 : 3 \xrightarrow{\times 3} = 3 : 9$$

Solve Real-World Problems

Glossary

Acute triangle

A triangle with all angles measuring less than 90°.

Algebraic expression

An expression that contains at least one variable.
$2x$, $x + 3$, $5 - x$ are algebraic expressions in terms of x.

Angle

An angle is formed by two rays with the same endpoint.

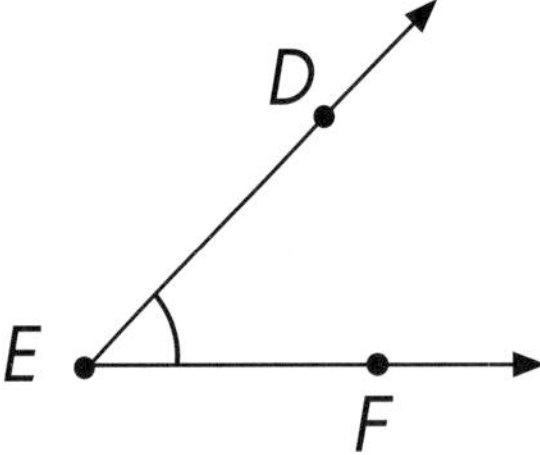

Area

The amount of surface covered; commonly measured in square units, such as square centimeters (cm^2) or square inches ($in.^2$).

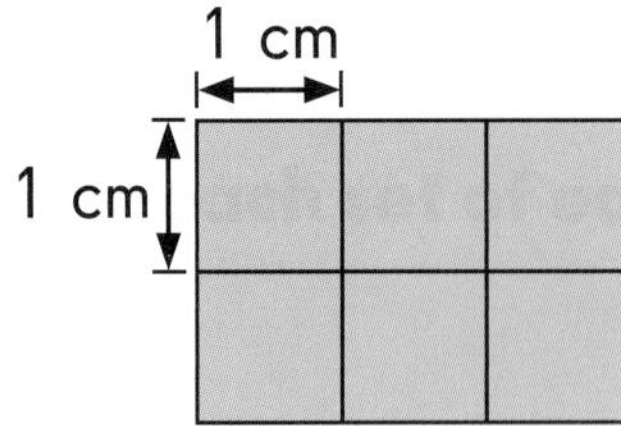

Area of the rectangle = 6 cm^2

B

Base

The face or side on which an object lies.
In a triangle, any one side can be the base.

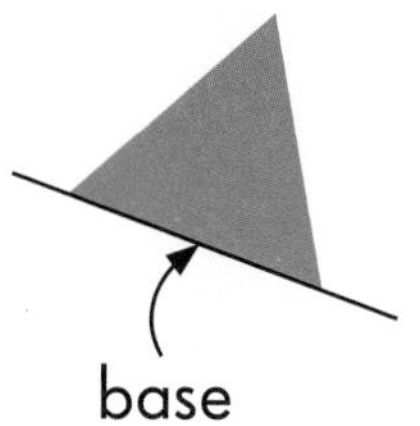

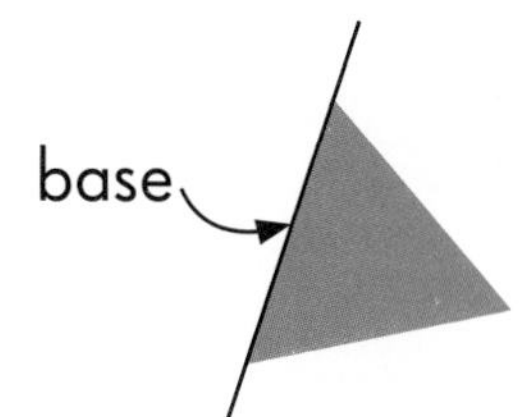

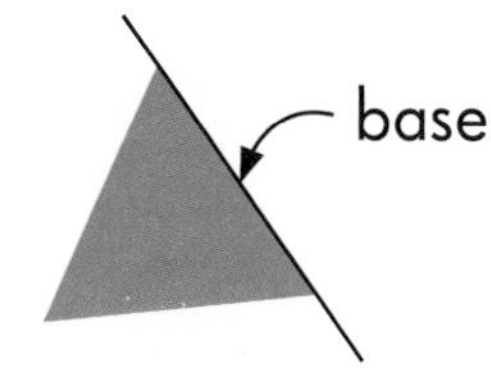

Benchmarks for fractions

Numbers which are easier to work with and to picture than others.
Common benchmarks for estimating with fractions: 0, $\frac{1}{2}$ and 1.

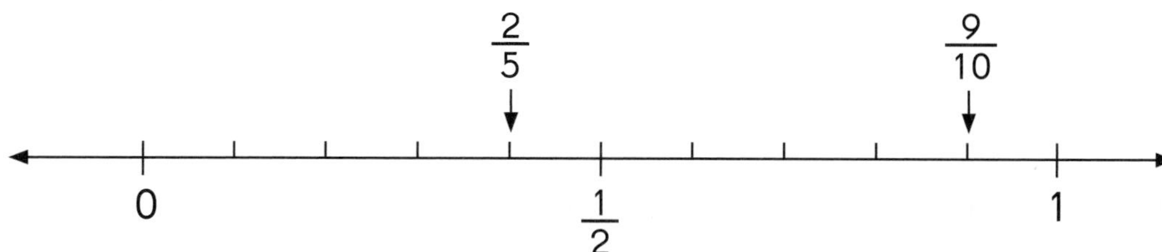

$\frac{2}{5}$ is about $\frac{1}{2}$.

$\frac{9}{10}$ is about 1.

C

Common factor

A number that is a factor of two or more numbers.
Factors of 8: 1, 2, 4, 8
Factors of 12: 1, 2, 3, 4, 6, 12
1, 2, and 4 are common factors of 8 and 12.

Compatible numbers

Pairs of numbers close to the original number pairs that are easy to add, subtract, multiply or divide mentally. Used to estimate sums, differences, products and quotients.

The numbers 240 and 6 are compatible numbers used for estimating 248 ÷ 6.

D

Dividend

The number that is being divided.

$8\overline{)128}$

dividend

Division expression (in arithmetic)

An expression that contains only numbers and the division symbol. 2 ÷ 3 is a division expression.

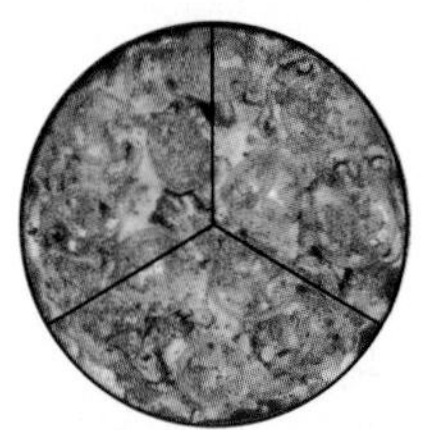
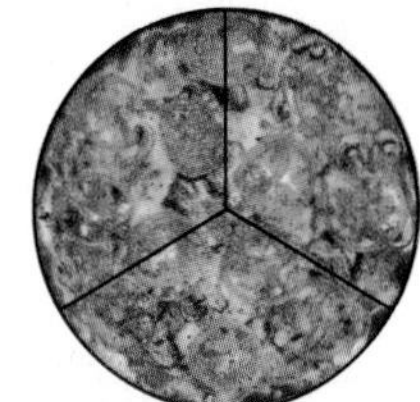
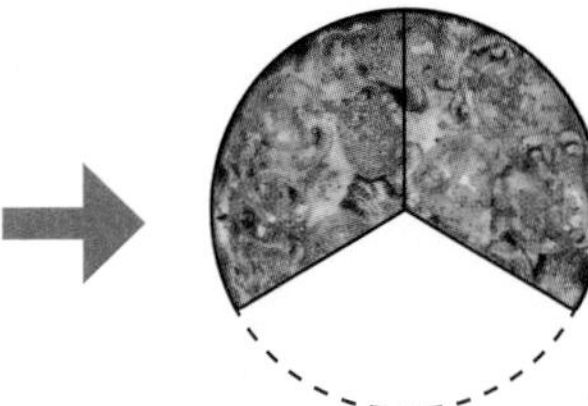
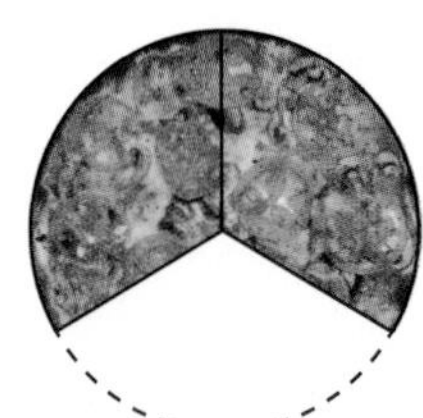
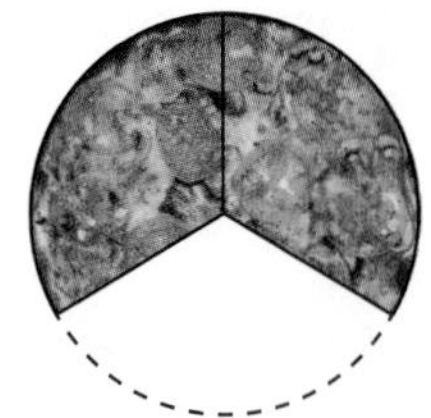

$2 \div 3 = \frac{2}{3}$

Divisor

The number the dividend is being divided by.

$8\overline{)128}$

divisor

E

Equality Property

You can add the same number to or subtract the same number from both sides of an equation. The new equation will still be true for the same value of variable.

Look at the balance.

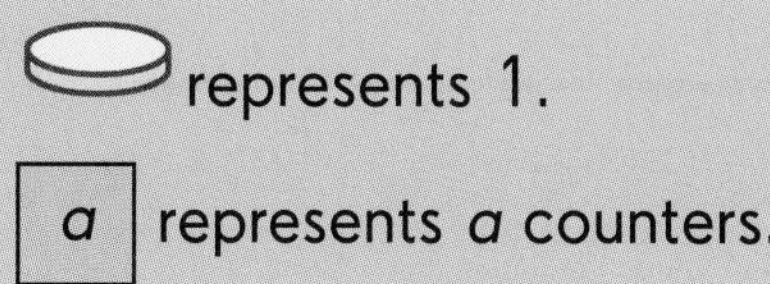

a counters together with 4 counters on the left side balance 5 counters on the right side.

You have the equation $a + 4 = 5$.
This equation is true for $a = 1$.

Add 2 counters to both sides of the equation.
The two sides still balance.

You have a new equation, $a + 6 = 7$.

$a + 6 = 1 + 6 = 7$

The new equation $a + 6 = 7$ is still true for $a = 1$.

You can multiply or divide both sides of an equation by the same number. The new equation will still be true for the same value of the variable.

Look at the balance.

$4a$ counters on the left side balance 8 counters on the right side.
You have the equation, $4a = 8$.
This equation is true for $a = 2$.

Multiply the number of counters on both sides by 2.
The two sides still balance.

You have a new equation, $8a = 16$.

$8a = 8 \times 2 = 16$

The new equation $8a = 16$ is still true for $a = 2$.

E

Equation

The statement that two expressions are equal.
$x + 5 = 10$, $x - 8 = 3$ and $2x = 4$ are equations.

Equivalent fractions

Fractions that have the same value.
$\frac{1}{2}$, $\frac{2}{4}$, and $\frac{3}{6}$ are equivalent fractions.

Equivalent ratios

Ratios that show the same comparison.

The ratio of the number of green beads to the number of pink beads is 4 : 8 or 2 : 4 or 1 : 2.

4 : 8, 2 : 4 and 1 : 2 are equivalent ratios.

Evaluate (an algebraic expression for a value of the variable)

To substitute the value(s) given for the variable(s) of the expression and then find the value of the expression.

Expanded form

768,540 = 700,000 + 60,000 + 8,000 + 500 + 40 in expanded form.

Expression

A number or a group of numbers with operation symbols.

Factor

2 × 9 = 18
2 and 9 are factors of 18.

Front-end estimation with adjustment

Take the value of the front-end, or leftmost, digits.
Then add or subtract the values.

$$\begin{array}{rcr} 3{,}815 & \rightarrow & 3{,}000 \\ 2{,}298 & \rightarrow & 2{,}000 \\ +1{,}972 & \rightarrow & +1{,}000 \\ \hline & & 6{,}000 \end{array}$$

Estimate what is left over to the place of the leading digit of the sum or difference obtained.

$$\begin{array}{rcr} 815 & \rightarrow & 800 \\ 298 & \rightarrow & 200 \\ +\ 972 & \rightarrow & +\ \ 900 \\ \hline & & 1{,}900 \end{array} \rightarrow 2{,}000 \text{ (to the nearest thousand)}$$

Adjust the estimate.

6,000 + 2,000 = 8,000

G

Greater than (>)

Hundred Thousands	Ten Thousands	Thousands	Hundreds	Tens	Ones
5	1	2	3	7	4
4	1	2	3	7	4

$512{,}374 > 412{,}374$
512,374 is greater than 412,374.

Height (of a triangle)

The perpendicular distance from the base to the opposite vertex.

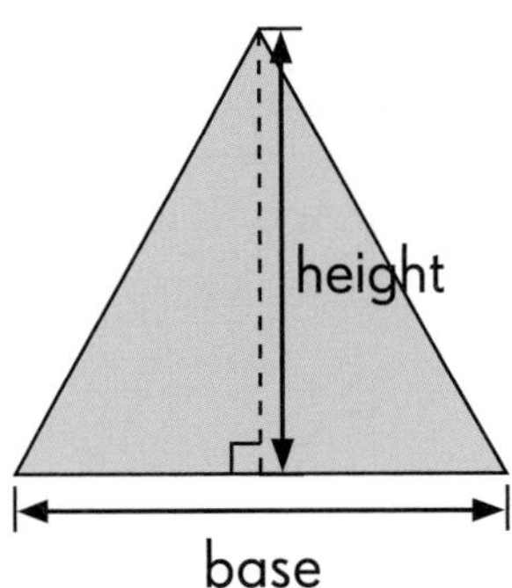

Hundred thousand

10 ten thousands or 100,000

I

Inequality

A statement that two expressions are not equal.
$8 > 2$, $2x < 8$, $8 \neq 13$ and $3y \div 9 > y - 1$ are inequalities.

Improper fraction

A fraction with a numerator greater than its denominator.
Its value is greater than 1.
$\frac{3}{2}$, $\frac{4}{3}$, and $\frac{6}{5}$ are improper fractions.

L

Least common denominator (LCD)

The least common multiple of the denominators of two or more fractions.
The LCD of $\frac{2}{3}$ and $\frac{3}{4}$ is 12.

Least common multiple (LCM)

The least number among all the common multiples of a set of two or more numbers.
Multiples of 4: 4, 8, 12, 16, 20, 24, ...
Multiples of 6: 6, 12, 18, 24, 30, 36, ...
12 is the LCM of 4 and 6.

Less than (<)

Hundred Thousands	Ten Thousands	Thousands	Hundreds	Tens	Ones
5	1	2	3	7	4
4	1	2	3	7	4

412,374 < 512,374
412,374 is less than 512,374.

Like terms

a and $2a$ are both multiples of a.
a and $2a$ are like terms.

M

Million

10 hundred thousands or 1,000,000

Mixed number

A number made up of a whole number and a fraction.

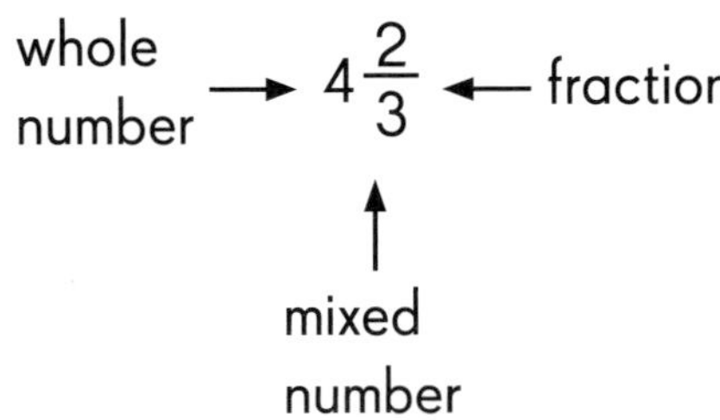

Multiple

The product of a given whole number and any other whole number.

$2 \times 4 = 8$

8 is a multiple of 2 and of 4.

N

Numeric expression

An expression that contains only numbers and symbols.

O

Obtuse triangle

A triangle with exactly one angle measuring greater than 90°.

Order of Operations

Set of rules stating the order in which to perform the operations, '+', '−', '×' and '÷' when simplifying any expression involving two or more operations:

1. Work inside the parentheses.
2. Multiply and divide from left to right.
3. Add and subtract from left to right.

Period

A group of three places commonly used for reading numbers that are 1,000 or above.

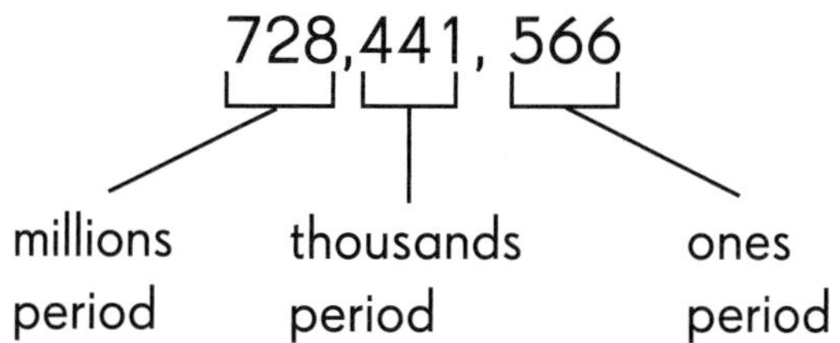

Perpendicular lines (⊥)

Lines that form right angles.

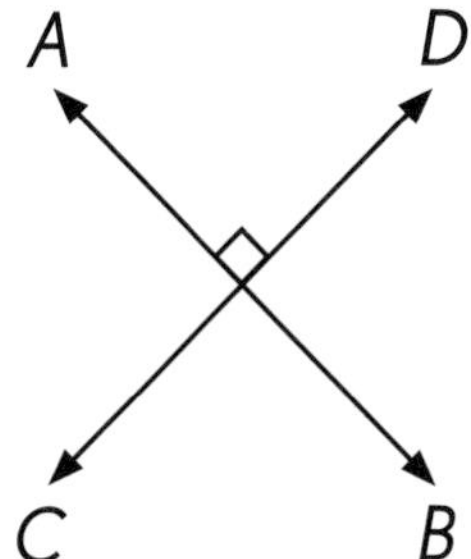

$\overleftrightarrow{AB}$ is perpendicular to $\overleftrightarrow{CD}$.

Place value

The value of a digit as determined by its place.
In 5,873, the digit 8 is in the hundreds place, so it stands for 800.

Product

The result of multiplication.

$$2 \times 9 = 18$$

factor (2), factor (9), product (18)

Proper fraction

A fraction with a numerator less than its denominator. Its value is less than 1.

$\frac{3}{4}$, $\frac{5}{6}$, and $\frac{7}{8}$ are proper fractions.

Quotient

The result of division.

$$8\overline{)128} = 16$$

16 ← quotient

Ratio

A comparison of two numbers or quantities by division.

bran muffins

blueberry muffin

The ratio of the number of bran muffins to the number of blueberry muffins is 2 : 1 (in ratio form) or $\frac{2}{1}$ (in fraction form).

Reciprocal

$\frac{1}{5}$ is the reciprocal of $\frac{5}{1}$ or 5.

Remainder (in whole number division)

The number that is left over when a divisor does not divide the dividend exactly.

```
     1 5
  8)1 2 8
     8 0
   -----
     4 8
     4 0
    ----
       8  ← remainder
```

Right triangle

A triangle with exactly one right angle.

Round

To approximate a number to the nearest ten, hundred, thousand (and so on).
To round any number:
Look one place to the right of the digit you want to round to.

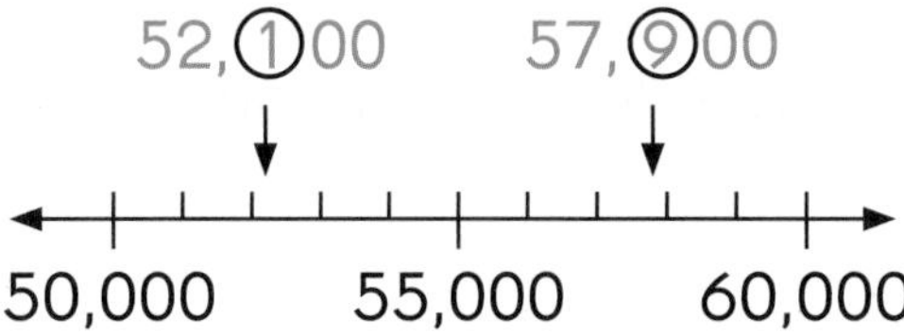

If the digit is less than 5, do not change the number in the rounding place.
52,① 00 rounded to the nearest thousand is 52,000.

If the digit is 5 or more, add 1 to the digit in the rounding place.
57,⑨ 00 rounded to the nearest thousand is 58,000.

S

Side

One of the line segments that form the polygon.

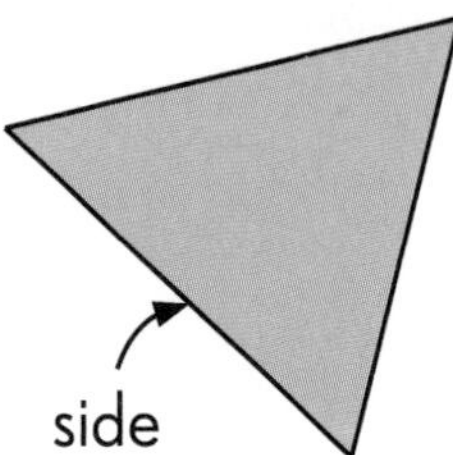

Simplest form (of a fraction)

The form in which its numerator and denominator have only 1 as a common factor.

Simplest form (of a ratio)

The form in which its terms have only 1 as a common factor.

Simplify

Combine like terms and apply number properties to an expression.
$9 + 5 - 4 - 1$ simplifies to 9.
$9s + 5 - 4s - 1$ simplifies to $5s + 4$.

Solve

To find the value of the variable that will make an equation true.

Standard form

3 million 5 hundred in standard form is 3,000,500.

T

Term (of an expression)

Any one of the numbers, variables, products or quotients which together make up the expression.
x, 1, $3x$ and 2 are terms of the expression, $x + 1 + 3x + 2$.

Term (of a ratio)

Any one of the numbers that make up the ratio.

Ratio Form	Fraction Form
2 : 1	$\frac{2}{1}$

1st term

2nd term

True

In $x + 5 = 9$, if $x = 4$,

Left side:
$x + 5 = 4 + 5$
$= 9$ (from right side)

$x + 5 = 9$ is said to be true for $x = 4$.

V

Variable

A symbol, such as a letter, representing an unknown number in an algebraic expression.
In the expression $m + 11$, m is the variable.

Vertex (of an angle)

The point at which two line segments, or rays meet to form an angle.

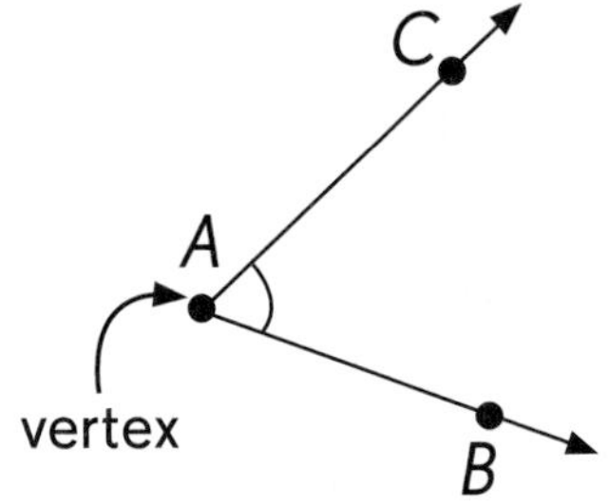

Vertex (of a polygon)

A point on a polygon where two sides meet to form an angle.

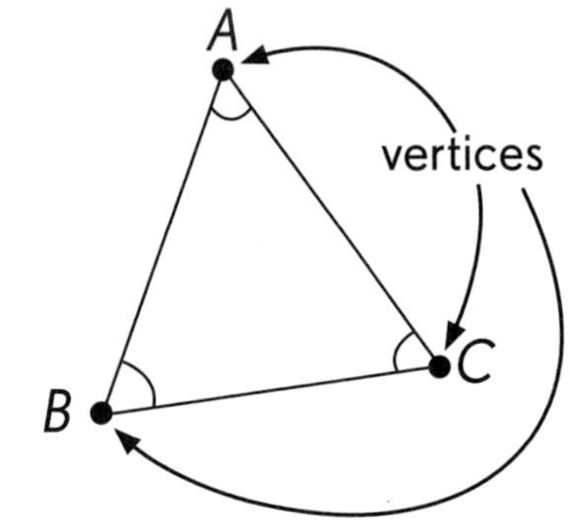

W

Word form

The word form of 7,010,000 is seven million ten thousand.

Index

A

Pages listed in black regular type refer to Student Book A.
Pages in blue type refer to Student Book B pages.
Pages in *italic* type refer to Workbook (WB) A.
Pages in *blue italic* type refer to Workbook (WB) B pages.
Pages in **boldface** type show where a term is introduced.

Pages listed in black regular type refer to Student Book A.
Pages in blue type refer to Student Book B pages.
Pages in *italic* type refer to Workbook (WB) A.
Pages in *blue italic* type refer to Workbook (WB) B pages.
Pages in **boldface** type show where a term is introduced.

Pages listed in black regular type refer to Student Book A.
Pages in blue type refer to Student Book B pages.
Pages in *italic* type refer to Workbook (WB) A.
Pages in *blue italic* type refer to Workbook (WB) B pages.
Pages in **boldface** type show where a term is introduced.

Isosceles triangle, 186–188, 190, 195, 197–200, 202–204, 224–228; *WB 121, 127–128, 131–132*

Pages listed in black regular type refer to Student Book A.
Pages in blue type refer to Student Book B pages.
Pages in *italic* type refer to Workbook (WB) A.
Pages in *blue italic* type refer to Workbook (WB) B pages.
Pages in **boldface** type show where a term is introduced.

M

Pages listed in black regular type refer to Student Book A.
Pages in blue type refer to Student Book B pages.
Pages in *italic* type refer to Workbook (WB) A.
Pages in *blue italic* type refer to Workbook (WB) B pages.
Pages in **boldface** type show where a term is introduced.

Pages listed in black regular type refer to Student Book A.
Pages in blue type refer to Student Book B pages.
Pages in *italic* type refer to Workbook (WB) A.
Pages in *blue italic* type refer to Workbook (WB) B pages.
Pages in **boldface** type show where a term is introduced.

Q

R

Pages listed in black regular type refer to Student Book A.
Pages in blue type refer to Student Book B pages.
Pages in *italic* type refer to Workbook (WB) A.
Pages in *blue italic* type refer to Workbook (WB) B pages.
Pages in **boldface** type show where a term is introduced.

Pages listed in black regular type refer to Student Book A.
Pages in blue type refer to Student Book B pages.
Pages in *italic* type refer to Workbook (WB) A.
Pages in *blue italic* type refer to Workbook (WB) B pages.
Pages in **boldface** type show where a term is introduced.

Photo Credits

5: ©iStockphoto.com/Thomas Perkins, *6*: ©iStockphoto.com/Jennifer Conner, *9l*: ©iStockphoto.com/Ana Abejon, *9r*: ©iStockphoto.com/Irina Shoyhet, *10*: ©iStockphoto.com/Quavondo Nguyen, *11bl*: ©Dreamstime.com/Erdosain, *11br*: ©iStockphoto.com/Jacom Stephens, *17*: ©iStockphoto.com/Pathathai Chungyam, *20*: ©iStockphoto.com/Jose Manuel Gelpi Diaz, *22t*: ©iStockphoto.com/Jani Bryson, *22b*: ©iStockphoto.com/Ana Abejon, *28*: ©iStockphoto.com/Andrey Shadrin, *33t*: ©iStockphoto.com/Eileen Hart, *33b*: ©iStockphoto.com/Tracy Whiteside, *34*: ©iStockphoto.com/Ana Abejon, *48t*: ©iStockphoto.com/Ana Abejon, *48b*: ©iStockphoto.com/Jennifer Conner, *49*: © iStockphoto.com/Ana Abejon, *50*: ©iStockphoto.com/Jani Bryson, *51*: ©iStockphoto.com/Andrey Shadrin, *52t*: ©iStockphoto.com/Lisa Howard, *52b*: ©iStockphoto.com/Tracy Whiteside, *53*: ©iStockphoto.com/Quavondo Nguyen, *54*: ©iStockphoto.com/Jose Manuel Gelpi Diaz, *56t*: © iStockphoto.com/Pathathai Chungyam, *56b*: ©iStockphoto.com/Andrey Shadrin, *57*: © iStockphoto.com/Tracy Whiteside, *58l*: ©iStockphoto.com/Ana Abejon, *58r*: ©iStockphoto.com/Lisa Howard, *59*: ©iStockphoto.com/Irina Shoyhet, *64t*: ©iStockphoto.com/Irina Shoyhet, *64b*: © iStockphoto.com/Jose Manuel Gelpi Diaz, *65*: © iStockphoto.com/Jani Bryson, *66*: ©iStockphoto.com/Tracy Whiteside, *67l*: ©iStockphoto.com/Ana Abejon, *67m*: ©iStockphoto.com/Jani Bryson, *67r*: ©iStockphoto.com/Andrey Shadrin, *68*: ©iStockphoto.com/Jennifer Conner, *70t*: ©iStockphoto.com/Eva Serrabassa, *70b*: ©iStockphoto.com/Jose Manuel Gelpi Diaz, *71t*: ©iStockphoto.com/Lisa Howard, *71b*: ©iStockphoto.com/Ana Abejon, *72t*: ©iStockphoto.com/Jennifer Conner, *73*: © iStockphoto.com/Ana Abejon, *75t*: ©iStockphoto.com/Irina Shoyhet, *75b*: ©iStockphoto.com/Andrey Shadrin, *76l*: © iStockphoto.com/Eva Serrabassa, *76r*: ©iStockphoto.com/Jose Manuel Gelpi Diaz,

77: ©iStockphoto.com/Eileen Hart, *79*: ©iStockphoto.com/Pathathai Chungyam, *80*: ©iStockphoto.com/Tracy Whiteside, *82*: ©iStockphoto.com/Jacom Stephens, *83tl*: ©iStockphoto.com/Jani Bryson, *83ltl*: ©iStockphoto.com/Tracy Whiteside, *83ml*: iStockphoto.com/Ana Abejon, *83bl*: ©iStockphoto.com/Irina Shoyhet,

84tl: ©iStockphoto.com/Jacom Stephens,*84ltl*: ©iStockphoto.com/Eileen Hart, *84ml*:©iStockphoto.com/Eva Serrabassa, *84bl*:©iStockphoto.com/Ana Abejon, *85t*: ©iStockphoto.com/Pathathai Chungyam, *85b*: ©iStockphoto.com/Ana Abejon, *86*: ©iStockphoto.com/Jose Manuel Gelpi Diaz, *87*: ©iStockphoto.com/Jani Bryson, *88*: ©iStockphoto.com/Jennifer Conner, *91*: ©iStockphoto.com/Eva Serrabassa, *92*: ©iStockphoto.com/Jani Bryson, *98t*: iStockphoto.com/Ana Abejon, *98b*: ©iStockphoto.com/Lisa Howard, *99*: ©iStockphoto.com/Ana Abejon, *100l*: ©Rudolf Stricker/Wikimedia Commons, *100r*: ©iStockphoto.com/Jennifer Conner, *101tr*: ©iStockphoto.com/Jose Manuel Gelpi Diaz, *101br*: ©iStockphoto.com/Eva Serrabassa, *104*: ©iStockphoto.com/Jacom Stephens, *105*: ©iStockphoto.com/Jani Bryson, *106t*: ©iStockphoto.com/Ana Abejon, *106b*: ©iStockphoto.com/ Jennifer Conner, *107*: ©iStockphoto.com/Tracy Whiteside, *109*: ©iStockphoto.com/Irina Shoyhet, *115t*: ©Wikimedia Commons/MECU,.com/Pathathai Chungyam, *122t*: ©iStockphoto.com/Ana Abejon, *122b*: ©iStockphoto.com/Pathathai Chungyam, *123*: ©iStockphoto.com/Eva Serrabassa, *124*: ©iStockphoto.com/Thomas Perkins, *127t*: ©iStockphoto.com/Jennifer Conner, *127b*: ©iStockphoto.com/Ana Abejon, *128*: ©iStockphoto.com/Pathathai Chungyam, *131t*: ©iStockphoto.com/Andrey Shadrin, *131b*: ©iStockphoto.com/Eileen Hart, *132t*: ©iStockphoto.com/Tracy Whiteside, *132b*: ©iStockphoto.com/Jennifer Conner, *134t*: ©iStockphoto.com/Tracy Whiteside, *134b*: ©iStockphoto.com/Lisa Howard, *140*: ©iStockphoto.com/Eileen Hart,

141: ©iStockphoto.com/Jennifer Conner, *145*: ©iStockphoto.com/Jani Bryson, *146*: ©iStockphoto.com/Ana Abejon, *150*: ©Wikimedia Commons/Przykuta, *152t*: ©iStockphoto.com/Pathathai Chungyam, *152b*: ©iStockphoto.com/Ana Abejon, *154*: ©iStockphoto.com/Eva Serrabassa, *155*: ©iStockphoto.com/Tracy Whiteside, *166*: ©iStockphoto.com/Jani Bryson, *171*: ©iStockphoto.com/Jacom Stephens, *172*: ©iStockphoto.com/Pathathai Chungyam, *175*: ©iStockphoto.com/Tracy Whiteside, *177*: ©iStockphoto.com/Lisa Howard, *178*: ©iStockphoto.com/Ana Abejon, *179*: ©iStockphoto.com/Jacom Stephens, *Jennifer Conner, 185*: ©iStockphoto.com/Jose Manuel Gelpi Diaz, *190*: ©iStockphoto.com/Pathathai Chungyam, *191*: ©iStockphoto.com/Lisa Howard, *192*: ©iStockphoto.com/Jacom Stephens, *194*: ©iStockphoto.com/Jani Bryson, *198*: ©iStockphoto.com/Jani Bryson, *209l*: ©iStockphoto.com/Irina Shoyhet, *209r*: ©iStockphoto.com/Ana Abejon, *211*: ©iStockphoto.com/Lisa Howard, *212bl*: ©iStockphoto.com/Jacom Stephens, *212bm*: ©iStockphoto.com/Lisa Howard, *212br*: ©iStockphoto.com/Tracy Whiteside, *213*: ©iStockphoto.com/Tracy Whiteside, *214l*: ©iStockphoto.com/Jennifer Conner, *214r*: ©iStockphoto.com/Ana Abejon, *221t*: ©iStockphoto.com/Lisa Howard, *221b:* ©iStockphoto.com/Jennifer Conner, *223*: ©iStockphoto.com/Irina Shoyhet, *224*: ©Image Source, *228*: ©iStockphoto.com/Eva Serrabassa, *230l*: ©iStockphoto.com/Jacom Stephens, *230r*: ©iStockphoto.com/Lisa Howard, *231*: ©iStockphoto.com/Tracy Whiteside, *232*: ©iStockphoto.com/Jose Manuel Gelpi Diaz, *233tr*: ©iStockphoto.com/Pathathai Chungyam, *233br*: ©iStockphoto.com/Tracy Whiteside, *234*: ©iStockphoto.com/Jose Manual Gelpi Diaz, *235*: ©iStockphoto.com/Ana Abejon, *251l*: ©Dreamstime.com/Ivonne Wierink, *251m*: ©Dreamstime.com/Jamie Duplass, *252*: ©iStockphoto.com/Irina Shoyhet, *256*: ©iStockphoto.com/Tracy Whiteside, *257*: ©iStockphoto.com/Jose Manuel Gelpi Diaz, *258*: ©iStockphoto.com/Ana Abejon, *269bml*: ©iStockphoto.com/Jose Manuel Gelpi Diaz, *269bmr*: ©iStockphoto.com/Pathathai Chungyam, *270tr*: ©iStockphoto.com/Andrey Shadrin, *270bm*: ©iStockphoto.com/Thomas Perkins, *271tr*: ©iStockphoto.com/Ana Abejon, *271mr*: ©iStockphoto.com/Jani Bryson,, *271br*: ©iStockphoto.com/Ana Abejon, *272mr*: ©iStockphoto.com/Irina Shoyhet, *272br*: ©iStockphoto.com/Tracy Whiteside, *273*: ©iStockphoto.com/Jani Bryson, *276*: ©iStockphoto.com/Jacom Stephens, *277*: ©iStockphoto.com/Tracy Whiteside, *279ttr*: ©iStockphoto.com/Quavondo Nguyen, *279mtr*: ©iStockphoto.com/Andrey Shadrin, *279tbr*: ©iStockphoto.com/Irina Shoyhet, *279br*: ©iStockphoto.com/Ana Abejon, *280tl*: ©iStockphoto.com/Lisa Howard, *280tr*: ©iStockphoto.com/Ana Abejon, *280bl*: ©iStockphoto.com/Eva Serrabassa, *280br*: ©iStockphoto.com/Tracy Whiteside, *283tr*: ©iStockphoto.com/Jani Bryson, *283br*: ©iStockphoto.com/Pathathai Chungyam, *284*: ©iStockphoto.com/Lisa Howard, *287*: ©iStockphoto.com/Andrey Shadrin, *288*: ©iStockphoto.com/Jennifer Conner, *293*: ©iStockphoto.com/Jani Bryson, *296*: ©iStockphoto.com/Jennifer Conner, *297tr*: ©iStockphoto.com/Jose Manuel Gelpi Diaz, *297mr*: ©iStockphoto.com/Ana Abejon, *297br*: ©iStockphoto.com/Eva Serrabassa, *298*: ©iStockphoto.com/Jacom Stephens, *299tm*: ©iStockphoto.com/Irina Shoyhet, *299br*: ©iStockphoto.com/Jani Bryson, *303tr*: ©iStockphoto.com/Quavondo Nguyen, *303br*: ©iStockphoto.com/Ana Abejon, *307*: ©morguefile.com/mconnors, *308*: ©iStockphoto.com/Ana Abejon, *312br*: ©iStockphoto.com/Tracy Whiteside

Blank